JOHN BROWN—the Cost of Freedom

This sketch of John Brown was done by Selden J. Woodman, an artist who met Brown in New York City in early 1858. In the 1880s, Woodman rendered this image, largely inspired by a tintype in the Kansas Historical Society. Widow Mary Brown was highly pleased with Woodman's portrait sketch, which appeared in *The Century* magazine in July 1883.

JOHN BROWN

THE COST of FREEDOM

LOUIS A. DeCARO JR.

INTERNATIONAL PUBLISHERS, New York

For my son, Louis Michael DeCaro,
whose birth wonderfully interrupted
the writing of this book

© 2007 by Louis A. DeCaro, Jr.
First edition, 2007
Published by International Publishers, New York
All rights reserved under International and
Pan-American copyright conventions
Printed in the USA

ISBN-13: 978-0-7178-0742-0
ISBN-10: 0-7178-0742-8

Library of Congress Control Number (LCCN) 2006932607

CONTENTS

Acknowledgments vii

1. The Man and His Times 3

2. The Real Story of Businessman Brown 16

3. The Hard Lessons of Capitalism 28

4. The Making of a Radical Reformer 38

5. Kansas 43

6. The Road to Virginia 55

7. The Raid Reconsidered 70

8. John Brown—for the Record 90

9. John Brown's Body Revisited 95

Appendices
    Appendix-A: Key to Sources 111
    Appendix-B: Documents 112

Index 157

End Notes 159

Illustrations
    Sketch of John Brown, Frontispiece ii
    Sketch of John Brown w/group 2
    Other illustrations 101-110

APPENDICES

Appendix-A: Key to Sources
Appendix-B:
A Note on John Brown's Writing and the Style of Transcription Employed
Documents: Selected Letters of John Brown
1. John Brown, Red Rock, Iowa, to Henry L. Stearns, Medford, Massachusetts, July 15,1857, and an appended letter from John Brown to George L. Stearns, Aug. 8, 1857.
2. John Brown, Randolph Township, Pennsylvania, to Frederick Brown, Hudson, Ohio, Nov.21, 1834.
3. John Brown, Franklin Mills, Ohio, to H. J. Huidekoper, Meadville, Crawford County, Pa., July 5, 1838.
4. John Brown, Franklin Mills, Ohio, to George Kellogg, Vernon, Connecticut, Sept., 20, 1839.
5. John Brown, Springfield, Massachusetts, to Mary Brown, Akron, Ohio, Mar. 7, 1846.
6. John Brown, Akron, Ohio, to A. B. Allen, editor, Feb. 15, 1846, in *American Agriculturist*.
7. John Brown, Burgettstown, Pa., to John Brown, Jr. and Wealthy Brown, New York City, Apr. 12, 1850.
8. John Brown, Springfield, Massachusetts, to Mary Brown, North Elba, New York, Nov. 28, 1850.
9. John Brown, Springfield, Massachusetts, to Mary Brown, North Elba, New York, Jan. 17, 1851.
10. "Words of Advice," January 1851.
11. John Brown, Osawatomie, Kansas Territory, Jan. 19, 1856, to Owen Brown, Hudson, Ohio.
12. John Brown, Osawatomie, Kansas Territory, to T. W. Carter, Massachusetts Arms Company, Chicopee Falls, Massachusetts, Feb. 20, 1856.
13. John Brown, "Near Browns Station," Kansas Territory, to Mary Brown, North Elba, N.Y., June 24, 1856.
14. John Brown, Albany, New York, to George L. Stearns, Boston, Mass., Apr. 28, 1857.
15. John Brown to Mary Brown [and Ruth Brown Thompson], Jan. 30, 1858. Post-script by Frederick Douglass.
16. "Old Hundred," Chicago, Illinois, to Frederick Douglass, Rochester, New York, June 22, 1858.
17. John Brown to "E.B.," Nov. 1, 1859.
18. John Brown to Mary Brown, Nov. 10, 1859.
19. John Brown to H. L. Vaill, Nov. 15, 1859.
20. John Brown to Heman Humphrey, November 25, 1859.

Acknowledgments

Although I do not identify with my publisher's ideology, I have great respect for International Publishers' longstanding commitment to providing readers with excellent scholarly works, especially materials relating to the black struggle in the United States. My first copy of W. E. B. DuBois's *John Brown* was International Publishers' 1962 Emancipation Centennial edition which was reproduced from the book's first edition in 1909, along with a new preface by DuBois. Another wonderful addition to my library was International Publishers' 5-volume set of *The Life and Writings of Frederick Douglass*, edited by Philip S. Foner. Considering the home that International Publishers has made for Brown and Douglass, I am honored to have my work also included in their catalogue. In this light, many thanks go to Betty Smith, editor, for kindly and patiently working with me, especially when family developments demanded a change in plans.

In the pursuit of John Brown, I have gained a number of friends whom I hold as respected allies in the work as well as the meaningful reflection due his phenomenal life story: Thomas Vince, archivist and historian at the Western Reserve Academy, Hudson, Ohio, has been most kind and helpful. Also in Hudson, Gwen Mayer of the Hudson Library and Historical Society has been a great encouragement during both of my research forays there. Over in Meadville, Pennsylvania, Anne Stewart and Ed Edinger, both grassroots researchers on John Brown and Crawford County, have proven to be great friends to my work. Anne's criticisms and generous sharing of her own years of research have proven particularly helpful correctives for my work at key points. Up in Canada, Gwen Robinson and her associates at the Chatham-Kent Black Historical Society in Chatham, Ontario, were wonderful hosts and likewise shared generously of their materials.

Surely my friend Jean Libby of Palo Alto, California, deserves special mention. For thirty years Jean has been pursuing John Brown as a grassroots researcher and activist, and her pioneering labors have benefitted the study of his life in major ways. Indeed, after Boyd Stutler, no researcher has contributed so importantly to this study.

A few other friends of John Brown also deserve salutation: Susheel Bibbs, biographer and portrayer of abolitionist Mary E. Pleasant; Martha Swan of John Brown Lives!; Larry Lawrence of the John Brown Society; the actor Norman Marshall, portrayer of John Brown; and the superlative illustrator John Hendrix (a former parishioner of mine). They have all shown a zeal for Brown's legacy that have been personally uplifting and important to the currents flowing through the "John Brown community" today. Among my clergy brethren, I must also acknowledge the great kindness and support of Rev. Dr. Raymond Rivera of the Latino Pastoral Action Center and the Sanctuary Church of the Bronx, New York, Rev. Dr. Luis Carlo of the Alliance Theological Seminary, New York City campus, and Rev. Dr. Paul de Vries of the New York Divinity School. They have proven to be friends indeed, not only in the support they have extended to me and my family, but in their ongoing commitment to a Christian orthodoxy inclusive of justice and liberation.

Finally, to borrow from the words of Old Brown himself, "I do not forget the firm attachment of her who has remained my fast, & faithful affectionate friend," my wife Michele Sweeting DeCaro. In a very real way, she has graciously permitted John Brown to permanently reside in the house with our family, even when the expansive volumes, files, and demands of the study have tried her patience. Of course this book is dedicated to our young son who, no doubt, has gotten all his charm and sweetness from his mother.

Lou DeCaro, Jr.
Cathedral Parkway, New York City
July 12, 2006

Has John Brown no message—no legacy, then? He has and it is this great word: the cost of liberty is less than the price of repression . . . even though that cost be blood.

W. E. B. Du Bois (1909)[1]

This sketch of John Brown speaking with an elderly black man appeared in *Lippincott's Magazine of Popular Literature and Science* in August 1877, in a story by Lizzie W. Champney. This fictional account represents Brown's legendary forays into the South to move among black people. Of course this illustration could just as easily represent his factual associations in Ohio, Pennsylvania, New York, and other northern states.

1. The Man and His Times

As a boy growing up in the early 1800s, John Brown, who would one day raise a storm over the entire nation, raised a lot of dust and feathers on the Ohio frontier. Young John chased wild turkeys, hung around local Indians, played pranks, and always preferred his pet squirrel and livestock to his school books. His pious father and mother, Owen and Ruth Brown, had moved westward in 1805, taking their young family to settle on Connecticut's reserve lands in northeastern Ohio. As one of the first citizens of Hudson, Ohio, Owen embarked on a long and successful career as a tanner, real estate investor, and public servant. Like many Yankee settlers in Ohio, the Browns brought a strong sense of their Puritan tradition with them, including the spirituality of English Calvinism, the priority of education, and the centrality of family life. John would become a rough-hewn, wind-blown child of the frontier, but underlying his buck-skinned, calloused exterior was a strong sense of the literary and religious heritage that connected him to Puritan theologians and Pilgrim patriots.[2]

To understand Brown and his contemporaries, one must appreciate the degree to which religious ideas shaped the context of their lives and thinking. His own world was one of farms, fleeces, and hides, but it was also one of lengthy, well-studied sermons, high-minded theological debates, and informed political criticism. Most of all, his world was *theocentric*, a world where the existence of God was assumed—where the eyes of the divinity were thought to run "to and fro over the whole earth," and divine sovereignty was believed to have set the course of all that lives and dies, from the rise of the smallest ant hill to the fall of man's greatest empire, not to mention the eternal destiny of every living soul. Historians have often made negative remarks about Brown's religious ideas, implying that his faith was somehow twisted and inclined toward abuse. One such cynic writes that predestination "had dominated his behavior since adolescence," and that Brown thus "fashioned his life

after the Old Testament, interpreting its mysteries in his own way, trans-
lating them into his own acts through signs and omens, and often tor-
menting himself and others with his own indecision."[3]

Not only is this the stuff of fiction, but it overlooks the fact that many
of Brown's Protestant contemporaries held the same religious beliefs,
including the pious, slave-holding Presbyterians of the South. Indeed, if
John Brown has a militant Christian counter-part in the battle over slavery, it is Thomas "Stonewall" Jackson, one of the heroic Southern figures
of the Civil War. A devout Calvinist like Brown, Jackson was no less
convinced of divine sovereignty and predestination, though historians
have yet to suggest that he was warped because of it. (Prior to his famous
role as a Confederate military leader, Jackson was an eyewitness to
Brown's hanging in 1859, and afterward wrote a letter to his wife in
which he recounted watching him on the gallows, fervently praying for
the abolitionist just before the trap door swung open. "I sent up the peti-
tion that he might be saved," Jackson declared. "I hope that he was
prepared to die, but I am doubtful."[4] Of course Brown had no doubts
whatsoever.) Calvinists like Brown and Jackson were not slaves to deter-
minism or victims of fatalism. Nor did they believe in the violent, angry,
and loveless so-called "Old Testament God" often cited by historians.
Rather, John Brown's Calvinist theology was based on the idea of progressive revelation in Scripture, consisting of love and justice, law and
grace, and human responsibility as well as divine sovereignty.

We live in a society where religious culture is increasingly diverse,
though often tolerated more than celebrated. In Brown's time, however,
the United States was still quite centered in the evangelical Protestant
themes of its Puritan forebears. Not only was a majority of the population quite regular in church attendance, but the Bible was the thesaurus
of social and cultural discourse, and it was even common among scholars and orators to justify their arguments with biblical references. Abraham Lincoln was not unique in drawing ideas from the Bible, and his
audience would have immediately recognized that the theme of his
notable "House Divided" speech was a direct appropriation of the words
of Jesus in the Gospel of Matthew. Even opponents of orthodoxy, such
as spiritualists, were far more immersed in this biblical thought style
than are their modern counterparts. As Neil Postman observed, the
world of John Brown's era was yet a print-based society. Everything from
religion to advertisement was framed and defined by the written word.[5]
Like so many other prairie farmers in his era, he collected books and

journals as much as tools and trades. In 1845, Brown's favorite agricultural journal thus described the "model farmer"not only as a success in the field and fold, but as one with a "selected library" of several hundred well-read books, as well as subscriptions to literary, religious, and political publications.[6] Brown's resemblance to the "model farmer" was not unusual, essentially because his generation was steeped in the printed word, especially the Bible.

Just as the United States in the 19th century was brimming and bubbling with religious debates and camp meeting "revival" preaching, it was in a hot simmer over the dilemma of its own moral contradictions, specifically regarding the issue of black enslavement. Along with the pervasiveness of religion, John Brown grew up in the shadow of this smoking, political Vesuvius. Indeed, while 19th century religion was concerned for a variety of social and moral issues, the volcanic threat of slavery was the greatest challenge to the church. Whether or not conservative clergy or laity chose to acknowledge it, slavery was the issue of all issues, and it divided communities and religious denominations North and South long before the bloody schism of 1861.

To be sure, just as all southerners were not slave masters or abusive racists, most northerners were adamant racists, being quite hostile toward any kind of black presence in their communities. Our history teachers have not sufficiently informed us that black enslavement also existed in the North at one time, and some of the most racist attitudes prevailed in northern communities where slavery was being phased out by law in the early years of the 19th century. "The effacement of the memory of northern slavery has skewed American regional identities by exonerating white northerners and blaming white southerners," writes Nell Irvin Painter.[7] John Brown's native state of Connecticut was slow in ending slavery (it was not finally abolished there until 1848), and even slower in developing any kind of liberality toward black people.[8] Nevertheless, as he grew from boyhood to manhood, slavery was solidified as a southern political and economic institution. The growing debate regarding its expansion would rage throughout his formative years, and with each passing decade it actually seemed things were worsening for the prospect of black freedom.

Although it would take many years before the crisis came to an explosive conclusion in the Civil War, the preceding years were filled with fits of strife and bloodshed, as well as the high-pitched sermonizing and oratory of moral outrage on both sides of the issue. In an ongoing debate over the legitimacy of slavery, anti- and pro-slavery preachers clenched the Bible in a furious contest of tug-o-war. Meanwhile, southern statesmen were becoming increasingly loud, aggressive, and determined to have their way, ever pushing for the expansion of slavery's territory while threatening to rebel or secede. The prevailing inclination of northern politicians was to placate the South and seek compromises and conciliation toward the preservation of the Union. Furthermore, slavery also had many allies in the northern business community, who considered any criticism of the "peculiar institution" to be inflammatory. For instance, after the passing of the Fugitive Slave Act in 1850, one fugitive named Henry Long was captured in New York City, and eventually shipped back to the South in chains. Yet Long's alleged master first had to prove his case in court, and did so with the financial support of many from the New York City business community [Document 9].[9]

Slavery had its enemies too, particularly the abolitionist movement, which began as a besieged minority of unrelenting activists, often shouted down by those who advocated gradual emancipation and the colonization of blacks in other lands. Abolitionists were especially loathed for their incessant call for the immediate end of slavery. With few exceptions, they were advocates of the "moral suasion" doctrine, an ideology quite similar to the philosophy of non-violent resistance which prevailed among civil rights activists in the 20th century. Moral suasion suggested that slave holders were to be persuaded by moral conviction and by the tireless preaching, propagandizing, and suffering of the abolitionists. It was an idealistic, strongly religious movement that upheld the goodness of man and the belief that selfishness, oppression, and racism could be debated, disproved, and defeated according to the sheer force of righteous words and the example of martyred lives. John Brown may have flirted with these beliefs as a young man, but he never married them to his convictions. Indeed, throughout the years he grew increasingly critical of the pacifist philosophy, believing that the slave power would never be persuaded except by force.

While most northern states had devoted friends of black liberation, Ohio produced some of the most formidable and fiery enemies of slavery in the history of the United States. This was particularly true of the Western Reserve section, known for anti-slavery schools like Western Reserve College and the Oberlin Institute, and for the brilliant political gadfly of slavery, Congressman Joshua Giddings. Yet even in the more unlikely section of southern Ohio, there was a strong anti-slavery movement among Presbyterian ministers in the first half of the 19th century. This dynamic movement was personified by the Rev. John Rankin, who left the South to serve in the pastorate at Ripley, Ohio. Throughout the antebellum years, Rankin led vigorous campaigns against slavery, and was even immortalized as the abolitionist figure in Harriet Beecher Stowe's bestseller, *Uncle Tom's Cabin*.[10]

Though he never attained the stature of an anti-slavery leader, John's father, Owen Brown, was a humble but influential abolitionist in Ohio. He had been converted to Christianity and to the anti-slavery cause while still a young man in Connecticut, and brought his strong personal faith and uncompromising hatred of slavery with him to the frontier, settling in the blossoming community of Hudson. In its infancy, Hudson was a town of log cabins, exposed to the raw vibrance of the wilderness, and quite conscious of its vulnerability to attack from enemies as well as diseases that could suddenly sweep through a village without mercy. But Hudson, like the rest of the Western Reserve, grew quickly into a thriving image of its New England origins, always centered around church, education, and the determined pursuit of profit.

John Brown inherited his father's passion for independence in business, just as he emulated Owen's piety and commitment to Calvinist religion. Yet both were bound up with his father's pronounced anti-slavery convictions. In fact, except for his later determination to use force of arms, John was never more than his father's equal in terms of anti-slavery conviction. Owen's humble beginnings as a tanner and shoemaker, as well as his pronounced speech impediment, might have diminished him in the sight of some, but he was not to be underestimated. Even his writing, though fraught with spelling errors, belied a sharp mind, capable business style, savvy sense of humor, and a bold commitment to racial justice. According to Owen's memoir, in the early days of Hudson's settlement, he enjoyed friendly relationships with local Native Americans who traded venison, turkey, and fish for the white settlers' meal and bread. However he did not share the prejudice of some whites, of whom he wrote that they "seemed disposed to quarrel with the Indians," and was critical of policies that pressured their relocation, just as he deeply resented the hypocrisy of local whites who traded intoxicating beverages for Indian furs.

From the time of his conversion in the 1790s, Owen was nurtured in abolitionism through the influence of Congregational ministers in Connecticut who were the successors of the renowned Puritan preacher and scholar, Jonathan Edwards. Although they deviated somewhat from Edwards's Calvinist orthodoxy, it was their abolitionism, not their theological alterations, that marked young Owen's thinking. Having embraced traditional Puritan religion in a non-traditional way, his self-effacing piety and high reverence for God became inseparable from his devotion to black liberation. For Owen Brown, as it would also be for his son John, abolitionism was not simply about the end of slavery, but also the peace and well-being of black people. "I have no hatred to Negroes," he wrote many years later in his memoir—a significant statement in the mid-19th century, considering that many anti-slavery whites actually disdained black people.[11]

During John Brown's formative years, the most popular "solution" to the problem of slavery put forth by whites was the mass relocation of blacks to Africa and other lands. Led by the American Colonization Society (ACS), whites who held this view insisted that colonization was fair and benevolent, especially since blacks faced insurmountable inequities and injustices as long as they lived among whites. While black nationalists would later use a similar premise to justify a return to Africa, the prevailing sentiment of the colonization movement was essentially racist. The ACS not only held that the gap between whites and blacks was ordained by God, but they were also opposed to blacks receiving education and other equitable opportunities in society, measures they dismissed as hopeless. Far worse, many supporters of colonization even supported anti-black restrictions and other measures of disenfranchisement in the name of "inevitable necessity." In order to appease the prevalent racism of white society, colonizationists never supported civil rights in North America. Instead they held that slavery should be gradually abolished in deference to the economic interests of the slave holders.

The colonization philosophy was upheld by many antebellum statesmen, including James Madison, Andrew Jackson, Daniel Webster, Henry Clay, and Francis Scott Key, who penned the lyrics that later became the national anthem of the United States. Given his personal views on race, it is no surprise that even Abraham Lincoln was far more a colonizationist than he ever was an abolitionist, despite the Emancipation Proclamation and the 13th Amendment. In the antebellum years, when John Brown was still specializing in fine sheep and wool, the man who would be President was specializing in social segregation and his views fell in line with other anti-slavery colonizationists.[12] In light of the popularity of colonization, it is no wonder that abolitionists were so hated and vilified during in the first half of the 19th century, especially when they called for immediate emancipation and complete civil rights for black people. Although many of them were hardly egalitarian in practice, at least the abolitionists posed a provocative challenge to the racism of white colonizationists.

In Owen Brown's Hudson, most anti-slavery folks were sympathetic to colonization well into the late 1840s. However, abolitionism was steadily gaining strength, especially through the writings of Boston's William Lloyd Garrison, the flaming advocate of immediate emancipation and black equality. Garrison's *Liberator* and other abolitionist papers were often read by Ohio's abolitionists, including the Browns. In opposition to conservative colonization supporters, the Browns and a small number of families in Hudson stood firmly in the community as abolitionists, and Owen increasingly distinguished himself as an immediate emancipationist. He not only had some of his children enroll in the abolitionist Oberlin Institute, but served on the school's board despite his dissatisfaction with its semi-Calvinist innovations. Deeply devoted to the cause of black equality, he was far more active within the anti-slavery movement than his son John, who quietly refrained from joining the Ohio Anti-Slavery Society or any other abolitionist group.

As a youth, Owen had embraced immediate emancipation after reading an abolitionist pamphlet written by the son of his Puritan hero, though books and tracts alone cannot explain the zeal of conversion. In Owen's case, abolitionism seems to have found a connection to his own experience, particularly the brief but memorable childhood affection that he held for a solitary African. As Owen recounted the story, after his father had gone off to fight against the British in 1776, his mother was left alone to support the family and farm. Things only worsened when news came that her husband had died of illness in the field. Amidst her struggles to sustain the family, a slave holding neighbor loaned out a Guinean man, known only as Sam, to do the seasonal plowing for the Browns. Not more than five years old at the time, little Owen immediately attached himself to the friendly African. Strong and kindly, Guinean Sam would hoist the boy upon his shoulders, carrying him about while the child surveyed the world with a sense of wonder and security. "I fell in love with him," Owen wrote of his affection for Sam. Yet their bond was as brief as it was sweet, for he also recalled how Sam had become deathly ill after completing the plowing. When the boy finally called on him, the sickly man declared that he was going to die and was preparing for his journey home to Guinea. Owen recalled how Sam specifically asked to be buried with sufficient food for the sojourn, and remembered this incident as the first funeral that he had ever attended.[13] But along with the memory of this humble burial, he carried the poignant memory of this unfortunate African, who came to represent far more than a single victim of slavery. Again and again, Owen Brown would survey the world from the tired black shoulders of the oppressed and thus would ride upon the memory of Guinean Sam for the rest of his days as an outspoken, unrelenting enemy of slavery.

In his later years, John Brown also wrote a memoir of his childhood, although solely as a favor to the adolescent son of George L. Stearns, one of his greatest financial supporters [Document 1]. Some historians have labeled the 1857 essay as largely being a work of cunning, based upon the unflattering presumption that Brown was trying to manipulate the wealthy father through his impressionable young son. However, the evidence shows that Brown was asked to compose the memoir by the younger Stearns, and had to be further prodded by the elder Stearns before he completed the requested sketch. Had Brown been motivated by a selfish agenda, he would hardly have needed such prompting; and only after six months had passed did the younger Stearns finally receive Brown's autobiographical reminiscence.[14]

Writing of himself in the third person, John Brown tells a selective story of his early life, here and there granting glimpses of his childhood sins and sorties, from lying and theft to snowball fights and rambling "in the wild new country" of Ohio. Dressed in buckskin, young John could tan his own leather from any number of animal hides and soon overcame his fear of Indians, now preferring their company and even learning "a trifle of their talk."

Despite the negative reading of some scholars, the greatest motivation of his memoir was essentially evangelism John Brown style, since he wanted to encourage the young man's religious conversion as well as his devotion to the anti-slavery cause. Like other documents that Brown wrote, his autobiographical sketch is inevitably a Puritan work, focused upon the central themes of family, education, and religious life. Indeed, while entertaining his reader with snips and bits of his boyhood years, Brown eventually hones in on two major themes, the first of which is the great personal value of the Christian religion. Using the thread of spiritual discipline, he weaves a story of personal loss—especially the death of his mother when he was eight-years-old—that leads to an early conversion and a sober approach to life thereafter. Young John not only becomes an avid reader of good books, but a "firm believer in the divine authenticity of the Bible."

The other theme is the vocation of abolitionism, and like his father's reminiscences, John also carries a solitary black figure in the painful memory of his childhood. He thus writes that at the time of the War of 1812, John bravely herds some cattle about one hundred miles from home by himself, probably into the wilderness of Michigan. In fact, during the war, his father regularly sold "beef cattle" to the army and the episode that Brown recounts is undoubtedly related to Owen's business venture. Finding himself in the home of a kindly white host, young John is flattered and doted upon, while the same man turns ruthlessly upon an enslaved black youth. He is thus caught in an emotional and spiritual dilemma, since every "little act of kindness" toward him is matched by the violence, abuse, and insult heaped upon the black youth. The "*negro boy* (who was fully if not more than his equal)," Brown recalls, "was badly clothed, poorly feed, and *lodged in cold weather* and beaten" before his eyes. Paralyzed by the moral contradiction of the episode, John returns to Hudson contemplating "the wretched, hopeless condition of *Fatherless and Motherless slave children*," as he explains to young Stearns, "for such children have neither Fathers or Mothers to protect and provide for them." Indeed, young John then interrogates the very depths of his own soul by asking, "*Is God their Father?*"

Brown's intention is clear enough: he did not need to win young Stearns over to the anti-slavery cause because his parents were already die-hard New England abolitionists, and undoubtedly young Stearns was already exposed to the anti-slavery sentiments of his prosperous family. Yet as an abolitionist document, Brown's memoir was essentially challenging his young reader to take personal ownership of the cause. Like young Stearns, John had also been reared in a devout anti-slavery homestead, and just as he had been converted to Christianity for himself, he needed to embrace abolition for himself too. According to Brown, this tragic episode thus made young John "a most *determined Abolitionist* . . . and led him to declare or *Swear Eternal war* with slavery." Brown not only wanted young Stearns to buy into the abolitionist faith, but he wanted to remind him that blacks were not simply victims of whites, but equals to whites as well. "Now some of the things I have been *telling* of were just such as I would recommend to you," Brown adds, "and I would like to know that you had selected those out and adopted them as part of your own plan of life."

Although he overlooked the rigorous abolitionism of his home life in telling his story, Brown's autobiographical sketch rings true. The boy he portrays is much like the adult observed in so many scattered reminiscences of John Brown the abolitionist. Highly reserved but never unfriendly, he was comfortable in solitary moments, fond of Bible reading and prayer, largely self-motivated as a learner and worker, and quite drawn to fine livestock. He portrays young John as having a temper, which at its worst could be "haughty" and "obstinate," and also a tendency "to speak in an imperious or dictating way." Brown was honest enough in his self-portrayal, showing that along with his tendency toward reticence and sobriety, he also struggled with an inclination toward a kind of usurping arrogance. However much he was aware of this negative tendency in himself, it was a strong personality trait that he carried throughout life, and one that his critics have found easy to exaggerate to the detriment of his legacy.

In keeping with their determination to portray Brown as a troubled figure, those who have misrepresented his religious beliefs have also exaggerated his serious temperament to the point of suggesting he was a sociopath. One such critic thus describes him as having "no sense of humor, only a determined and self-righteous sense of justice straight out of the Old Testament." These kinds of cynical descriptions are often the mainstay in popular narratives, even though they are more like the distorted images of a trick mirror at an amusement park than sound reflections of historical fact. To be sure, John Brown was hardly a jovial man, nor was he given to outbursts of hilarity. In keeping with his reserved temperament, he tended to mute his own laughter, as observed by one of his hosts, Nellie Russell, the wife of a Boston judge. Recalling a particular moment when his amusement mounted, she said that he made "not the slightest sound, not even a whisper, or an intake of breath, but he shook all over," rocking and quaking with mirth "in utter silence."[15]

Like his manner of laughter, his sense of humor was equally peculiar, being both subtle and dry. Brown delighted in anecdotes but seems also to have liked word play, which allowed him to drop hints and make innuendos, the kind of humor that his black friends referred to as "signifying." His daughter Sarah long remembered an incident from her childhood, when Brown bought her a small patch of worsted scarlet for a doll dress. Ever the Puritan, her father made no secret of his dislike of bright-colored apparel, even on dolls. "I have heard of *crewel*," Brown said as he put the fabric against her doll. "I think *this* must be *murder*." Such were John Brown's puns, Sarah recalled, particularly in his inclination toward sarcasm. Nellie Russell from Boston recalled that Brown had "the keenest possible sense of humor, and never missed the point of a joke or of a situation," and was especially amused "by the blunders in the speech of uneducated tongues."[16] In one case he liked to tell the story of a simple country preacher whose sermon text was an obscure biblical verse about the use of badger skins as a covering for Israel's sacred tabernacle. As Brown's story went, the simple preacher mistook "badger" for "beggar," announcing that the poor man's skin was torn off and used to "*kiver that cussed* tabernacle!" Like Abraham Lincoln's celebrated sense of humor, Brown's enjoyment of fractured English was not condescending or malicious, but rather folksy, "jocose and mirthful."[17]

Examples of Brown's humor are also found in his correspondence, such as in a brief letter to Frederick Douglass, the African American abolitionist, with whom he had become quite close from the late 1840s. In 1858, after he had become engaged full-time in the anti-slavery cause, Brown wrote to Douglass requesting that he assist Harriet Tubman, the hero of the underground railroad, in raising one hundred dollars for family concerns. In jest, Brown signed the letter "Old Hundred," no doubt playing on his Kansas sobriquet, "Old Brown," and the name of a popular hymn based on the 100th Psalm [see Document 16]. Douglass could hardly have missed the fact that his blue-eyed amigo was doing a little "signifying." Far more interesting is the underlying humor of one of the pseudonyms used in his correspondence when he had become both a wanted man and a celebrated Kansas freedom-fighter. Throughout 1857, Brown used the name "Nelson Hawkins" to prevent pro-slavery agents and government officials from tracking and reading his mail. While historians have long recognized "Nelson Hawkins" as a *nom de guerre*, they have been oblivious to its underlying humor, the point of which probably raised a chuckle in the Brown family circle. In fact, the Browns realized what historians have heretofore missed, namely that Nelson Hawkins was a real person, an Ohio associate of Brown's elder married sons, Jason and John Jr. The real Nelson was a carpenter who lived in the vicinity and a made social visits to the Brown household in Akron. When Junior received letters from places like Iowa, Kansas, and Nebraska, all of which were signed, "Nelson Hawkins," he could hardly have missed the humor of his father's ploy.[18]

Just as many writers have wrongly denied Brown his sense of humor, they have mistaken his reserved, reticent manner for a kind of cold, hard nature, as if he were driven only by an obsessive, narcissistic hatred of slavery. Quite to the contrary, Brown's personal flame burned low but warm with human kindness, and it was as certain that he would show himself as compassionate as he was stern and stubborn. His Kansas associate James Blunt put it best in his description of Brown being "dignified and modest in manner" and never indulging in levity and "seldom seen to laugh." Yet in daily interaction "with all classes of people," he concluded, "he was as mild, kind, and sympathetic as the most refined and delicate woman." Blunt believed that no man had a "keener sense of right and justice" than John Brown.[19]

Indeed, he was far less inclined to raise a fist on his own behalf than he was to fight on behalf of the underdog. One episode from his Ohio years has become convoluted and somewhat untrustworthy, but the core narrative seems truthful enough as a witness to Brown's character. According to the story, when he was supervising the Perkins farm and flock in Akron in the early 1840s, he had a run-in with a local ruffian and thief. The man had stolen some fine sheep and Brown had confronted him about the crime. Resentful, the thief later came upon him unawares in the field and attacked him with some kind of lash or goad, wounding him to the point of drawing blood. But Brown suffered the abuse without fighting or seeking revenge, doing nothing except to file a complaint with a local constable after the fact.[20] Self-defense was a sacred calling, and one day he would go so far as to supervise the splitting of skulls in order to protect the innocent. Yet throughout his life, John Brown never fought, brawled, or retaliated out of prideful self-interest or political prejudice.

In autobiography, he portrayed young John as having been something of a tough prankster, who was *"excessively* fond of the *hardest & roughest* kind of play," such as wrestling, snowball fights, foot races, and knocking "old seedy Wool hats" off the heads of his playmates. Yet when Brown wrote that he was *"never quarrelsome"* as a boy, he was muting another aspect of his childhood temperament. In fact, from the time of his youth, he tended to manifest an intolerance toward bullying and other expressions of childhood injustice. He may not have been quarrelsome, but he did not stand passively aside amidst such tense but typical school yard incidents. His younger half-brother, Edward Brown, later recalled that his famous sibling "could never bear to see an older or larger boy bulldoze a smaller one, and has many times had fights over such cases." According to Edward, as John matured into young manhood, he "was noted in his neighborhood as a man who took up ever on the weaker side." Another sibling, one of his younger half-sisters, likewise spoke of Brown's "chief characteristic" as being a "remarkable sensitiveness to wrong and injustice." In later years, Brown would not only take up the cause of the fugitive slave, but would also involve himself in matters pertaining to justice for frontier settlers and farmers. No doubt, his siblings were put off by his ultimate resort to violence at Harper's Ferry, just as they were shocked into despair by his failure and execution. Yet it was no surprise that their brother John so despised the monstrous system of black enslavement that he would give his life in fighting it. "He saw in slavery simply an opportunity to exercise the characteristic of his nature," Edward later concluded. "He felt that it was a great duty that was incumbent upon him to fight this in every way he could."[21]

2. The Real Story of Businessman Brown

Few notable figures in the history of the United States have had their pre-public lives so distorted, exaggerated, and subjected to caricature as has the businessman who became John Brown of Harper's Ferry. To be sure, this is reflective of the unstudied liberties that historians have become accustomed to taking with his story, largely because there is no consensus of fairness with respect to Brown in either the academy or the media. For instance, a noted scholar recently accused him of manifesting an "unslakable thirst for violence" as well as a "rage at the modern."[22] In fact, neither charge is true, nor do such claims reflect a responsible approach to the historical record, but rather an inclination toward the game of rhetoric-and-innuendo born of personal bias. Of course, the dubious charge that Brown manifested a thirst for bloodshed has been an obvious staple of many white scholars for over a century, and is easily disproven in any responsible biography. However the notion that he manifested a "rage at the modern" is about as novel as it is inane.

Certainly, as belief in human equality goes, John Brown was not only modern, he was far in advance of most white people in his age.[23] But even as a farmer and businessman, it is also true that he was *essentially modern* and in his own way greeted scientific and technological developments with interest. Perhaps the popular but erroneous notion that Puritans were backward and narrow-minded people is partly to blame here.[24] To the contrary, they were essentially forward-looking people with a robust appreciation for life and an interest in advancements in business and culture, as reflected by their many accomplishments as institution-builders in North America. It was no accident that the second astronomical observatory in the United States was constructed in Brown's hometown of Hudson, Ohio, on the campus of Western Reserve College.[25] The so-called "rage at the modern" that allegedly typifies anarchists and fundamentalists was not an issue for 19th century Calvinists, including John Brown. Notwithstanding his three-hundred-year-old Protestant theology, he was typical of the vibrant interest in scientific progress which prevailed among the Puritan seed of the antebellum era. "I very much dislike the too common practice of undertaking to enlighten the world with the results of experiments not fully made, and of undertaking to instruct others before we half understand what we write about ourselves," he declared in 1846, in an article describing his successful experimentation in the treatment of infested sheep.[26] Despite the style of his appearance, which some found reminiscent of an earlier time, Brown was a forward-looking man who took advantage of whatever new developments emerged in the antebellum era. If the advent of the railroad, as Peter Drucker has written, "was the truly revolutionary element of the Industrial Revolution," creating a new "mental geography" in the United States, then Brown was a willing beneficiary of that revolution. Indeed, he was one of the first trans-continental activists to operate according to this new "mental geography," not only traveling on the railroads, but making good use of print and photographic media as well.[27]

Similarly, his business misfortunes have often been magnified as a pretense toward discrediting his character and later anti-slavery activity. Popular narratives have commonly included the notion that Brown's failures in business fed into his "rage" at slavery, and fueled his advance into abolitionism. "Every venture failed, for he was too much a visionary, not enough a businessman," goes one such version. "As his financial burdens multiplied, his thinking became increasingly metaphysical and he began to brood over the plight of the weak and oppressed." Another concludes: "But in fighting slavery Brown had one last chance to prove himself the consummate, albeit bloodthirsty, manager . . . he would control the destinies of others though he realized he'd lost control of his own."[28] In the 20th century alone such poisonous portrayals are so prevalent as virtually to have formed one long screed of hyperbole and sarcasm in the name of historical narrative.

To no surprise, Brown's business failures, as negatively portrayed by conventional historians, stand as the antithesis of Abraham Lincoln's personal and professional failures, which span employment loss and political defeats—the latter ranging from his failure to win a seat in the state legislature in 1832, to his disappointed senatorial campaign of 1858.[29] Invariably, the legend of "Lincoln's failures" has functioned as a model of personal upliftment and inspiration, and the mark of nobility and determination of character, while Brown's failures are rehearsed *ad infinitum* as a tale of flawed character and ill-starred destiny. In reality, Lincoln and Brown faced a number of setbacks and personal disappointments and both may be credited for strength of character and determination. However, Lincoln was a lawyer with aspirations to political advancement and access to influential people, and the trajectory of his career must be measured in terms of the resources and benefits that he increasingly enjoyed as a result of his political associations and alliances. In contrast to the Lincoln legend, businessman Brown was far more representative of the "common man" of the antebellum era, and the story of his struggles and failures should be appreciated for the determination, optimism, and energy it represents on behalf of a whole class of struggling farmers and prairie yeomen.

To be sure, Brown's business life was hardly brilliant, and one of his former associates was probably right to charge that he was a "visionary," which in the 19th century meant that he was a dreamer. Another admiring colleague wrote: "I don't think he would wilfully overstate his business, but he would likely build some air castles and thereupon through his enthusiasm set things up fully as high as they would stand." Furthermore, Brown could be quite hard-headed and not easily inclined toward taking counsel, and none of this served his interests as a tradesman. He was "hard and inflexible," recalled one of his associates, and despite his discipline and honesty, he was neither a "trader" nor "a regular-bred merchant."[30] Yet his business record is not all foible and failure, and it is evident that he had a Puritan's nose for opportunity. Under the right economic circumstances, and with the right kind of guidance and support, businessman Brown might actually have done fairly well. Unfortunately, historians tend to gloss over this significant phase of his life, preferring to summarize it in simplistic, unstudied terms reflective of presumption and prejudice—usually with the intention of diminishing the man's social and political judgment. The preeminent documentary scholar, Boyd Stutler, recognized this trend, writing in 1958 that no "adequate study" had been made of his affairs. "As a matter of fact," Stutler continued, Brown's "transactions followed the pattern of his time, plus, of course, the impress of his positive character. He lived in an age of speculation; bankruptcy was not uncommon, and was not considered a stain upon the moral character."[31]

Thus far even Brown's friendliest biographers (myself included) have not sufficiently placed him in the economic, regional, and social context of the antebellum agrarian and manufacturing arenas. Like a plot marked off for future archaeological study, we have only sampled the story of businessman Brown in small slices, and only now have begun to inquire about the extent to which his failures reflected conditions and forces outside of his control. Without denying his shortcomings and errors as well as the desperate groping that nearly took him off the course of his own moral charting, it is time that he be reassessed in a fair light. In fact, it is historically irresponsible to continue reiterating the traditional half-truths and distortions regarding Brown's failed businesses, particularly as they have been used as a pretense to misrepresent his later life and activities in opposition to slavery.

Brown's business life can be examined in three phases: The first phase entails his upwardly moving activities in Ohio and Pennsylvania between 1818 and 1835. During this period he emancipated himself from his father's household, established a tannery business, married and fathered children, and then ventured into northwestern Pennsylvania, where he spent most of a decade as a modestly successful and influential figure. The second phase, roughly from 1835–42, was typified by a variety of business ventures, many of them running concurrently and none of them successful. Although a time of lofty visions and bold forays, it proved to be a period of great difficulty, misfortune, and personal loss for Brown—undoubtedly a time of crisis which, in its most shadowed hours, even made death seem a sweet release.[32] Finally, the third phase (examined in the next section) was from 1844 through 1854, when he was the partner of the wealthy Simon Perkins of Akron, Ohio. In this final episode of his business life, he almost broke even despite the legendary failure of the Perkins-Brown venture.

Teenage John briefly pursued the pastoral calling of the church but ultimately found himself better fitted for the literal pastoral role of the flock and farm. After his conversion at fifteen, his brief stint as a pre-ministerial student in Connecticut was undermined by an economic downturn and an inflammation of the eyes, which plagued him off and on throughout his life. According to Brown's brief memoir, this problem had begun while he was still a minor, and had greatly inhibited his primary study.[33] No doubt believing that divine providence had redirected his path, instead John focused his youthful energies on tannery work, a craft he had eagerly learned from his father. In 1818, he moved out of his father's house and entered his first business partnership with Levi Blakeslee, his elder foster brother. The Brown-Blakeslee enterprise in Hudson went well, the two bachelors living in a cabin on what is now

Hinds Hill Road, which John later replaced with a frame house after marrying Dianthe Lusk in 1820.[34] Young Brown was ambitious and self-assured, and the promise of greener pastures undoubtedly compelled him to pull up stakes in Ohio and set off for the raw wilderness of north-western Pennsylvania. In 1826, probably against the preference of his ailing wife, he moved his family (now including three young sons) to Crawford County, settling about twelve miles from the burgeoning town of Meadville.[35]

The move to Pennsylvania in 1826 was perhaps based upon the encouragement of a kinsman from eastern Ohio named Seth Thompson, both men believing that the wilderness offered good opportunities for the enterprising and the godly. The Brown-Thompson venture was an interstate effort that involved the establishment of a formidable tannery and leather business in Pennsylvania, as well as a depot for the conveying and sale of livestock from Ohio's Western Reserve. It was no small undertaking for a man of twenty-six years, and Brown carried it off quite well. In a short time he cleared, settled, and established his home and business on a 200-acre tract of densely-wooded forest land in New Richmond Township, near Clark's Corners, a stage stand on a simple state road running up from Meadville. Close proximity to the thriving town gave him the best of both worlds—the natural timber resources of the wilderness so necessary for his tannery operation and the commercial networking and social connections that would allow him to rise to a respectable position in the vicinity. Over the nine years that Brown lived in Crawford County, he sustained a reasonably good business profile despite the challenges and uncertainties of the national economy in the 1830s. His difficulties in this period have also been exaggerated by his recent biographer, who says Brown was a "bumbling capitalist" with no head for business of any kind, but mainly enjoyed tanning hides because it gave him the opportunity to "live around animals and have the sense of being a shepherd like the prophets of old." To the contrary, Brown not only had strong professional ability but he was hardly playing the role of the shepherd in Pennsylvania, where he was dealing mainly in hides and cattle.[36]

Local scholars have fairly well documented Brown's accomplishments in conquering the wilderness land and setting up his tannery operation in northwestern Pennsylvania, particularly his business leadership and endowment of learning, religion, and civic contribution in his rural township.[37] For the record, he not only managed and trained employees, but promoted their cultural upliftment by reading and intellectual exchange (an exercise he would always promote among his anti-slavery guerillas in later years). Brown likewise organized a Congregational church (1832), served as a trustee for the keeping of state road maintenance (1833), and was the postmaster and mail carrier for the Randolph stop (from January 1828 to May 1835), which entailed a weekly round-trip of about thirty-five miles on horseback. He effectively juggled the demands of business and home along with these obligations, and likewise was responsible for introducing fine blooded livestock into the region as well as additional acts of charity and religious service.[38]

As an upwardly mobile figure in Crawford County, Brown consistently traded on his high character ratings, which almost became legendary in the community.[39] Although he never became wealthy during his Pennsylvania years, it was an era when reputation and character were a kind of collateral in the business community and his good reputation extended into neighboring Meadville, which was hardly a one-horse town. Historian Anne Stewart points out that in Brown's era, Meadville was a well-established center for the northwestern part of the state, hosting the seat of the Sixth Judicial District, a state arsenal, a number of schools (including a college), and three major libraries.[40] Those who take Brown for a "bumbling capitalist" need to take a closer look at the record, particularly the fact that the local Democratic Party actually nominated him as their candidate for county auditor in 1834. In keeping with a pattern of stubborn independence that characterized his life-long *modus operandi*, Brown declined the nomination; it seems he never supported a party or a presidential candidate after John Quincy Adams, who was a strong opponent of slavery.[41] Yet the point remains that businessman Brown's intelligence, honesty, and professionalism qualified him as a worthy community figure, and one who frequently worked at the grassroots level of civic and religious service.

Like many others in the western states during the mid-1830s, when John Brown got caught up in the land speculation boom, he overestimated the economy and relied too heavily on credit. He had never intended to be reckless. In fact, the most likely reason for his return to Ohio in 1836 was the flattering invitation of Zenas Kent, a prominent figure in Franklin Mills [present day Kent], who knew of Brown's solid reputation and solicited him to become a business partner in a proposed tannery operation. Given the exciting canal developments in Ohio, Brown quite reasonably saw greater chances for success back in his home state, and he probably returned with a strong interest in the high-profit arena of land speculation. However the partnership with Kent was dissolved before it had even begun. Just as Brown completed the construction of the tannery site, Kent decided to rent out the facility to his son instead.[42]

Rather than being terribly disappointed, he threw himself eagerly into land speculation and construction in Franklin Mills, primarily intent upon canal-related projects. Public transportation projects were booming in the frontier states in this period, and private stock companies were formed to undertake these new ventures with state funds. A major endeavor in this era involved linking the Pennsylvania and Ohio canal systems, and he was undoubtedly talking up the possibilities of investing in related projects to his family and associates in Ohio, including partner Seth Thompson. A number of sources attest to the fact that Brown took some kind of construction contract on the Pennsylvania and Ohio canal system and that he was also looking to invest in "wildcat" projects, such as an extension of the canal from Akron to Franklin Mills.[43] Having borrowed a significant sum of money, he also purchased a large farm that he intended to parcel out for sale, as he had done with his Pennsylvania property.[44] He also bought land and erected office buildings in Franklin Mills that would turn a fine profit once the canal was operative.[45]

Initially, Brown seems to have succeeded in these projects, but in 1838 he wrote to a Meadville associate that he had "made money rather too quickly" in 1835–36. Indeed, his wealth was essentially based on bank notes and credit, and with the Panic of 1837 (which Brown called "the change in the times"), his efforts were considerably stunted. Still, he pressed on, further and further into credit debt, anticipating a breakthrough in the economy and a harvest of wealth with the completion of his canal and construction projects. "We in this country feel now in hope that another year will effectually relieve us," he wrote in mid-1838 [Document 3].[46]

Unfortunately, the financial situation only worsened, not just for Brown but for many others hoping to have made their fortunes in the ill-fated boom of the 1830s. As monies for canal projects dried up, other real estate ventures likewise suffered, and he was left with debt and lawsuits for unpaid notes, wages, and money due on accounts. According to one source, the records of the Common Pleas Court at Ravenna, Ohio, showed twenty-one different law suits in which Brown was the defendant, either by himself or with partners. Ever the optimist, he pushed forward, along with partner Thompson, hoping to redeem himself by marketing western cattle in Connecticut. Meanwhile he was devising other means for a successful business start-up, such as the purchase of a mill in the town of Franklin Mills. In late 1838, Brown was in Connecticut, hopeful of obtaining funds. "I am useing [sic] every exertion to obtain a loan in this quarter and have considerable hope of final success," he wrote to Thompson. "There is no want of money here for good names, for any length of time." Writing from Connecticut the following spring, he reported that cattle sales had only been moderate, and now he was looking toward banks in Boston to obtain much-needed cash. By the summer of 1839, however, things had only gotten worse. Brown returned from New England empty-handed, with fading hope of obtaining money from eastern banks. "The prospect is rather dark however," he wrote to Thompson. "I have made every exertion in my power to extricate ourselves from the difficulty we are in, but have not yet been able to effect it." Still, he had not given up, although admitting he felt "rather more depressed than usual."[47]

From this point, Brown's story spirals downward with increasing speed and sorrow. Facing overwhelming debt and legal challenges, he became desperate. In 1839, beside his taxes and business expenses, he had ten children to feed and clothe, including three teens and seven other children ranging from newborn to ten years of age. Having obtained a sizable cash purse from a New England firm expressly for the purchase of western cattle, Brown convinced himself that he could use this money to pay debts and taxes and then return it from the bank loan he expected from Boston. This was his moral nadir as a merchant. Despite his good intentions, he lost control and nearly wrecked his reputation, which was the one great asset that had remained intact. His resort to what Boyd Stutler called "very questionable expedients" only made matters worse, and he continued to juggle other people's money until the least of his worries was debt. Fortunately for Brown, his associates in Ohio and in the east trusted him; when he finally owned up to his abuse of funds, he was treated with leniency [Document 4].

All in all, the record of John Brown's loans, debts, and lawsuits is overwhelming and complicated for the historian. What makes this chapter of his life all the more difficult is the fact that he continued to knock on virtually any door of opportunity, from cattle sales to breeding race horses, and from tannery partnerships to land settlement schemes and other ventures, always expecting something of a break-through. "Notwithstanding all our difficulties," Brown preached to an ailing Thompson in a letter written in 1840, "let us trust in him who hears the young ravens when they cry, & hath sustained us, & our families hitherto."[48]

Historians thus blame Brown for his misfortunes in 1837–42, rather simplistically concluding that his ruin was largely due to his own folly. In his defense, however, we have not paid sufficient attention to his economic context and have therefore erred in three ways. First, his financial difficulties have been presented almost as in a vacuum, as if his failure was the unfortunate exception among his peers. Yet financial failure and bankruptcy were quite common in Brown's time, especially in the western states where specie was limited, counterfeit bank notes were common, and credit-based speculation prevailed in the later 1830s. According to Thomas Vince, an authority on the history of Ohio's Western Reserve, almost every wealthy family in Hudson had business problems in the 1830s. For instance, Harvey Baldwin, the son-in-law of Hudson's founder, failed in business. "He invested great money in railroads in the early 1850s," says Vince, "but Baldwin and every important family in Hudson lost money in this endeavor." All too often, Brown is not viewed in relation to these peers and contemporaries, but instead is held up as if he was the only one to fumble and fail in business endeavors. "Nobody points a finger at Baldwin and every prominent family," concludes Vince. "There were hundreds of lawsuits due to this failure. Yet the Hudsons are not dismissed as failures."[49]

Secondly, those who diminish Brown often overlook the fact that modern businessmen have access to more federal resources, safeguards, and legal protection than businessmen in the antebellum era could ever have imagined. For instance, between 1836 and the Civil War years there was no national banking system, no single currency, and far less security with respect to the integrity of paper money. As Larry Lawrence, chairman of the John Brown Society has observed, modern business people have access to valuable safety nets, such as insurance and limited liability corporations and partnerships. "Even deposits in banks were not protected until the 20th century," he concludes. "It's highly unfair to single out any one individual for criticism in the context of the pre-Civil War world." Indeed, the sharp contrast between Brown's era and our own goes to the very marrow of economic assumption, including how the value of money is determined. "In our society today, money's value is measured by what it can buy—its purchasing power," writes an official from the Federal Reserve, "not by its material worth."[50] Finally, economies and economic essentials varied widely according to region, not only according to the availability of banks and specie, but also with respect to how regional banks and markets experienced crisis and comeback in this era. While biographers have passingly acknowledged the Panic of 1837 in recounting Brown's misfortunes, they have not adequately developed antebellum economic history, thus failing to differentiate the Panic from the later Crisis of 1839, which was Brown's real undoing.[51]

According to economic historian John Wallis, the Panic of 1837 and the Crisis of 1839 were two very different downturns in Brown's world. The Panic occurred as a result of domestic and foreign influences, and was largely felt in the eastern states, but especially in New York City and New Orleans, the major ports for the international cotton trade. Wallis says that while the Panic was felt throughout the nation, a decline in specie, loans and discounts, and deposits was much worse in the east than in the south and west. In nearly every aspect, it was more severe for northeastern banks than for western banks in 1837. On the other hand, the Panic was quickly remedied by federal measures, which then elicited remedial measures from the British banks with respect to the cotton markets of the United States, further encouraging a quick recovery. In fact, due to the regional impact of the Panic, as well as the successful manner in which the eastern economy bounced back in 1837–38, many businessmen in the west, including John Brown and his associates, did not actually experience a real financial "panic" as historians have supposed.

Wallis shows that as the economy made a comeback between 1837 and 1839, there was a tremendous amount of state borrowing of money in order to build canals, banks, and railroads in the western states. This casts "substantial doubt on the idea that Americans thought the Panic of 1837 was the beginning of a serious economic downturn," Wallis observes. "States throughout the country went right on borrowing, Panic or no Panic." Brown's home states of Ohio and Pennsylvania were already among the heaviest borrowers, and while the east was experiencing an economic trauma in 1837, these and other states in the south and west were experiencing a boom. As the government sold millions of acres in the farthest western states, this increased federal grants returned to the states, which then stimulated even more state investments. John

Brown's Ohio, like other heavy-borrowing states, expanded its substantial investments, which attracted both domestic and foreign lenders. Consequently, after 1837, the land boom was further bolstered by canal and railroad construction, which in turn engendered greater public confidence. In this light, it is understandable why Brown neither felt the crunch of the Panic nor perceived the dangers that lay ahead. The eastern banks had come back quickly, and Brown could write to his partner back in Ohio by late 1838 with an air of confidence. There was money enough in the east, there was a boom in the west, and there was yet every reason to believe that he and Thompson could make a good thing despite the setback since things were bound to improve.

Rather than improve, however, things turned ugly in 1839 as a result of what Wallis calls "an American cycle of events." Along with a number of other states, Ohio had formerly issued bonds through various agencies, such as canal boards or land companies (including John Brown's Franklin Land Company). These agencies then placed the bonds in banks or with individuals, which were then sold for cash on commission. However, after the Panic of 1837, tightening markets for bonds in western states made them harder to sell at par, which Brown himself noted late in 1838, while trying to raise funds back in Connecticut. Writing to partner Thompson, he complained that "the only difficulty is in useing our Western securities." When banks in Ohio and other western states found it difficult to redeem their bonds, they increasingly began to deal in credit, an economic pattern which seems to have filtered downward into the business economy, proving to be a snare for Brown and other merchants. The state of Ohio had borrowed heavily and now found itself with enormous debt. Unable to meet their obligations, western banks overreached and defaulted on their obligations to the states, which "set in motion the events that became the Crisis of 1839."

Since banks in the south and west were too closely tied to state government finances, when state governments began to suffer, the money supply also declined sharply, resulting in a loss of confidence in the banks. Without depositor confidence, "banks collapsed in the south and west, but not in the northeast." In contrast to the Panic two years before, Ohio and other western states experienced heavy losses in specie holdings, loans and discounts, and deposits in 1839–40. As banks in the northeast were on their way to recovery, banks in the outlying states were now struggling with reductions. The huge fall in deposits was particularly ominous since deposits "are the measure that best captures public confidence in the banks." In fact, between January 1839 and January 1841, the national money supply declined by 22-percent, and banks in the south and west bore the brunt of this loss, since 80-percent of the decline was regional.[53] These factors, and not mere bad judgment, brought John Brown's business venture crashing down in 1839, and the dark prospects of which he wrote that year were only the beginning of a downturn in the frontier economy of the United States.

Furthermore, other circumstances, all of them out of his reach, were significant in shaping the outcome. For instance, an Ohio historian claims that his plans for canal-related ventures in Franklin Mills were inadvertently undermined by special interests based in Akron. Another source connects Brown's misfortunes with the failure of a broader program that was calculated by community leaders to make Franklin Mills into an industrial center. Yet another points out that Brown's plans were simply in advance of the times, and that had he come along in the railroad era of the 1860s and 70s, his speculations "would probably have made a fortune for him and those who invested with him." Whatever the case, John Brown was bankrupt by 1842. As he described it later, this was a time of "poverty, trials, discredit, & sore afflictions." Years later he wrote to his wife Mary, saluting her faithfulness in the shadowed days "when others said of me, 'now that he lieth, he shall rise up no more'"[53] [Document 5].

3. The Hard Lessons of Capitalism

Virtually flattened, nevertheless he arose, hoisting himself up with the tools and skills that he knew best, as well as his amazingly well-preserved reputation. In fact, the key figure in Brown's come-back was one of his unfortunate former lenders, the wealthy Heman Oviatt of Richfield, Ohio, who invited him to keep his vast flock of sheep. Despite having lost $6000, Oviatt maintained that Brown was "thoroughly honest" and that his failures in business were not as significant as his abilities and character. Brown seized upon the opportunity, which also included the development of a productive tannery operation in Richfield, and their partnership began to prosper. Redeeming himself from economic despair, Brown was increasingly attentive to the care and breeding of quality livestock, an interest he had somewhat neglected while in Pennsylvania. Indeed, from the early 1840s, he became quite passionate about improving breeds of fine sheep and wool. As he studied and experimented, the Oviatt flock began to prosper in productivity and reputation, which proved more than a balm to Brown's bruised ego. It was during this period that he began to travel to other counties and states, looking up various sheep farms to interview the wool-growers and study their flocks, often purchasing quality livestock for his partner or himself.[54] Yet there were greener pastures before him.

In late 1843, the magnate Simon Perkins Jr. of Akron, Ohio, contacted Brown with a proposition. Perkins had heard of his reputation and success and wanted Brown's expertise for his own farm and flocks. For one so embarrassed and bankrupt two years before, this must have seemed like a promotion of biblical proportions to Brown, one which virtually erased his former misfortunes in the minds of all but his worst critics. The new partnership afforded him a substantial income and rent-free housing on the Perkins estate. "I think this is the most comfortable and the most favorable arrangement of my worldly concerns that I have had," Brown wrote to John Jr. in January 1844. Oviatt was an extremely prosperous businessman, but Perkins was virtually Ohio royalty. Having inherited a fortune, he had also married into the renowned Tod family and had a number of business ventures and speculations under his belt, including part ownership of a multi-site wool manufacturing establishment in Akron. An alliance with such a man not only empowered Brown to expand his research and development of fine sheep and wool, but inevitably broadened his exposure and heightened his dreams. Throughout 1844–46, he looked beyond the immediate concerns of management and concentrated on improving the Perkins flock through an extensive and carefully studied plan. No doubt persuaded by Brown's strategy, Perkins funded his partner's travels throughout eastern Ohio, western Pennsylvania, western Virginia, and finally into the northeast and New England. In 1845–46, Brown repeatedly declared that he had "traveled Tens of Thousands of miles in the search after the best flocks," covering much of the country "time after time, beginning with Vermont and New Hampshire, and ending with Virginia."[55] Later in life a grumpy Simon Perkins expressed contempt for Brown's militant efforts against slavery and also blamed him for the failure of P&B. But these claims run contrary to the evidence of his warm support of Brown at the time.

Brown's contribution to the sheep and wool-growing industry in the antebellum era is all but forgotten in the annals of agricultural history in the United States. This is likely because of his subsequent controversial role as an anti-slavery guerilla, which no doubt scandalized many former business colleagues and associates, including the conservative Perkins. Yet Brown's leadership in the 1840s, especially among the thriving wool-growers in the western states, is a matter of record. Besides references to his partnership with Perkins, many of his letters and evaluations are published in a variety of agricultural journals from that period including the *Maine Farmer*, the *American Agriculturalist* and the *Cultivator* (New York), the *Ohio Cultivator*, the *Prairie Farmer* (Illinois), *The Plough, the Loom, and the Anvil* (Pennsylvania), and undoubtedly others [Document 6]. When an influential sheep farmer published his proposal for a national convention and competition, the editor of *The New England Farmer* advised that John Brown should sit as one of the three principle judges. He not only conducted experiments for cures and treatments but prescribed improved techniques for preparing wools for market, always leading by the example of his own hard work and success. In September 1847, M. B. Bateham, editor of the *Ohio Cultivator*, included a report of his own traveling inspection of flocks in the Buckeye State, concluding that the "Perkins & Brown sheep . . . are without doubt the finest in staple of any large flock in Ohio, if not in the Union." To underscore the point, Bateham added a glowing letter from Samuel Lawrence of Lowell, Massachusetts, perhaps the foremost wool manufacturer in the nation. "Mr. Brown's wool has ever been of the highest character, since he first brought it here; but this year it has amazed us," Lawrence declared. "I have said to Mr. Brown, what I sincerely believe, that if he will go on a few years more, he will have a better breed of sheep than are now in existence."[56]

But as he waded knee-deep through an ocean of North American wool, it did not take long for him to observe and evaluate the system operating below the surface. Ever the reformer, his interaction with wool-growers throughout the nation left him increasingly disturbed by the common complaints and criticisms they expressed toward the manufacturers. Even though he fairly recognized that the betterment of the wool industry would require efforts and sacrifices on both sides of the issue, Brown began to suspect that factory owners like Lawrence were talking more about cooperation between growers and manufacturers than they were actually promoting it with real policy. Indeed, he had not only waded into a sea of wool, but was now caught in the depths of a problem that was well over his head. His attempt to resolve that problem on behalf of the wool-growers would prove to be both his foremost contribution to the industry as well as the beginning of his final failure in business.

After the Revolutionary War, the wool manufacturers of the United States were determined to control their own destinies and recoup the losses resulting from British colonialism, and often did so to the disadvantage of the wool-growers. Initially, sharp price differentials were enforced against poorly prepared domestic wools; then the government enacted tariffs which protected the manufacturers but exposed the sheep farmers to low-cost competition from other wool-producing nations. These disparities engendered cynicism, distrust, and a lack of cooperation among the wool-growers, and a legacy of tension and a lack of cooperation between them and the manufacturers developed. One source of this conflict centered around the time-consuming and costly process of cleaning and preparing wools for market. When the growers provided clean wools, the manufacturers did not compensate them for the expense of labor and the loss due to wool shrinkage. In order to evade these losses many wool-growers simply packaged dirty and ill-prepared wools for market, enjoying better profits up-front. However this practice increasingly diminished the reputation of domestic wools abroad, which ultimately weighed against them when new wool-producing nations began to enter the market in the 1840s. These new foreign wools were stringently cleaned and packaged, presenting a substantial market alternative to buyers and manufacturers in the United States and in Europe.[57] As Brown undoubtedly realized, the rise of these new market sources was a serious blow to the often embarrassed wool-growers of the United States.

Prominent leaders among the wool-growers, including Brown, recognized that they had to address the problematic manner in which domestic wools were sent to market before they could make demands of the manufacturers. Consequently this was one of the major issues of a significant convention of producers which met in Steubenville, Ohio, in February 1847. This historic series of discussions and reports was the first interstate meeting of its kind and included extensive presentations and inquiries into a variety of themes. As a driving force of the convention, Brown prepared a detailed report describing an expedient method of washing and preparing wools without impurities. This was neither quaint nor trivial, but a significant factor in the minds of the most progressive leaders among the wool-growers. "A disregard of these little things," Brown preached to farmers from Ohio, Pennsylvania, and western Virginia, "is the greatest hindrance to the sale of American wools in England or France." He lectured further that they did not realize the injury that many wool-growers had done to their own cause by the "shameful, dishonest" practice of sending out wools loaded with dirt and foreign matter as a means of increasing the weight at market. To underscore the urgency of the theme, this report was published along with other convention matter in the *Ohio Cultivator*. Unfortunately for Brown and other activists in the wool-growing community, this problem continued to prevail for generations afterward.[58]

As partners, Perkins and Brown are unacknowledged forerunners in the efforts of the sheep and wool industry of the United States, particularly in their having founded one of the "three principal wool depots" in the country in 1846. Like his social views, Brown's attempt to organize the wool growers was well in advance of his peers. For instance, there was no state association of wool-growers until 1860, when they were effectively organized in California. Nor was there a national organization until just after the Civil War, when sheer necessity prompted the

wool-growers to unify in order to meet with the well-organized manufacturers. In fact, the 1846 venture of Perkins and Brown into the wool
commission business, though famously failed and often misrepresented
by scholars, was a visionary attempt to organize and advocate on behalf
of wool-growers across state lines, and apparently the first effort on
behalf of the burgeoning western sheep farmers. Unfortunately, prejudice and the failure of historical memory have slighted Brown's efforts
on behalf of wool-growers in Ohio, Pennsylvania, and West Virginia. It
was not until 1918 when producers from this region were collectively
mature enough to envision and accomplish what he had attempted over
seventy years before.[59]

The "Perkins & Brown Commission Wool House" (P&B) was
announced in fliers and advertisements in agricultural journals during
the spring and summer of 1846. P&B offered to receive clients' wool
shipments, sort and class their product, and then seek out the best buyers and markets on their behalf on a cash-only basis. As Boyd Stutler
writes, "Brown was deeply in earnest about the wool reforms" and threw
himself into the effort sincerely believing that he would find the manufacturers cooperative for the benefit of the nation, just as he expected the
wool-growers to be supportive and disciplined on behalf of their own
cause. This was an error, especially with respect to the paternalistic manufacturers who had lauded his wool and pretended an affinity to, if not
a dependence upon, the wool-growers.[60]

One of the major criticisms applied to Brown, even by his warmest
biographers, has been his hard-headed and inflexible manner of grading
the wools for sale. "He made his gradings, fixed his prices and that was
it," wrote Stutler. "[T]he buyer could take the wool or leave it." His critics, like the prosperous merchant Aaron Erickson of Rochester, New
York, went further by making light of Brown's belief that the wool-
growers were being undermined by improper grading. Erickson likewise
ridiculed his judgment and ability as a wool-grader.[61] Notwithstanding
his shortcomings as a merchant, grading wools for pricing was both an
economic and political issue, and it is clear that Brown had taken the
manufacturing bull by the horns. The idea that the wool-growers themselves might assume the task of grading and pricing their product was a
fundamental threat to the system upon which the manufacturers had
built their industry.

Despite his self-assured claims to having had ample experience in the
industry, nothing could have prepared Brown for the high level of stress

and anxiety that accompanied his work. Having to effectively sort, grade, and move his clients' product was challenge enough; but trying to satisfy their desire for immediate gratification in profits was much worse, and their "incessant calls" began to distress him by the end of 1846. When economic and political unrest in England and the European continent "produced an alarm amongst wool holders," who then flooded P&B with their wools, Brown somehow remained confident that he could keep the operation stable as long as they could give "moderate advances" to the growers. His optimism proved to be ill-founded, especially as it became clear that the "manufacturers and buyers had no intention of permitting P&B or any association of wool growers to grade raw wool for them and to fix prices." It was clear to them that Brown and other leaders had not sufficiently united the wool-growers into a dynamic movement and that the farmers were not fully committed to a cooperative venture. Brown also began to realize that the wool-growers preferred short-term profits to long-term reform and prosperity. It would not be the last time that advocates for the wool-growers would feel betrayed by the "conservatism, timidity, or prejudice"of the very people they represented.[62]

Contrary to what has often been written, the ultimate failure of P&B was only secondarily about Brown's lack of market mastery. Primarily, the wool-growers were simply outdone by the organization, propaganda, and resources of the manufacturers. These factors made it more than difficult for them to function within the lopsided economic structures that favored the industrialists over against the growers of the United States. Savvy manufacturers and international merchants like Samuel Lawrence and Aaron Erickson were probably laughing up their sleeves at the floundering wool-growers, even as they whispered and chuckled about "plain John Brown . . . the great reformer of the wool trade at Springfield." In public discourse, Lawrence had effectively pulled the wool over the eyes of the wool-growers, having established himself within the industry as a kind of wise and benevolent father who somehow transcended the interests of the manufacturers in his dealings with them. For instance, writing in *The Plough, the Loom, and the Anvil*, Lawrence audaciously placed the onus of success upon the wool-growers themselves, declaring that "the paternal care of American industry" was actually in *their* hands. "It depends upon the wool-growers of this country how far the business of fabricating shall be carried," he challenged. "[G]ive us the wool at German prices and we shall supply ourselves."[63]

Brown soon realized that the manufacturers had hastily moved to oppose P&B and the wool-growers' efforts. At best, this opposition simply entailed their taking advantage of any alternative market in order to avoid enabling the producers in their quest to become an economic force. When they could not find agreeable prices on the foreign market, the manufacturers might slow down production, lay off workers, and "nibble" (as Brown described it) around the domestic wools without buying. Brown felt that if the manufacturers had their way, the producers would have to sacrifice their profits by selling "at prices that would tickle," and by granting "long credit without interest." At worst, some manufacturers were not above stalling on payments until P&B threatened to drag them into court. By 1849, Brown spoke of Springfield as "the seat of war," referring to the "hostile feeling existing towards" P&B on the part of the manufacturers.[64]

Secondly, P&B was vulnerable to the whims and demands of the farmers and was frustrated by what Brown called "the wants of our friends," and by trying to "save them from disappointment." He increasingly felt that the wool-growers did not really understand the complexity of P&B's efforts, nor did they appreciate that their concerns went beyond the immediate sale of wool. In February 1849, he wrote that even when a small sale was made, every wool-grower hearing about it demanded full payment. When they did not receive immediate satisfaction, some had even sent their wools to other dealers. Nor did he feel confident in sharing the greater concerns of the wool commission operation with them, lest their criticisms degenerate into blind demands that P&B be closed down. "As to wool Depots," Brown vented to another colleague, "we do not believe any man living can so conduct one as to avoid the most bitter reproaches, & injurious insinuations." In the end, he felt himself "goaded to desperation" by many of the wool-growers, even while he was contending "with all the obstacles" that the ingenuous manufacturers had placed before him.[65]

Thirdly, P&B was launched at a time of unprecedented growth in the industrial realm, particularly among the wool manufacturers. Between 1845 and 1849, essentially the years of P&B's operation, the number of wool manufacturing establishments grew from around one thousand to well over fifteen hundred, predominately in New England. This kind of industrial leadership was linked to the rise of eastern cities and the wholesale clothing trade in the same region, as well as the vanguard development of textile machine industries in Massachusetts. Manufacturers were also benefitted by an expansive pool of immigrant laborers as well as the burgeoning wool buyers trade, both of which enhanced and empowered their interests while the producers were still struggling with issues of organization. During P&B's tenure, New England buyers dominated the nation's wool dealing by controlling a third of domestic wools and forty percent of imported wools.[66] In the midst of such circumstances, Brown was increasingly stymied by the gall of the manufacturers. "Many of the fine wool manufacturers are determined to keep away from us as long as possible, & will go elsewhere & pay higher prices rather than buy of us," he wrote to some of his clients in March 1849.[67]

In 1840–50, the decade encompassing P&B's operation, there was increasing competition in the United States from foreign wools. There was some domestic exporting, but hardly sufficient to counter the producers' losses to foreign imports. What further disadvantaged P&B and its clients was the market's shift away from fine wools, associated with traditional broadcloth production. As Brown recognized, it was not that the manufacturers did not want domestic wools or have use for them in their increasingly diverse production capacity; but the availability of a variety of wool sources allowed them to successfully compete with foreign manufacturers while at the same time they could purchase domestic products according to expedience.[68]

Encouraged by the interest that European agents had shown in P&B's wools, Brown saw his last hope in establishing relationships with foreign firms such as Thirion Maillard of France and H. W. T. Mali of Belgium. Limited sales made stateside were fine, but Brown was proposing something far more audacious: he hoped that by forming a working alliance with foreign manufacturers, P&B could effectively break the grip of the manufacturers back home. "I am hinting that I intend going to Europe to make *permanent arrangements* in regard to the wool trade," he wrote to Perkins in the spring of 1849.[69]

Brown was thus in Europe from late August until mid-October 1849, spending most of the time in England. His brief tour of France, Belgium, and Germany between August 29 and September 8 availed little despite his previous contact with European firms. The rest of the time he was in England, but whatever pleasure he derived from touring, Brown was ultimately disappointed by the flattened interest in his wools. As it turned out, only a small amount of wool was taken and sold quite badly, far beneath the price he expected. He withdrew the rest from public sale, writing home in complaint of the obstinate prejudice displayed by the English buyers toward "American wools." However he must have been quite disgusted to find that some of P&B's bales were actually loaded with filth and waste matter, apparently justifying European prejudices. Even the formerly enthusiastic Belgian and French buyers proved disappointing when he realized that they wanted P&B's wool at the same prices that they paid for their own colonial wools. Brown realized it was time to go home. He had done everything within his power and nothing remained but to return to Springfield and acknowledge defeat.[70]

Over the next few years, Perkins and Brown were entangled with lawsuits in several different cities pertaining to manufacturers and wool-growers. The P&B cases varied, sometimes making Brown and his partner into plaintiffs and other times defendants. In the long run they were neither overwhelmingly victorious nor entirely defeated, and one noteworthy case even reached "an amicable settlement" out of court. Of course, had they enjoyed the benefit of the modern limited liability corporation, Perkins and Brown would probably have fared better. But unlike his business failures in the late 1830s and early 40s, the breakdown of P&B neither ruined Brown nor brought his partnership with Simon Perkins to an end. Perkins had absorbed the lion's share of the losses anyway, and he genuinely wanted his partner to remain on with him, not only to see the lawsuits concluded but to permanently manage his flocks and farm in Akron. In the spring of 1850, Brown happily reported that Perkins had "met a full history of our difficulties, *& probably losses* without a frown on his countenance" and spoke only with "words of comfort, & encouragement." Indeed, he wrote further, Perkins was "wholly averse" to breaking up their partnership or separating their interests, and "gave me the fullest assurance of his undiminished confidence & personal regard"[71] [Document 7]. To be sure, the subsequent legal proceedings initially threatened to strain relations between the partners, and Brown worried that their "confidence and cordiality" would be lost if Perkins blamed him. Assuming his expressed concerns were real and not imagined, it was quite unrealistic for Perkins to expect the lawsuits to end quickly, and certainly unfair to hold his partner responsible when they proved otherwise. But even these concerns were evidently short-lived, Brown quickly writing to his family that Perkins had reaffirmed a "very kind spirit" toward him and that "the fog [*was*] clearing away from our matters a little." Indeed he probably counseled his wealthy partner "to remain resolute and patient," and although P&B

proved a failure, neither partner was devastated. Years later, Perkins—who resented Brown's anti-slavery militancy and disdained the Harper's Ferry raid—changed his tune and blamed Brown for P&B's failure, but John Brown Jr., who had worked closely with his father in the wool commission house in Springfield, remembered that Perkins himself had "heartily" supported his father's efforts. Contrary to Perkins's later claims, the firm's letters, along with Brown's personal correspondence, verify his uncritical support and certainly make him equally culpable for the demise of P&B. They also attest to the fact that the downfall of the wool commission venture was not primarily due to Brown's lack of business ability as is commonly supposed, but rather to the successful combining and boycotting strategy of the manufacturers.[72]

While Brown undoubtedly walked away from the wool commission business defeated and disappointed, he was neither personally nor financially ruined. His role at the Perkins estate sustained him until 1854, when his partner apparently suffered another financial loss due to investments entirely separate from their association. According to Brown family testimony, he cleared about $1000 in his last year with Perkins and afterward did some farming and livestock sales to pay for his final move in 1855. By the end of the following year, however, businessman Brown would become a Kansas guerilla. Thereafter these troublesome ventures would be all but forgotten, except by prejudiced historians in the 20th century, most of whom were bent on fashioning the wool business into another kind of noose for John Brown. Thus, a century after P&B folded, the eminent Civil War historian Allan Nevins presumptuously opined that Brown's effort on behalf of the wool-growers primarily spoke to "the question of his sanity or insanity."[73]

4. The Making of a Radical Reformer

John Brown's radical struggle against slavery was undoubtedly rooted in his family's unique blend of conservative theology and abolitionism. The former not only shaped his personal spirituality but probably led him to distrust the religious innovations so preponderant in the abolitionist movement. This may have been one reason for his lack of participation in prominent anti-slavery organizations. Brown certainly questioned pacifism for both practical and theological reasons, especially as the crisis over slavery was coming to a head in the 1850s. As one source contends, he may have been passingly influenced by the non-resistant approach (perhaps through his association with Quakers in the wool business and underground railroad), but even this is doubtful.[74] More likely, Brown was simply a conservative Christian by outlook and thus wary of the resort to violence. Indeed, in the first twenty years of his adult life even his activism was irregular, marginal, and politically mild-mannered.

While it is apparent that he was a life-long participant in underground railroad activity, his anti-slavery militance was not significantly manifested until the mid-to-late 1840s, particularly after he moved to Springfield, Massachusetts, and began to interact with blacks in that city. In prior years, such as his decade in northwestern Pennsylvania, there is only slight evidence that Brown was involved in the underground railroad, and no reason to believe that he engaged in any overt anti-slavery activity. Brown was clearly thinking about the plight of blacks and probably had some association with free African Americans in northwestern Pennsylvania. It is a matter of record that he contemplated starting a school for young blacks in Crawford County in the 1830s [Document 2]. But even granting that John Brown quietly supported fugitive slaves from time to time, his fiery profile as an enemy of slavery did not emerge during his Pennsylvania years.

On the other hand, some might assume that Brown was so conservative as to have been quite a different man than he became later in life. Such a mistaken view overlooks the facts of his upbringing and beliefs as well as his personal political evolution from a justice-oriented conservative to a radical reformer. Even in the early phases of his career, for instance, there were hints of things to come. At the onset of his move to Crawford County in 1826 he was caught up in the dissatisfaction of settlers in nearby Erie County who had a long-standing dispute with the Pennsylvania Population Company (PPC) over property rights. The conflict dated back to the late 18th century, and even though the PPC had eventually won claim to settlers' lands, some of these disenfranchised families continued to seek opportunities to make legal reclamation. According to an agent of the PPC, around the time Brown settled in Pennsylvania he became so inflamed by the settlers' cause that he had ridden about Erie County urging them to keep up their disputes in the certainty of an ultimate victory. While this effort proved vain, he won the loyal friendship of Morrow B. Lowry, from one of the disenfranchised settler families. In turn, Lowry, a future Republican state senator, visited Brown in his Virginia jail cell in November 1859, thereafter lauding his memory. As noted above, the otherwise conservative Brown was similarly stirred by the injustices faced by the sheep farmers of Ohio, Pennsylvania, and western Virginia. Like the powerless settlers of Erie County, the wool-growers won Brown's support because their cause spoke to basic issues of justice and fairness. While he made no illegal attempt to attack the PPC or the wool manufacturers of New England, his efforts reflect an inclination toward activism and intervention on behalf of the underdog—an inclination increasingly haunted by the reality of the monstrous institution of chattel slavery. With the passing of years and the growing defiance of pro-slavery leaders, Brown's bent, both spiritual and political, grew more intense. "I have never known a man," recalled Lowry his Pennsylvania friend, "who had a deeper sense of the claims of God and man upon him than John Brown." It was this deepening sense of divine vocation and political responsibility that ultimately drove him toward anti-slavery militancy.[75]

Another aspect of his emerging militancy as a businessman was the well-known impact of the killing of abolitionist Elijah Lovejoy, in Alton, Illinois, in November 1837. During a public prayer meeting in response to the killing, Brown made an open vow to "devote my life to increasing hostility toward slavery." Some have questioned whether Brown set aside his vow in pursuit of financial gain, while others have gratuitously questioned the historicity of the incident itself. However there is no evidential reason for such skepticism, and the open vow incident itself is well supported in the annals of Hudson, Ohio, where it took place. Although Brown was clearly detoured by subsequent setbacks and failures in business, even his family recognized that "his spirit was constantly struggling with the problems of the National life." Remembering these years, Mary Brown later told a journalist that many nights her husband had lain in bed, awake and praying over the plight of the slave.[76]

However it was his unusual bonding with black people that ultimately pushed him over the boundary of pronounced anti-slavery sentiment into the realm of a peculiarly extraordinary zeal, the nature of which was unfamiliar even to many anti-slavery whites. Residing in Springfield, Massachusetts (1846–49), and then subsequently relocating his family to live nearby a colony of free blacks in New York's Adirondacks (1849–51, 1855), Brown enjoyed meaningful associations with black laborers and professionals, many of whom were fugitives. In Springfield, he hired blacks as employees, became a *de facto* member of the Sanford Street Zion Methodist Church, and interacted with visiting African American activists, including the abolitionist Frederick Douglass. While Springfield was hardly a black metropolis, it featured a vibrant African American context, the likes of which Brown had never known living on the western frontier. That he favored attending a black non-Calvinist church over the prominent Congregational church in Springfield not only suggests his disdain toward racial prejudice in the white church, but also that Brown was drinking in the cultural and political environment of the black community. His relations within that community—not his later exploits in Kansas—mark his initial radicalization and incipient "Black Orientation" (as Benjamin Quarles called it). It was in Springfield that Brown began to formulate plans for some kind of raid upon the South, and it was here that he attempted to organize local blacks into a militant organization designed to resist agents of the Fugitive Slave Law of 1850. As Brown recognized, Springfield's blacks were deeply disturbed and fearful about the impact of the Law, although his writing reflects a distinctly Calvinistic and militant approach to its passing. "It really looks as if God had his hand in this wickedness also," he wrote to his wife. "I of course keep encouraging my friends 'to trust in God and keep their powder dry.'" One reminiscence from this period states that he had supplied knives to members of the church, encouraging them to trust God and prepare for war [Documents 8–10]. Reticent, reserved, and somewhat old-fashioned in his attire, Brown was a peculiar figure among blacks. In time, however, his genuine piety, quiet warmth, and obvious comfort in their presence—not to mention his outspoken tendency on their behalf—won him a trusted place within the community.

After speaking at Springfield's Town Hall on February 1, 1848, Frederick Douglass met him and afterward described him in an open letter. Recalling that he had encountered Brown within a huddle of notable black leaders, Douglass ascertained that although "a white gentleman," he was "in sympathy a black man" who so identified with African Americans that it seemed "his soul had been pierced with the iron of slavery." Thus commenced a blissful friendship that continued until 1859, when it became strained over strategic differences pertaining to the Harper's Ferry raid. It was during the 1840s that Brown likewise became acquainted with other prominent blacks, including Douglass's rival and critic, Henry Highland Garnet, as well as Jermain Loguen, Willis Hodges, James Gloucester, and other prominent free blacks. Despite the stylish nature of his final autobiography (1881), Douglass was probably quite factual in recalling that black leaders tended to whisper Brown's name when talking about him among themselves. Whether or not they actually believed that he would take action, or whether they ever intended to join him, they clearly took comfort in his unusual zeal.[77]

In 1849, even as P&B's wool commission operation was crumbling, Brown had his eyes on the chilly Adirondacks, where he intended to settle his family in the midst of a black colony that had been established by land grantees from New York State. When the wealthy abolitionist Gerrit Smith donated thousands of acres to New York freemen, there was an initial thrust of interest from black leaders who advocated using the wilderness opportunity to build a self-supporting community as an alternative to the racist context of northern cities. Brown loved mountain living and eagerly sought a place nearby the black settlement in Essex county, known affectionately as "Timbucto." His intention was to assist them in making the difficult adjustment from urban to agrarian living, especially in the cold and difficult climate. In the spring of 1849, the Browns were duly relocated to the town of North Elba, and became integrally involved in the struggling "Timbucto" community. While Smith's black colony experiments in Essex and Franklin counties ultimately declined, the Adirondacks became Brown's favored residence, even after an obligatory four-year removal to Ohio, ending in 1855.[78] It is no mystery that he preferred North Elba to Springfield or any other city since he was essentially agrarian and bucolic in his orientation. In the lofty Adirondack region, John Brown could feel close to God, the good earth, and black people. However, in the winding down of P&B's wool commission business, Brown commuted back and forth between his family and Springfield [Document 8].

The shift that took place from disappointed businessman to anti-slavery guerilla in the mid-1850s was one of evolving necessity, not desperation or delusion. Politically and socially radicalized by the late 1840s, Brown was still a determined family man who could not yet embark upon a militant course of activism. He had faithfully provided for his family through the worst of times, and even death's violations had undoubtedly rendered his family ties all the more firm. Like others in the era of pre-modern medicine, he had helplessly watched as many of his loved ones were swept away by sickness and accident. Widowed at thirty-two-years of age, he also lost two young children while living in Pennsylvania. After remarrying, he lost four more children in one fell swoop of dysentery in 1843 and another toddler in a household scalding accident in 1846. As if the conquering worm had not its fill, another baby girl was taken by sickness in 1849, and a one-month-old boy succumbed to illness in 1852.

By 1855, Brown was intent on settling his family back in the Adirondacks, where he planned on building a solid if not humble home for his wife and younger children. In these waning years he was earnestly contemplating a radical move upon the South and was constrained to build his family a home, though openly wondering if he himself would "live to occupy it."[79] Ironically, it would be Brown's concern for family welfare that would lead him away from this mountain farmhouse, along an inadvertent pathway into full time activism. Shortly after moving them into the simple, barely-finished structure, he answered a call that led him to Kansas. Thereafter his visits home were but brief and fleeting rehearsals of his former days as a hardworking and devoted husband and father.

5. Kansas

In 1854 the Kansas and Nebraska territories were opened to settlement by the government and a fiery debate ensued as to the expansion of slavery in these forthcoming states. When "Popular Sovereignty" was determined as the way to resolve the issue (that is, according to the votes of the settlers themselves), southern and northern leaders began to urge westward migration and settlement. Although it was assumed that Nebraska would enter the union as a free state, Kansas became an imbroglio that would surprise and horrify the nation. Guns, not votes, would nearly decide the fate of the territory.

Brown clearly hoped to gather his grown children and their families around him, but instead of following him to the Adirondacks, they chose to go westward with other free state settlers. No doubt, the father was also attracted to the idea of Kansas settlement, although he clearly made the choice to return to his mountain paradise and formulate his own plan to attack slavery. Although the town of North Elba (near present day Lake Placid, New York) was not an underground railroad stop as some have assumed, Brown undoubtedly hoped to recruit volunteers through the black colony and its connections with free men in the northeast. According to Frederick Douglass, Brown was already sketching and revising a plan for such an effort from the 1840s. His intention was to take a small force of men into the South, gradually drawing away enslaved people and arming them in a guerilla movement. Instead of killing slave masters and their families, his intention was to destroy the monetary value of slavery as an institution by causing it to collapse under the very nose of slaveholding society. While violence would be necessary for self-defense, Brown's plan actually was premised on diminishing violence. He and his soldiers would make clandestine raids, gather recruits and subsist by seizing supplies from slave holders, and evade counterattack by exploiting the mountainous terrain of the Appalachians.[80] Brown may have considered variations of his original plan before going to Kansas; according to Martin Delany, a black leader who collaborated with him in Canada, the abolitionist even considered using the new territory as a base of his operations against slavery.[81] Ultimately, Brown's involvement in Kansas was parenthetical to his designs and his western adventure proved to be a life-changing detour on the road to Virginia.

In May 1855, Brown had hardly unpacked in North Elba when he received a long letter from John Jr. in Kansas. After providing extensive details about their new dwelling and life in the territory, Junior began to discuss the intrusions of "lawless bands of miscreants," heavily armed and financed by pro-slavery forces in "[e]very Slave holding State from Virginia to Texas." According to one anti-slavery Southerner whom he had met, some Southerners had formed an "Annoyance Association" whose objective was to use means of stealth and outright attack in ridding the territory of free state people. The younger Brown explained that they would need pistols and field rifles, as well as heavy swords and bayonets. The Brown boys were ready to be armed, but this letter shows that Junior was thinking more broadly of arming other free state men and wanted his father to seek out the help of the wealthy abolitionist Gerrit Smith and others to fund these arms.[82] To no surprise, the elder Brown answered this call with action, fully supported by his wife Mary, both of them seeing this as a matter of family security as well as anti-slavery devotion. Leaving their twenty-year-old son Watson and a hired hand to care for the farm, Brown enlisted his son-in-law Henry Thompson and left for Kansas, stopping en route to attend an abolitionist convention in Syracuse, New York. Junior had also written similar letters to abolitionist leaders, some of which were read at the convention on June 28; Brown himself took the podium to inform the audience that he was on his way to Kansas and asked them for money to buy guns. His request nearly split the convention, some abolitionists speaking in favor of offering support, others counseling against it. Frederick Douglass, no doubt in an attempt to salvage some support for his friend, spoke in favor of soliciting individual assistance from the attendees as a compromise solution. Having received a modest sum from some of the abolitionists, Brown and Thompson moved westward, stopping in Ohio before setting out for the territory. In Akron, he found more support, receiving clothing, weapons, ammunition, and money. After seeing his father Owen in Hudson for the last time, he left the old man in a state of concern. It seemed to him that his son was already in a militant frame of mind, and afterward he sent a letter admonishing him to avoid taking an offensive posture—counsel that Brown would follow until it became clear that terrorism, not conventional warfare, defined the struggle in Kansas. Years later, Lucy Brown Clark recalled that when her Uncle John left Hudson, the weapons were loaded onto his wagon in a large wooden box shaped like a casket. Before pulling out of town, Brown scooped her up on his lap, gently explaining why he was taking the guns to Kansas. "He said his boys had gone out there to live, and that they had little children of their own. They had been attacked in their own homes, their cattle had been driven away by the border ruffians, and that he was going there with these guns to help them."[83]

It seems that most people with an interest in (or dislike of) John Brown are less concerned for the story of Kansas than they are his role in the bloody "Pottawatomie massacre" of 1856. Certainly the story of "Bleeding Kansas" is an expansive narrative that far outreaches Brown's role. In a real sense he is a secondary figure with respect to the political developments that ultimately brought the territory into the union as a free state. He had little to do with issues of legislation and statecraft, and when the territory was finally free of fighting and subjected to peaceful political operation, he was neither needed nor interested in Kansas. War-torn, broken-hearted, and exhausted, his family would finally quit the territory and return to Ohio, and John Brown himself would turn toward the South.

Brown's initial letters from Kansas suggest that he was guardedly optimistic concerning the future of the territory as a free state. Indeed by late 1855, free state settlers had become the majority and the only way that pro-slavery forces could sustain power was by intimidating voters and stuffing ballot boxes with illegal Missouri votes. With an increasing number of settlers opposed to slavery (albeit also to black settlement), pro-slavery "leaders were quick to feel their power slipping from their hands." In July 1855, before Brown's arrival, a fraudulently elected pro-slavery state legislature had enacted laws that promised heavy penalties to free state settlers and anti-slavery activists. The free state majority responded with an overwhelming vote for their own legislature in October (the same month that Brown and Thompson arrived), creating a counter-legislature in the territory. Despite the presence of pro-slavery thugs, the majority held a reasonable hope that democracy would rule in Kansas. But in November 1855 the climate of assurance began to shift when a free state man was murdered by a Missourian and territorial civil war threatened. After another anti-slavery settler was murdered, the free state bastion of Lawrence was nearly assaulted by pro-slavery forces. The town escaped, however, because of the cunning of free state leaders and the cowardice of the pro-slavery governor, and the constitution of the anti-slavery legislature was passed in mid-December. At this point even Brown believed that Kansas would enter the union without slavery if the majority could hold their ground in the territory. In early 1856, however, Brown and other free state people began to recognize that the pro-slavery side was not going to accept the reality that "popular sovereignty" had not worked in their favor. News of "shocking outrages" committed against anti-slavery people in Leavenworth alarmed the majority, as did a renewed threat upon Lawrence. As Brown saw it, only the winter snows and a heavy spring thaw separated them from an onslaught of pro-slavery terrorists. "It is likely that when the snow goes[,] such high water will prevail that it will be difficult for the Missourians to invade," Brown wrote in February 1856, "and that by God, by this element, may protect Kansas for some time . . . . My judgment is; that we shall have no more general disturbance until warmer weather."[84]

Between his sons' unabashed pro-black sentiments and the younger John's election to the legitimate territorial legislature, pro-slavery neighbors were unhappily aware of the Browns [Document 11]. With "Old Brown" (nicknamed to distinguish him from his namesake) now resident, there was no doubt that their settlement "was to become known on both sides of the border as a centre of violent resistance to all who wished to see human slavery introduced into the Territory." Even when he made forays into nearby Missouri for supplies, Brown did not hide his political orientation. "*I always* (when asked) frankly avow myself a *Free State* man," he wrote to a relative back east. To annoy the pro-slavery element even more, Brown and his sons surveyed the southern boundary of the Native American Ottawa nation, with whom they enjoyed friendly relations. (It was probably the Ottawa whom grandfather Owen Brown had befriended back in Ohio before they were driven out in the early 1800s.) Their actions were both pro-Native and anti-slavery in sentiment, since most of the interlopers upon Indian lands were pro-slavery settlers. "The Surveying of the government lands seems under Divine Providence to derange the plans of the pro Slavery men here much more than of any others," Brown wrote to his father in March 1856. "They have been exceeding greedy of the timbered lands; & great numbers of them have intruded upon the Indian reservations. Some Slave holders near us[,] we are informed[,] have become quite discouraged; & are about to clear out."

The Ottawa council were undoubtedly pleased to have such helpful neighbors, especially after the Brown boys evicted one squatter from his cabin at gunpoint, tossing his belongs out the door behind him as he cursed and fled. In April 1856, Brown and his sons were further highlighted as dangerous opponents when they openly spoke against pro-slavery domination during a settlers' meeting in their vicinity—Brown senior declaring that he was an "Abolitionist of the old stock . . . and that negroes were his brothers and equals." When the Browns and others supported resolutions to reject the pro-slavery legislature, they caught the eye of a judge who issued warrants for their arrest. Rather than waiting to see what would come of the "bogus" warrants, Brown went out of his way to confront the court, undoubtedly hoping the judge would try to enforce the pro-slavery laws. After filling the courtroom with free state volunteers, Brown drafted a document in resistance to the court and had it delivered to the judge. Thoroughly intimidated, the judge and local pro-slavery collaborators "completely backed out . . . without doing anything"; then the judge made a hasty retreat to Lecompton, a pro-slavery town in the territory. Brown happily wrote home to his wife about the incident, describing how the pro-slavery magistrate had been "most effectually routed."[85]

Not long afterward a company of armed southerners from Georgia, Alabama, and South Carolina arrived in the vicinity, and Brown entered their camp posing as a pro-slavery surveyor in order to discover their intentions. Ostensibly recruited as settlers, these men were intent upon terrorizing and driving out free state people from their claims. Yet Brown was far more concerned to learn of their collaboration with local pro-slavery neighbors like Henry "Dutch" Sherman, a former slave hunter, and James Doyle and his sons, William and Drury. As he discovered from the unwitting southerners, it was their stated intention to clear out "the damned Brown crowd" and it was all too clear who would act as their guides in the vicinity. In retrospect some have claimed that the southerners had made an empty boast, but given the political climate and the real lack of governmental protection for anti-slavery settlers, Brown could not afford to underestimate these threatening statements. Despite a free state majority, the territory was under the boot of pro-slavery domination, financed and guided by the most militant Southern leaders and protected by the administration of President Franklin Pierce in Washington, D.C. Only two months prior, Pierce issued a proclamation denying any support to the free state cause in Kansas and placing the U.S. military at the disposal of pro-slavery territorial officials. Brown's response was to seek additional weapons from free state allies in the east while lamenting the prospects of having to shoot down "the poor soldiers of the country" [Document 12]. Emboldened by the government's tacit sanction of terrorism and fraud in the spring of 1856 (two more anti-slavery men were murdered), free state politicians were arrested and the town of Lawrence was shelled, invaded, and ravaged by southern terrorists on May 22. With little impetus toward militancy, Lawrence's timid leadership surrendered to the onslaught, some of the invaders being the same southern "settlers" who had planned on rooting out the "damned Brown crowd."[86] News of Lawrence's defeat quickly reached outlying free state settlers, although the cowardly surrender (as Brown saw it) left no time for them to come to the aid of the town. Now the only question was whether the "Border Ruffians" would make good their threats against Brown and other free state men. In a worst case scenario, there is little doubt that the outspoken Browns would be the primary target of pro-slavery terrorists. According to John Brown Jr., his father's "surveying" expedition in the southern camp had taken place only a few days before the assault on Lawrence, and by then his father had "abundant and entirely satisfactory evidence that our family were marked for destruction." Junior's wife, Wealthy Brown, recalled that her husband and brothers-in-law were particularly distinguished from other free state neighbors by their outspoken opinions in favor of abolition and black equality. Nor could the Browns hope for militant support from many free state people, since most were "decidedly timorous" and generally preferred to avoid confrontation with pro-slavery antagonists. Under such conditions it is likely that John Brown felt himself cornered. The resulting violence, known as the "Pottawatomie massacre," shows the degree of desperation and vulnerability he and others felt in the shadow of unchecked terrorism.

Since the late 20th century it has become fashionable to refer to the Pottawatomie killings in terms of terrorism, although the often presumptuous and unstudied comparisons drawn between Brown and contemporary terrorists fail to address what Eldrid Herrington calls "comparable cause." She points out that to "call Brown a terrorist is still to believe that the antebellum United States was the United States as it should be." This is particularly true of those writers who have rushed to condemn Brown's actions while overlooking the fundamental terrorism of a nation that sustained and protected slavery. Similarly, to refer to

Brown in Kansas as a terrorist is to assume that the political situation in the territory was essentially equitable, safe, and democratic, when in fact it was a place overrun by pro-slavery terrorism and lawlessness, and no actual protection from territorial and federal governments existed for those marked as extreme opponents to what was essentially a racist regime. Certainly historians and journalists who represent the prevailing thought style in the United States have never been troubled over the notion of using violence to counteract real threats to *their* world. "Terror campaigns provide their own antidote," the late Michael Kelly wrote after the terrorist attacks of September 11, 2001. "They provide the people who are supposed to be terrorized with a powerful new duty—to save themselves, to destroy those who would destroy them." Certainly the Browns were living within a context of terrorism and were well aware of what their "powerful new duty" required if they wanted to save themselves. "Now something *must* be done. We have got to defend our families and our neighbors as best we can," John Brown told neighbor Theodore Wiener, a German Jewish settler who had already tangled with a local pro-slavery thug. "Something *is going to be done now*. We must show by actual work that there are two sides to this thing and that they cannot go on with impunity." In retrospect, Governor John Andrew, testifying before Congress on behalf of the State of Massachusetts, declared that "there was no law, nor official of the law, to protect, or who did protect, the free-State settlers," and in fact Kansas settlers generally suffered due to lack of law enforcement from the pro-slavery regime. Although Andrew did not believe that Brown had perpetrated the Pottawatomie killings, even he understood that the bloody outburst was "an action of necessary self-defense."[87]

As the foremost targets of neighboring pro-slavery collaborators in the vicinity, it is understandable that the Browns predominated the killing party, including sons Owen, Frederick, Salmon, and Oliver, and devoted son-in-law Henry Thompson. Neither John Jr. nor Jason Brown supported their father and brothers' response, probably more from trepidation than conviction. Unlike their brothers, neither man was distinguished by militance, and their faint-heartedness was sometimes a point of criticism from those within and outside the family. Yet both sharpened the swords for their father's expedition; it is likewise hard to believe Jason's later claim that he did not know the intention of his family's violent outing along the Pottawatomie. With the exception of the driver who transported them, the killers were all willing and bold enough to hack their enemies to death with broadswords, weighing the charge of murder against their own lives as well as the free state cause. Nor were they lured into the violent venture by John Brown's unbreakable "spell," a paltry notion undergirding the most influential biography to date. As I have argued elsewhere, the myth of Brown's "spell" over his men is the only means to explain their solidarity without acknowledging that *they had an evidential and experiential basis for believing themselves in danger of an imminent terrorist attack.* Certainly Theodore Weiner, who had already been assaulted on his own property, had a good reason to join the killing party too—thus adding more weight to the argument that the strike was preemptive and counter-terroristic, not an unprovoked act of unbridled anti-slavery rage or terrorism as it is often portrayed.[88]

The grotesque killings themselves are written about at length in Brown's biographies and need not be reiterated here in all their gory details. During the night of May 24–25, 1856, five men—a father and his two adult sons (known activists in a terrorist organization euphemistically called the "Law and Order" party), along with another local thug and a free state turncoat with real political ties to the pro-slavery establishment in the territory—were seized from their homes and hacked to death in the darkness along Pottawatomie Creek. Although no deliberate mutilation occurred beyond the purpose of execution, the carnage of severed limbs and split skulls is sickening even to contemplate. The executioners, at least Thompson and the Browns, were otherwise benign, principled men who thereafter lived with scarred memories of the bloody episode. Indeed, Brown's son-in-law wielded the sword with deathly precision and then carried the memory of Pottawatomie throughout his long life. Interviewed in 1908, the 86-year-old Thompson still maintained that it was "a necessary and righteous act," though in his private thoughts he worried about the ultimate judgments of God. As Thompson's granddaughter attested, he always believed that Pottawatomie had been a case of "kill or be killed." But like others who have taken life in time of war, Thompson was hardly comfortable with the thought of facing the God of heaven with blood on his hands.[89] As for Brown himself, novelist Russell Banks presumes that he "was terribly troubled by the Pottowatomie Massacre . . . and bore the weight of it with extreme difficulty." However Banks must be confusing his own fiction with history, for there is no evidence that Brown ever articulated any regrets for having supervised the Pottawatomie killings. Whatever personal sorrow he may have felt was never expressed, only the convenient claim that he had not wielded the sword although approving of the act. Of course, even in Brown's eyes this would not excuse him from culpability before God if the killings were actually unjustified, nor is there any evidence that he ever doubted the course he had chosen. On the other hand, he knew that the action was homicidal and had no confidence that free state supporters would understand the bloody strike or support him if they learned about his role. Furthermore, Brown was so disgusted by the passive surrender of Lawrence and the "trouble and fuss" he had experienced from its submissive leaders that he disliked even visiting the town thereafter. All the more then, Brown knew the ideological distance between himself and the conservative free state patrons was far greater than the distance in miles between Kansas and the east. The free state settlers' passivity and naive trustfulness toward the federal government explains how they were so easily terrorized in Kansas. As the outcome in the territory further illustrates, the free state mind set was not only conservative and timid in the face of pro-slavery militancy but also Negrophobic, the fact of which made egalitarians like the Browns at times seem as alien to their allies as to their enemies. As Anne Brown wrote in retrospect, it was easy enough for "the carpet knights and quill-drivers" of the post-Reconstruction era to criticize her father; yet the same can be said of many of Brown's anti-slavery contemporaries, who did not understand his militancy until secession and civil war blew up in their faces. For instance, when he later visited the office of Samuel Lawrence in Lowell, Massachusetts (his former competitor in the wool business and a supporter of the free state cause), Brown expressed strong opinions about militancy and radical abolition, telling the magnate that "he would prefer a dissolution of the Union to a continuance of slavery." Offended by Brown's excited, militant expressions, Lawrence promptly dismissed him from his office. The leading free state patron of New England, Amos A. Lawrence, may have supported Brown as a Kansas guerilla, but even he turned against him when learning that he had "stolen" slaves by force from their masters and carried them to freedom. Brown could hardly rely on such friends to support his militant efforts, let alone expect them to appreciate the actions that he and others had taken in the desperate hours of May 1856.[90]

Writing a month after the killings, Brown scrawled a four-page letter to his wife and family back in New York [Document 13] in which he described the events of May-June 1856, including the assault and havoc wreaked upon the passive inhabitants of Lawrence, the arrest of his two sons, John Jr. and Jason, and his victorious battle against pro-slavery forces. As a guerilla in the field, "dwelling with the serpents of the Rocks, & wild beasts of the wilderness[,] being obliged to hide away from our enemies," Brown wrote in pencil, no doubt suggestive of the hard circumstances he was enduring. More interesting, however, is the message written "between the lines" concerning the Pottawatomie killings—a message conveyed in three disparate parts that form an inherent communique.

On page one Brown thus wrote: "On the 2d day & Evening after we left John[']s men we encountered quite a number of pro Slavery men & took quite a number prisoner. Our prisoners we let go; but we kept some Four or Five Hordes. We were immediately after this accused of murdering Five men at Potawatomie [sic]; & great efforts have since been made by the Missourians & their ruffian allies to capture us." Taking Brown at his word, he and his men had apparently encountered and captured some pro-slavery men (probably settlers) and then released them, except for several "Hordes," by which Brown meant "Border Ruffians." He does not say what transpired except that he and his men were afterward accused of committing murder—a charge he does not deny. It seems that these "Hordes" were probably interrogated, further affirming the Browns' sense of imminent danger. On the second page he suddenly interjected: "I had omitted to say that some murders had been committed at the time Lawrence was sacked," awkwardly flagging the killings for his readers again. Finally on page four, and once more without obvious reason, Brown wrote: "God who has not given us over to the will of our enemies but has moreover delivered them into our hand; will we humbly trust still keep & deliver us. *We feel assured that he who sees not as men see does not lay the guilt of innocent blood to our charge*" (author's emphasis). Clearly Brown was signaling something within this letter and his subtlety should not be mistaken for deception or double-talk. Without declaring that he was responsible for the killings, he made two peculiar allusions to the Pottawatomie incident, followed by a subtle acknowledgment of his role in those killings and an appeal to God's judgment instead of man's charge of "the guilt of innocent blood." This manner of allusion not only reflects Brown's natural reticence but also the need to protect himself and his sons. He is not confessing to murder in principle, but rather owning up to what others have taken to have been cold-blooded murder. As a wanted man on the run, propriety had not permitted him to give the blatant facts of the case. But he was clearly gesturing to his wife and family, asking them to believe that these "murders" were necessary and thus morally justifiable before God, having been committed under duress and threat and not from mere vendetta or political malice.

It is impossible to separate the broader political implications of the killings from matters of immediate concern to the Browns. Certainly there is ample testimony to the fact that Brown had an eye on the proslavery movement's activities in Kansas and knew that the killings would have a political impact beyond the immediate context. However Paul Finkelman rightly differentiates this impact from contemporary terrorism, noting that Brown was operating in a politically dysfunctional context where "violence and fraudulent elections were the rule," where *de facto* war was a reality and militant action was "the only way to significantly challenge slavery." Brown understood and welcomed the political implications of the killings, but had he been a terrorist as so many have labeled him, his record in Kansas would have been far more ruthless and his violence far less qualified. When Brown marched James Doyle and his two sons into the bloody darkness at Pottawatomie, even the victim's wife blurted out a fearful rebuke to her husband: "I told you [that] you would get into trouble for all your devilment"—no doubt an admission that her conspiring husband and sons had instigated the violence that had now come home to their door. Even so, the woman's appeals won the life of her fourteen-year-old son, who very likely was involved in his father's conspiracy along with his brothers. Had Brown been a terrorist, he might not have shown such mercy.

Three years later, after the Harper's Ferry raid had failed and Brown was about to be hanged in Virginia, he received a letter from the widow Doyle, reminding him of his role in the deaths of her husband and two sons. Her third son was all grown up now, she wrote, and very much wanted to come to Virginia and put the noose around his neck. Young Doyle never made it to Virginia, although he used the life that John Brown had spared to fight on behalf of slavery during the Civil War. In the 1880s, when Reconstruction was undermined and anti-slavery radicals had become old and disdained by white society, a writer named David Utter located the widow Doyle while preparing an anti-Brown article for *The North American Review*. To no surprise, she mentioned nothing of the "devilment" of her late husband and sons, instead claiming that she had no idea why Brown had killed them.[91] Of course, this was exactly what Utter was hoping for, and like so many current writers he made no effort to consider the Browns' side of the story.

John Brown would return to Kansas in the summer of 1858, just in time to witness the free state victory at the polls and the overwhelming defeat of the pro-slavery constitution on August 2. However pro-slavery terrorism proved recalcitrant, particularly in southeastern Kansas. Writing to John Jr., who was now safely settled back in Ohio, he reported the results of the free state victory, particularly describing the mood in Linn County where five anti-slavery men had been seized and executed under the leadership of Charles Hamilton (later a Confederate colonel). He described further how spies were still crossing into Kansas from Missouri and that he had successfully sniffed out one who finally "avowed himself a Proslavery man." Brown wrote that he gave the man "the most powerful abolition lecture" that he could muster, promising that "not a 'hair should fall from his head' so long as we knew of no active mischief he had been engaged in." In fact, this was precisely the strategy that Brown had taken two years before in his own Kansas neighborhood. Had his neighbors merely been pro-slavery in their convictions, no harm would have befallen them. But when a handful of his neighbors distinguished themselves as men of lethal "mischief" in conspiring against the Browns and others, they paid dearly for it along Pottawatomie Creek. The elder Brown concluded his letter by requesting the full facts and details of his family's efforts and experiences in Kansas for a publishable narrative, which he wanted to be written "with delicacy; & with fairness." Of course, he would not have included the horrible Pottawatomie killings in such a chronicle, though he seems to have been confident that history would rule in his favor when all the facts became known. In the meantime, Brown was irritated that his family's well-publicized role "in Kansas affairs" had often been "misstated by those who do[n']t know; & oftener [by those who] do not care to tell the truth." A century-and-a-half later, he would hardly be pleased that his actions at Pottawatomie have likewise been subjected to misstatement and misrepresentation, and certainly with neither delicacy nor fairness.[92]

6. The Road to Virginia

In August 1856, pro-slavery forces invaded the free state town of Osawatomie, in the vicinity of the Brown settlements and twenty-six-year-old Frederick Brown was gunned down in cold blood by a pro-slavery scout. His father refused to avenge the murder but continued fighting pro-slavery forces and raiding pro-slavery settlements into the fall of 1856, when he began to move eastward. Frayed and exhausted by the struggle, however, the Browns quit Kansas and their father joined them back in Ohio by December. Wearied, sickly, and financially broken, he spent Christmas in his boyhood hometown of Hudson, where he was reunited with relatives and children for a memorable holiday dinner. No doubt he strolled over to the old cemetery in town, solemnly examining the snow-covered grave of his father Owen, who had died not long before the assault on Lawrence that previous May. It was probably during this holiday respite in Hudson that Brown sat for a daguerreotype portrait, perhaps wearing a suit jacket borrowed from his younger half-brother Jeremiah. With sleeves short at the wrists and the portrait itself poorly lit, Brown's image seems dark and provocative—so much so that one imaginative writer erroneously concluded that Brown had deliberately made himself appear dark-skinned. However, as documentary scholar Jean Libby has observed, it was simply an inferior portrait, one which he chose to give away to an associate in Ohio rather than keep in the family.[93]

Although he was wanted by the law for his activities in Kansas, he was now a celebrated figure in the east. "Osawatomie Brown"—so named for the ill-fated free state town that he bravely fought to defend—thus spent much of 1857 touring and fund-raising in New England and New York state. But his was a poor celebrity. Despite the interest and enthusiasm he encountered along the way, Brown faced a level of distrust from officials of the National Kansas Committee, to whom he appealed in late January for arms and funds in support of the free state cause. Instead he got twelve boxes of clothes. Donations and pledges from individuals came inconsistently, a discouraging trend that was exacerbated by an economic panic the same year. Yet there were beneficial connections made too, especially with the renowned "Secret Six," a small circle of influential abolitionists who would continue to provide Brown political and financial support even when Virginia, not Kansas, became the focus of his plans [Document 14]. The object of several critical studies, this group of anti-slavery educators, philanthropists, and clergymen were key to Brown's successful movement among the abolitionist elites, especially the renowned literati of New England like Ralph Waldo Emerson and Henry David Thoreau. It was during this period that Brown visited the home of "Secret Six" supporter, George Stearns, thereafter writing an autobiographical sketch by request of his son. Likewise, Brown hid himself away in the home of Judge Thomas Russell, whose wife Nellie he entertained and awed with stories from the frontier and battlefield [see Chapter 1, n. 15]. He also made a number of visits home to see his wife and children, staying nearly two weeks in North Elba in early May 1857. With ample supplies, moderate funding, and a pocket full of promises, Brown set out for Kansas, stopping in Ohio, Wisconsin, Illinois, and Iowa along the way. When he arrived in the territory late in 1857, things had quieted considerably. This was no obstacle, however, because he was already preparing to recruit men for an expedition in another field.[94]

Had Brown's plans come to fruition as he hoped, the raid on Harper's Ferry would likely have taken place in the spring or summer of 1858, but the road to Virginia was full of obstacles, challenges, and detours. Certainly he had serious health concerns leading up to the time of the raid. He struggled repeatedly with bouts of "the Ague" (a form of malaria) that sometimes laid him out with chills, fever, and severe head and body aches. His family were suffering from this prairie sickness when he arrived in Kansas in 1855 and considering its prevalence along the Marais des Cygnes and Osage Rivers where they were encamped, it is no surprise that Brown eventually contracted the stubborn virus and suffered from its impact over the next few years. W.E.B. DuBois discerned this ongoing health crises when surveying Brown's letters of 1856–59, and rightly concluded that "there can be little doubt that it was an ill and pain-racked body which his indomitable will forced into the raid of Harper's Ferry." Yet he may have had far worse health concerns. For many years Brown's detractors have exploited an ill-faced daguerreotype that he had made of himself in 1858, claiming it to be proof of insanity. However as Libby reveals in discussing her careful research and consultations with forensic specialists, Brown's so-called "mad" portrait—with drooping check and mouth—actually suggests that he had experienced a mild stroke during this period too.

He left the United States in April and May 1858, crossing twice into Canada for the express purpose of seeking supporters for his intended raid on Harper's Ferry from among the black expatriates residing in various communities throughout Ontario. It was during this historic period that he met the liberator Harriet Tubman, who at that time was only beginning to be known by white abolitionists. After being introduced to Tubman by his black colleague Jermain Loguen, Brown was deeply impressed by the unsurpassed record of her brave deeds and accomplishments and wanted her for his Virginia plan. By 1858 Tubman had made numerous trips into the South on her bold missions of liberation, but found her enslaved parents wary of making the trip. According to one interview made in the early 20th century, the undaunted Tubman "bundled up feather bed, broad-axe, mother, father—all, and landed them in Canada." Tubman and Brown took to each other immediately, and the latter took it upon himself to solicit support for her in making a home for her parents [Document 16]. Meanwhile Brown was quite encouraged by Tubman's enthusiastic commitment to enlisting men for his cause.[95]

But enlisting strangers could be dangerous business, even when they were abolitionists. Brown brought great difficulties upon himself and his supporters by enlisting an English freedom-fighter named Hugh Forbes, then living in New York City. As he would painfully discover, Forbes's reputation as an associate of the Italian revolutionary Giuseppe Garibaldi belied an unsteady and mercenary character. Brown intended Forbes to bring his military expertise and abilities as a guerilla trainer to the struggle and promised him $100 per month; reticent to a fault when it came to his plans, Brown was surprisingly open to Forbes. Having caught the scent of Brown's prosperous backers, Forbes leapt at the chance, no doubt fancying himself, not Brown, as the one destined to become the liberator of the enslaved.

Brown's vulnerability to Forbes may be explained partly by his infatuation with military planning and strategy and partly by his tendency to impute the characteristics of other exotic liberators to the Englishman. Even when he had visited Europe as a wool commission executive in

1849, Brown had taken time to study military maneuvers and fortresses on the continent, paying close attention to earth-work forts that might be adapted to his own plans for a mountain-based campaign in the South. He was also a voracious reader of military history, especially regarding resistance movements. Around this time he had become "very familiar" with the successful military exploits of the dynamic religious revolutionary Schamyl (1797–1871), who united Muslim Caucasians and effectively resisted the Russians for thirty years in a mountain-based campaign that Brown wished to emulate (interestingly, both he and Schamyl were defeated in 1859). He had likely read one or both of the recently published works on the Muslim leader, the English translation of Baron August von Haxthausen's *Tribes of the Caucasus, with an account of Schamyl and the Murids* (1855), or Lascelles Wraxall's *Schamyl: The Sultan, Warrior, and Prophet of The Caucasus* (1856). Schamyl's militant devotion to the deity and to the freedom of his people undoubtedly attracted John Brown, especially his strong conviction that a small army of devoted, disciplined freedom-fighters could defeat a large army of oppressors. "The true believer has the faith in his heart, and the sword in his hand: for whoso is strong in faith, is strong in battle," Schamyl exhorted his warriors in a manner similar to Brown's own sentiments. "Believe not that God is with the many. He is with the good, and the good are always fewer than the bad." According to his own diary, Brown likewise pored over *The Life of Field Marshal the Duke of Wellington* (1854) by Joachim Siddon (written under the pseudonym Stocqueler), making careful note of "valuable hints" pertaining to the guerilla tactics of Javier Mina (1789–1818), who led the Spanish resistance to Napoleon's invasion in 1808. A fan of ancient slave revolts, works like Edward Gibbon's *The History of the Decline and Fall of the Roman Empire* (1816) also inspired Brown, especially his readings on the failed revolt of Spartacus and the successful opposition of Spanish chieftains against the Roman war machine. But he was even more enamored with the revolutionary leadership of Toussaint L'Ouverture (1743–1803), the liberator of Haiti, about whom he read everything he could get his hands on, having become "thoroughly acquainted with the wars in Hayti and the islands round about."

With his head and heart so full of these passionate examples, the discovery and enlistment of an authentic freedom-fighter like Forbes must have seemed like divine providence to Brown. Unfortunately, the Englishman was anything but heaven-sent, proving to be an opportunistic and ambitious adventurer instead of an impassioned liberator. Totally blind-sided by the man's arrogance and indiscretion, it did not take long before there was a clash of egos between the two strong-willed men. Forbes increasingly diminished Brown's plans, fell behind in preparing a training manual for his soldiers, and then griped and complained about the disruption of his pay—a matter that was actually out of Brown's control. After cajoling his leader to write a letter of recommendation that could be used to raise funds, ostensibly for his impoverished wife and children back in Europe, Forbes left Brown and returned to the east. To Frederick Douglass, the whining mercenary smelled like a skunk from the onset, but out of respect for Brown he gave him money and references to other associates, whom Forbes then exasperated "by his endless begging." Dissatisfied and convinced that he was being victimized, he began an abusive letter-writing campaign to John Brown's associates. Quickly evolving from a pest to a problem, Forbes then tried to force more money from Brown and the others by threatening to reveal the plans for the raid. Still bemoaning his alleged family's needs, he even informed Horace Greeley of the *New York Tribune* about Brown's plans. Spitefully determined to have his way, the Englishmen went even further by contacting and personally confronting a number of Republican leaders in Washington, D.C. When the "Secret Six" learned of Forbes's betrayal, most of them were thrown into a panic and decided—quite against Brown's opinion—that the best way to remedy the situation was to postpone the raid. While the unwelcome postponement worked to silence Forbes, it also had an unfortunate impact upon recruitment and support for the effort over a year later in 1859.[96]

The postponement took place in May 1858, following a "quiet convention" of Brown's followers and a number of expatriate black leaders and activists in Chatham, Ontario, a "muddy, busy little market town" with a population of four-thousand. A major Canadian terminus of the underground railroad, Chatham also attracted many professional and skilled blacks from the United States, and its vicinity was sprinkled with ambitious black town sites. The Chatham convention of May 8 and 10 was the climax of Brown's program of networking and recruitment among expatriate blacks in Canada and was intended as the launching point for the raid in the late spring or summer of 1858. The main focus of the convention was the review and ratification of Brown's *Provisional Constitution and Ordinances for the People of the United States*, which he had composed early in the year while sequestered in the home of

Frederick Douglass in Rochester, New York [Document 15]. The purpose of the *Provisional Constitution* was to provide a system of laws and guidelines for the guerilla nation that he expected to lead in the mountains of the South throughout his campaign against slavery. Some of Brown's defenders have seen the document as a positive effort, "an utopian, communal manifesto" akin to other marginal communities, from the persecuted Mormons in the United States to the determined maroons of the Caribbean. But others have bluntly criticized the document as entirely unrealistic and fanciful. While Brown clearly overreached himself in planning, at least he presumed that his movement's potential for growth required guidelines for law, moral instruction, and social conduct. That he intended to do so within the context of a guerilla state largely comprised of formerly enslaved people suggests a fundamentally high view of those he intended to liberate. This was no mere slave insurrection but an attempt to provide an alternative society based on democratic and egalitarian principles. Though he has likewise been wrongly scored for having lacked a plan, his *Provisional Constitution* shows that he intended to provide structure and leadership for a community that might very well exist on the margins of society for years until the issue of slavery was resolved. Brown may have been otherwise reticent concerning his plans, but he was clearly studying these matters. For instance, one of the books he read prior to the Harper's Ferry raid was *The Life of Jehudi Ashmun* (1835) by Ralph Gurley, the head of the American Colonization Society, the chronicle of a white leader's experience of colonizing formerly enslaved blacks in Liberia. To be sure, Brown was no advocate of colonization, at least not on white people's terms. Nor was the Liberian colony a guerilla state. However his interest in the book reflects the immediate concern of building what he intended to be a militant, egalitarian community comprised of formerly enslaved people, free blacks, white allies, and "proscribed" Native Americans and others victimized by white supremacy in the United States.

The *Provisional Constitution* clearly reflects the presuppositions of its author, from its Puritan emphasis on education and biblical morality to the arming of females and the use of capital punishment for soldiers guilty of rape or desertion. More importantly, the document's preamble reveals Brown's radical view of slavery as "a most barbarous, unprovoked, and unjustifiable War" inflicted upon black people by white society. He further contrasts the "eternal and self-evident truths" of the Declaration of Independence with the racist conclusions of the 1857 Dred Scott decision of the Supreme Court. Finally, Article VII of the *Provisional Constitution* provided for the office of Commander-in-Chief of the Army, which Brown undoubtedly designed for himself, as being separate from the office of the President. Boyd Stutler thus observed that while the *Provisional Constitution* was an instrument for the government of a nation of liberated slaves it also created the potential for a military dictatorship. No doubt aware of this issue, he wrote Article VII to provide for the democratic appointment, accountability, and removal of the Commander-in-Chief if necessary. Nevertheless, Stutler concluded, Brown was not above the seductions of power. Certainly many other well-intended leaders have been "carried away by the bright rainbow" of their own programs, only to become martinets and dictators.[97]

Brown's movements in Canada and the culminating convention in Chatham are a fascinating chapter in his story and he certainly received a supportive if not warm reception from the black male participants. It is not clear why Chatham's formidable black women were excluded from these meetings, and certainly Brown would not have chosen to do so of his own accord. However the "quiet convention" operated under the guise of being a Masonic meeting, and it may be that the exclusion of women was necessary to sustain this pretense. Among those present were clergymen, businessmen, craftsmen, writers, and other activists, the most notable being Martin Delany, the renowned abolitionist, physician, writer, and explorer who was a major organizing agent for the event. Perhaps Brown was disappointed that neither Frederick Douglass, Jermain Loguen, nor the "Secret Six" were in attendance; but he was generally pleased with the robust response of the thirty-four blacks who joined his own eleven men (only one of whom was black). According to the scant record of the convention, the *Provisional Constitution* met with support, except for Article XLI, which Brown had inserted to underscore that his movement was not revolutionary in terms of overthrowing governments or destroying the Union. His intention was rather to force an "amendment and repeal" of slavery while affirming allegiance to the flag of the United States. J. G. Reynolds, a veteran of the black convention movement in Ohio, resented this patriotic notion and wanted to have Article XLI struck from the constitution. Although Reynolds stood alone and was outvoted, there were probably other unspoken criticisms among the black expatriates, whose feelings of admiration and support for Brown were likely blended with a measure of skepticism and doubt. According to Delany, he repeatedly questioned and challenged Brown's ideas during the meetings, something that the abolitionist generally did not handle well. Brown responded with a low blow saying: "Gentlemen, if Dr. Delany is afraid, don't let him make you all cowards!" Delany appropriately defended himself, winning Brown's bow of respect. Such challenges, though typical of Brown's imperious attitude, may have quietly grated on the sensitivity of other black leaders. To be sure, the downside of his unusual egalitarian approach was that he could wound *any* man's dignity—white or black—if he felt it necessary for the sake of his mission. It is not clear to what extent his black associates recognized this at the time, especially since they were generally appreciative of his exceptional militancy. Every 19th century black narrative about him is salutary, although most of them were written in retrospective appreciation for his self-sacrifice on their behalf. The actual feelings of black male activists toward John Brown in the 1840s-50s, no doubt ranging from warm friendship and admiration to resentment and criticism, will never be fully known. Interestingly though, Vincent Harding, a leading narrator of the antebellum black experience, reflects his own sensibility by unfairly portraying Brown's harshness as racial condescension. Notwithstanding this in-depth dynamic, the overwhelming sentiment of the Chatham convention was supportive and the majority were genuinely convinced of Brown's absolute trustworthiness, including Osborne Anderson, the only attender who actually joined him at Harper's Ferry. Of course, individual trustworthiness was not their ultimate concern since the real issue to most of the men was the potential for the mission's success. The fact that Delany and others did not cling to Brown's efforts as a priority, but rather continued on with their own endeavors, may suggest that they had fundamental questions about the viability of the plan from the onset. As researcher Jean Libby has shown, at least seventeen of the black Chatham attenders returned to the United States to fight on the side of the Union during the Civil War. This suggests that their ultimate lack of support for Brown's efforts probably reflected their concerns over the unsteadiness, interruptions, lack of resources, and overwhelming challenges that daunted his movement. Brave though they were, it took far more pluck and resolution to follow John Brown in 1859 than it did to answer the call of "Father Abraham" in 1863.[98]

After visiting his wife and children in North Elba in June 1858, Brown departed westward for Kansas where he remained for the rest of the year. Now he appeared a very different man than the one who had first arrived in the territory with a wagon load of guns and swords. In 1855, John Brown stood straight and was clean-shaven, with a crown of thick, dark hair salted with gray. In 1858, he resembled the image that is most familiar to popular culture, an elderly man (though actually in his late fifties) with a slight stoop in his posture, a full head of gray hair, and a long prophet's beard that even frightened his grandchildren. Like his latest pseudonym, Shubel Morgan ("Shubel" is biblical Hebrew for "captive of God"), his beard was primarily a disguise, effectively altering his appearance from the earlier 1850s. However the beard may also have served to cosmetically diminish his drooping mouth and cheek. He also appeared different in other ways. According to William A. Phillips, who had met him twice before in Kansas, there was "in the expression of his face something even more dignified than usual; his eye was brighter, and the absorbing and consuming thoughts that were within him seemed to be growing out all over him."

The purpose for his move westward in 1858 was to assuage the concerns of the "Secret Six," who feared that the Forbes betrayal would not only endanger the mission but link them to Brown's plan. While Brown disdained this diversionary strategy and secretly resented his supporters for their timidity, he cooperated lest they consider him "reckless," particularly because "they held the purse" upon which he depended. The Six not only promised him a large sum of money if he would go west and remain there until the spring of 1859, but also that they would transfer their holdings of Kansas firearms to him with no further questions asked. All he needed to do was make a detour that would confuse Forbes, and afterward minimize the information about his plans so as to keep them safely outside of the circle of responsibility. Accepting this blend of disappointment and provision, he departed for Kansas and waited for an opportunity to "blind" Forbes with news of his exploits in the west. That opportunity arose at the end of 1858, when an enslaved man from Missouri, whose family was about to be auctioned at market, appealed to him for help. Brown and his men welcomed the chance to make a preliminary thrust into "Africa," while at the same time showing the Six that he was ready to move determinedly into the South. On December 20, 1858, Brown and his men invaded Missouri, liberating eleven enslaved people at gunpoint and killing one slave holder who resisted. In a feat of cinematic proportions, Brown's party evaded authorities in Kansas throughout the month of January 1859 and then embarked on a long, frigid trek from Nebraska that continued throughout February and early March.

Brown, his men, and the party of eleven (which grew to twelve after one of the fugitives gave birth) continued to evade the authorities, finally arriving in West Liberty, on the eastern end of Iowa. There the fugitives were placed aboard a train to Chicago and escorted safely to Detroit, Michigan, where they successfully crossed over to Windsor, Ontario, reaching Canadian freedom on March 12, 1859.[99]

Whether by chance or arrangement, Brown's arrival in Detroit coincided with the appearance of his friend Frederick Douglass, who was scheduled to speak in that city. According to biographer Richard Hinton, Brown and Douglass afterward attended an intimate meeting in the home of William Webb, along with a number of black leaders who had attended the Chatham convention in May 1858. Brown was undoubtedly congratulated within the circle of friends, and then began to discuss his renewed intention of raiding the South. To his dismay, Douglass— who had known had supported his plans from the late 1840s—now expressed objections, and a sharp disagreement took place between the two friends. When Douglass promised only financial support, Brown once again showed his worst side, accusing the orator of cowardice in the presence of his colleagues. Unlike the Chatham convention, there is no record of Douglass's self-defense during the meeting, although it is hard to imagine that he did not counter Brown's indiscrete remark with eloquence. The discerning Benjamin Quarles later wrote that "the Detroit meeting appears to have come to a close amicably in its personal relationships," but one suspects that Douglass was more than superficially wounded by his friend's insensitivity. He was no less a proud man than Brown, and it should not be forgotten that Douglass was the foremost black leader and a celebrated figure in his own right by 1859. Furthermore, he had already contended with the creeping paternalism and resentment of his former mentor, William Lloyd Garrison, who had tried to prevent him from spreading his own wings in the early 1850s when Douglass abandoned the nest of "moral suasion" and anti-Constitutionalism. As Henry Mayer concluded of the Douglass-Garrison fall out, it is similarly "tempting, but dangerous to discern a racial dimension in the conflict" between Brown and Douglass. On the other hand, it is possible that this incident soured their relations from this point, which may be why Douglass chose to overlook this episode in his stylized autobiographical recollections of Brown. In fact, when Richard Hinton inquired about the Detroit conflict in Douglass's later years, the aged leader insisted that "nothing of the sort occurred." As for Brown, whether or not he regretted the confrontation, he clearly wanted Douglass's help for his efforts and persisted in trying to persuade him. This is probably why he showed up in Douglass's printing shop in Rochester, New York, a month after the Detroit incident. According to one of Douglass's employees, Brown stopped in during the second week of April 1859, looking somewhat unkempt and restless, asking to speak to his famous friend. The two greeted each other happily, Brown's "keen piercing eye" fixed on Douglass the whole time they conversed. Perhaps the visit was Brown's way of smoothing things out with his friend, but doubtless it was also a vain attempt to woo the black leader over to his way of thinking.[100]

In his third and final autobiography published in 1881, Douglass wrote that he learned of Brown's intention of attacking Harper's Ferry during a secret meeting that took place within three weeks of the raid, although the meeting actually took place nearly two months before. Using a speaking engagement as a pretense for his visit, Douglass met with Brown in a quarry near Chambersburg, Pennsylvania in late August 1859. As Douglass fashioned the story, it was during this meeting that he first learned of Brown's determination to make an attack on Harper's Ferry as a preliminary move in his mountain-based campaign. Despite Brown's urging, Douglass wrote, he had refused to join the venture and warned the old man that he would be caught in a "perfect steel-trap." In his narrative he does acknowledge that Brown had previously spoken of raiding Harper's Ferry but had "never announced his intention of doing so" until the Chambersburg meeting, a claim that has never been questioned by scholars. In fact, Douglass seems to have conflated the developments of 1859 in his memoir, including the Detroit meeting, and probably knew about Brown's firm intention of attacking Harper's Ferry as early as March 1859. Furthermore it is likely that Douglass had supported Brown's plan as long as he had kept to the basic strategy of initiating raids on plantations and establishing a mountain-based campaign. Late in life, Douglass even contradicted his autobiography by telling a journalist that he had differed with Brown's plan all along and thought it "visionary." But considering the evidence of his words as well as the recollections and impressions of Brown's family, over the years Douglass had more than "assented" to Brown's plans. However, even more important than the change in strategy were the changes that had taken place in both men. Throughout the decade of their acquaintance, the two friends had evolved differently—Brown having become a radical reformer and militant freedom-fighter, and Douglass a celebrated orator and abolitionist leader with no intention of throwing himself headlong into any kind of danger, especially a meagerly supported effort in the South. Brown's friend and biographer Franklin Sanborn thus speculated in later years about the extent of Douglass's knowledge of the Harper's Ferry plan by the summer of 1859, "if not sooner."

Contrary to his stylized autobiography, then, it is more likely that Douglass knew from early 1859 that Brown had decided to initiate his endeavor by attacking Harper's Ferry and steadily opposed the strategy despite the appeals of his friend. Although somewhat cranky in her later years, Brown's daughter Anne, who was old enough to support her father's efforts, was probably honest in her claim that Douglass was "untruthful in his statements after the raid. He knew much that he denied having known." Furthermore, Douglass disappointed Brown not only because he opposed the Harper's Ferry plan, but especially because he refused to join him. Brown's children Anne, Salmon, Ruth, and son-in-law Henry Thompson all believed that Douglass had reneged on earlier promises to support their father's efforts. In fact, their resentment toward Douglass was so great that this sentiment persisted among Brown descendants into the 1970s.[101]

Worse yet for Brown was the fact that Douglass's refusal to underwrite his final strategy would inevitably undermine his efforts to gain significant black support. The leader's candor in resisting Brown was certainly no secret to the black community, especially in Philadelphia, where Brown had hoped to find a generous supply of men to join him. According to biographer William S. McFeely, Douglass stopped in Philadelphia en route to the secret meeting in Chambersburg [which took place on Saturday and Sunday, August 20–21], where he candidly discussed John Brown's efforts during a secret meeting in a local black church. McFeeley writes that Douglass found the attenders were fearful of bearing retaliation for what Brown might do, but misses the full meaning of the incident. In fact this episode followed events that had taken place in Philadelphia on August 15–16, when according to William Henry Johnson, a newly formed "colored military company" in that city had scheduled a parade which involved men who were already enlisted by Brown. Johnson recalls that Brown was disturbed by news of this public display of "armed and disciplined" blacks and feared that this would draw undue attention from authorities. Johnson says further that Brown came up to Philadelphia on August 15, 1859 in the hopes of discouraging the parade but was further undermined that evening, when a public meeting took place at the Shiloh Presbyterian Church on Lombard Street. The guest speaker was another one of Brown's black collaborators, J. J. Simons of New York City. Using more volume than wisdom, Simons "made a speech in which he commended the Negroes of Philadelphia for organizing a military company and stated there was a grand project on foot to invade the South with an army of armed northern Negroes" in order to liberate the enslaved. He then called for recruits from Philadelphia's black community who would "march through the South with a gun in one hand and a bible in the other." Johnson says that Brown was present at this meeting and was appalled by Simons's lack of discretion. Later that night Douglass and Brown called an emergency meeting at the home of Thomas J. Dorsey, a leading figure in Philadelphia's black community. Johnson was in attendance at this meeting and remembered Brown as having a "very kindly face" though shaded with "deep sorrow" because of Simons's indiscrete remarks at the church. Despite efforts at damage control, Johnson says that the incident created irreversible problems for Brown, who probably recognized that such public displays generally lacked substance anyway, especially since the black military company was "organized more for display than for actual service."

When the reality of Brown's concerns finally hit home to Philadelphia's blacks, it is understandable that some began to worry over the possible repercussions of their enlistment in his Virginia plan. Yet sufficient interest in Brown's effort persisted within Philadelphia's black community and according to Franklin Sanborn, "certain colored citizens" wrote a letter to Douglass urging him to support their efforts to join Brown in late September 1859. "We think you are the man of all others to represent us," they wrote, pledging to support Douglass's family if he joined Brown's efforts. "We have now quite a number of good but not very intelligent representatives collected," the letter concludes. These events thus provide a framework for further understanding Douglass's stylized autobiographical account of events in 1859. Clearly, Douglass had no intention of joining the raiders despite Brown's appeals and his demur undoubtedly damaged the confidence and enlistment of other blacks in the raid. Johnson concludes his narrative, claiming that he saw both leaders in Philadelphia once more just prior to the raid (on Thursday, October 13), which is quite possible from what we know of Brown's whereabouts. According to Johnson, Brown referred to the small number of raiders he had enlisted as "the forlorn hope of what might have been a grand expedition." Douglass stood nearby with a list of young black Philadelphians, none of whom apparently made it to Brown's headquarters in Maryland before the raid commenced. Johnson concluded that he was personally prevented from joining by Brown himself after the old man learned that he was a father-to-be. "'Then you can't go,' said he with a sad smile."[102]

That free blacks in the North failed to show significant support to Brown is obvious. While there may be evidence that some supporters set out too late to join him on time, the fact remains that most of the black leaders and their followers had an array of reasons for not going to Harper's Ferry. These reasons not only pertained to the 1858–59 Forbes hiatus and a general uncertainty regarding Brown's plans, but more likely the lack of substantial resources and martial reserves—things not lacking with respect to the Union cause during the Civil War. These uncertainties naturally fed into realistic apprehension and fear, especially since many potential recruits were fugitives from slavery and knew that their defeat and capture would elicit extreme measures of retaliation from white southerners, a concern that proved to be horribly true for black Union soldiers during the Civil War. Yet the fact that some black men and women risked their lives to support Brown does raise questions about those who opted for safety instead. As W. E. B. DuBois observed, when Brown's call came, "[m]ost of them said no . . . . They said it reluctantly, slowly, even hesitantly, but they said it even as their leader Douglass said it." The great black orator thus holds a special place in this regard because of his influential example, not to mention his probable secret counsels with influential leaders away from John Brown's hearing. Along with other high profile black men whose support appears to have been fairly thin or even hollow, Douglass's opposition to the raid in 1859 proved detrimental, no matter how highly he esteemed his unusual white friend. When all was said and done, the only recruit that Douglass contributed to the effort was a former slave known as Shields Green, whom he likely brought along to the Chambersburg meeting in an obligatory gesture of support. This explains why Douglass seems to have been surprised when, likely against his own private counsel, Green actually chose to stay with Brown. According to a second-hand account, the orator had persuaded Shields Green to stand as his paid "substitute," a notion that seems even more unfair to the courageous Green than to Douglass. Although the orator stylized his recollections of 1859, the spurious claim that he would have to pay someone to take his place seems ridiculous in light of the influence that Douglass exercised as a leader. Had he wished to send black recruits to join Brown, his emphatic word would have been sufficient to raise a small army.

In the 1880s, when Douglass still reigned as "the first great national Negro leader," John Brown Jr. privately mused over the orator's part in the Harper's Ferry episode. Unlike his siblings, Junior was not so certain that Douglass had ever made a firm commitment to join John Senior and drew no conclusion as to whether Shields Green was an intended substitute for the black leader. Still, he felt that it must have been "very disheartening" for his father when "the pinch" of Douglass's abandonment became final. "It may be the mist will never be cleared away respecting this actor in the Drama," he concluded. Other critics were less objective, including Nellie Russell, the cheerful wife and host of John Brown in Boston, who afterward went to Virginia with her husband to visit him in jail. Russell claimed that when her husband was discussing the "great opportunity lost" at Harper's Ferry, the old man blurted out: "*That* we owe to the famous Mr. Frederick Douglass" and then "shut his mouth in a way that made me know that he thought no good of Fred Douglass." Even granting that her views were probably tinged by racial prejudice and resentment toward Douglass's great success, it is hard to imagine that Russell fabricated the story entirely. As Junior recognized, the mist of history that surrounds this episode precludes drawing harsh judgments of Douglass. Certainly he and Brown deserve the benefit of the doubt considering the troubled age in which they sought to advance the cause of freedom. Nevertheless it is interesting that when Douglass was in Philadelphia to speak at a public meeting in 1863, twenty-year-old Anne Brown happened to be in attendance. She was disappointed that even though the renowned orator was aware that the daughter of his martyred friend was present in the audience, he avoided speaking to her and then was conspicuously absent from the after-party. Years later, Anne claimed that he "never wrote a word of sympathy to Mother or any other men of our family," and unfortunately her claim is thus far borne out in the archives. Not one post-Harper's Ferry letter from Frederick Douglass to the Browns has ever turned up.[103]

7. The Raid Reconsidered

In the spring of 1859, Brown's movements entailed making stops in Ohio's Western Reserve, where he saw family, friends, and anti-slavery allies, and in New England, where he met with his chief supporters. In particular, he stayed at Concord, Massachusetts, on May 9, where he passed his fifty-ninth birthday as a guest of "Secret Six" member Franklin Sanborn. In addition, he traveled down to New York City in early June, probably to confer with black leaders. He also stopped in Peterboro, New York, at the home of the abolitionist tycoon Gerrit Smith, another one of the Six. It may have been during this visit that Brown stood watching his host's son, Green Smith, who was outside with friends doing some target shooting for sport. After observing the young men's unskilled shooting, Brown selected a rifle, loaded it, and faced the target. "He pointed the weapon at the ground with his eye on the barrel, raised it rapidly, and the instant it came to a level he fired and hit the bull's eye right in the center." Handing the rifle to young Smith, the old man said "with a grim smile, 'Boys, that is the way to shoot,' and slowly returned to the house." Brown also spent some quiet weeks at home with his family in the Adirondacks in April and May, returning to them again in mid-June, just prior to his departure for the South.

It has sometimes been said that Brown left his family destitute. To the contrary, he had seen to it that money was raised to pay for their North Elba homestead and that Mary had sufficient livestock and resources. Nor were Brown's wife and daughters without help on the farm. Twenty-three-year-old son Salmon and thirty-seven-year-old son-in-law Henry Thompson remained in North Elba and were available to help, both men having opted not to join the raiders in the South. Black neighbors from the dwindling "Timbuctoo" colony also provided support, as did sixteen-year-old Byron Brewster, whom Brown had hired to work on the farm during his absence in Kansas in 1855–56. Before leaving for the South in June 1859, he took young Brewster aside and asked him to come back again to work on the farm since he was "going away for a while, and might not be coming back." To be sure, Brown's anti-slavery activities required sacrifices from the entire family, but they had long lived in a "simple manner" for the sake of the anti-slavery cause, as he told Frederick Douglass in the 1840s. Yet they were never impoverished, Brown having made every effort to send home food and supplies, if not money, throughout 1855–59. The late Edwin Cotter, the undoubtable authority on the Brown family in the Adirondacks, once noted that Mary Brown "faired well" in a context where farmers generally did not have a lot of cash and used the barter system instead. Even after her husband was hanged in Virginia, she was better off than most since she owned the house, farm, and livestock.[104]

In the summer of 1859, John Brown arrived in Maryland with his sons, renting the Kennedy farm near Sharpsburg for his headquarters. With his beard trimmed short and a new pseudonym, none of the locals could have imagined that he was "Osawatomie" Brown of Kansas. John Allstadt, a slaveholder who would become one of Brown's prisoners during the raid, remembered seeing him walking along the streets of Harper's Ferry in nearby Virginia. When he inquired as to the identity of "that old gentleman," he learned that the bearded elder was Isaac Smith, a farmer from New York state who had moved into the area on business. According to Anne Brown, her father always had an affinity for common names and once told her, "If I had not been John Brown I should have liked to be John Smith." Once or twice he even used the pseudonym "James Smith" in writing to Kansas colleagues. When it came to his most important *nom de guerre*, however, the choice of "Isaac Smith" was hardly an invention. Just as he had appropriated the name of Nelson Hawkins, a family friend from Ohio, it seems that he also took this name from an actual contemporary. The real Isaac Smith was a successful umbrella manufacturer whose self-named company had its main office in New York City and another in Boston, Massachusetts. Brown could not have missed Isaac Smith & Company's regular advertisements in the daily *Springfield Republican* during the years that he resided in Massachusetts. He was also a frequent business traveler in Manhattan and would hardly have overlooked Smith's trademark sign of three golden umbrellas when walking along Pearl Street. Whether or not his family knew the origin of this pseudonym, they willingly adopted it for the sake of the cause; even Mary Brown wrote to her husband after his arrival in Maryland, signing her name as "Mary D. Smith."

If Mary was cooperative in this regard, even wishing her husband "success in the good & great cause," she drew the line short of participating in his southern venture. The old man realized that the absence of his wife at the Maryland farmhouse was conspicuous and generally explained it by saying that "Mrs. Smith" had remained behind until their property could be sold in upstate New York. But Brown really wanted his wife to join him, along with teenage daughter Anne, and genuinely expected them to assist in the initial phase of setting up house in Maryland. When he wrote home on July 5, however, Mary refused to come, furthermore doing everything possible to discourage her daughter from going as well. Anne persisted, taking along her sister-in-law, Martha Brewster Brown, despite her mother's strong protest. When he greeted Anne at the hotel upon her arrival at Harper's Ferry, Brown embraced his daughter with a look of sorrow. When he asked if her mother had come, Anne could see that he was deeply disappointed by his wife's absence, so much so that she and her brothers never acknowledged the full extent of their mother's opposition. Although Anne did not reveal Mary's objections, it is evident that she was opposed to involving any of the Brown women in the raid. She had already sent off her sons Watson and Oliver, both young married men, to join their father, and evidently believed it was wrong for him to jeopardize the rest of the family. The Harper's Ferry raid thus tested the limits of the Brown family's determination and it is no surprise that daughter Ruth and husband Henry Thompson wrote to explain the latter's choice not to join him in Virginia. Nor did John Jr. and Jason choose to go. Kansas had proven too bloody and close a shave, including the loss of a brother. Undaunted, the old man kept his disappointments to himself and proceeded with his plans.[105]

The summer and early fall of 1859 were weeks of secrecy, evasion, and "arrangements were in active preparation for the work." As Isaac Smith, Brown proved a cordial and generous neighbor, often sharing cuts of freshly butchered meat with those in the vicinity. He also distinguished himself as a sincere Christian man who frequently attended services at the nearby Samples Manor Church of God, where the Reverend George Sigler knew him to be "an interested, attentive hearer." However Brown apparently attended other churches in the area, not only to avoid over-exposure in one congregation but perhaps also to give himself opportunity to study the area and contact local blacks. As Isaac Smith, Brown was also a supportive lay leader in collaboration with Episcopal minister William Heaton, who supervised services at Emmanuel Chapel, a small stone structure that still stands in Mont Alto, Pennsylvania. Local history records that Brown initiated a Sunday School for blacks at the chapel, likewise suggesting a dual religious and political agenda. Since he could not attend black churches without being conspicuous, he very likely relied upon some of the black raiders to visit those congregations, as they seem to have done in Chambersburg prior to the raid. Regardless, Brown was hoping to recruit within the free black community, not only to gain more hands and establish safe houses for other arriving black raiders, but also to enhance his contacts with enslaved people in the region. As Jean Libby has documented, Brown likely heard about the Reverend Thomas Henry of the African Methodist Episcopal Church through his interaction with church folk who worked on the underground railroad, and thereafter went to Hagerstown, Maryland, hoping to meet the minister in late June 1859. Although he was unsuccessful in his goal, Brown's notes and inquiries regarding this black minister illustrate that his investigations and networking went far deeper than many historians have assumed. Another local tradition, no doubt distorted by legend, shows that Brown had enlisted a local woman, probably of black ancestry, as a guide through the mountains and as a contact person for slaves in Maryland and Virginia. While the identity of this woman and the extent of her operations is open to question, there is sufficient testimony to her presence in the local histories of Pennsylvania and Maryland. Perhaps this same woman, or yet another agent of Brown, is the one who reportedly moved among the enslaved peoples of Talbot County in Maryland in advance of the raid.

As the numbers of arriving raiders increased in the Maryland farmhouse, it became more difficult to avoid inquiries and visits from curious neighbors. Another problem for Brown was the shipments of weapons that came concealed as tool freight for his supposed mining ventures. People talked about his heavy freight with curiosity, and even the Reverend Sigler thought the crates were somewhat mysterious. Shipped from Ohio by canal and river, the heavy load was then freighted on the Cumberland Valley Railroad to Chambersburg, Pennsylvania, where Brown had them stored until he could move them the last fifty miles of the way to his Maryland headquarters by wagon. No doubt the presence of Anne and Martha as housekeepers provided a suitable domestic appearance to most people as these young women also participated in the critical work of outwitting and evading intrusive neighbors. But as the growing presence of men, including blacks, became almost impossible to conceal in the Maryland farmhouse, real suspicions were aroused in the vicinity. Owen Brown, a stalwart among the raiders, later revealed that concerns over these suspicions forced his father to launch the raid sooner than planned.[106]

On the night of October 16, Brown and eighteen raiders entered Harper's Ferry, seized control of a railroad bridge, and entered the sleeping town without opposition. In the process, however, a night watchman escaped and a station baggage master, who turned out to be a free black man, was mortally wounded when he apparently refused to cooperate with Brown's men. In the very early morning hours of October 17, some of the raiders were then dispatched to capture and take slave holders in the vicinity as hostages. Afterward, two of Brown's black raiders went to a local farm to alert enslaved people. Back in Harper's Ferry, a train was stopped and held by unknown men armed by Brown, who by now had also seized the armory and arsenal. Wagons were then used to move men and arms back over to Maryland as well as from Brown's farmhouse to a school house on the Maryland side of the Potomac. As the night slipped away, Brown permitted the train to proceed—a tactical error, since the conductor subsequently telegraphed news of the attack on Harper's Ferry. Though the raiders had thus far been successful, Brown delayed in remaining in Harper's Ferry well into mid-morning, October 17, allowing for news of an "insurrection" to reach officials in Baltimore and giving local citizens and militia the opportunity to rally and fight back. This error in judgment proved lethal since militia arrived from nearby Shepherdstown by noon, launching a counterattack. As firing intensified, the townsmen and raiders, including the enslaved men fighting in support of the raiders, began to fall. Along with some of his men, Brown was forced to retreat to the armory's engine house where the hostages were held in an adjoining guard house. By early afternoon, large numbers of armed whites on higher ground began to fire down on the several raiders and slave allies who had not joined him in the engine house. Most of these were killed when attempting to escape, some having been murdered outright after being apprehended. By the afternoon, Brown and company, including slave collaborators, were holed up in the engine house and surrounded by a joint force of uniformed militia and armed citizens. At this point he made his first attempt to swap hostages for safe passage into Maryland with his men. Finding his terms rejected, Brown and his men faced a bold attack, including a nearly successful attempt to break through the doors of the engine house. Although effectively holding off the attack, Brown's opposition now thickened with the addition of militia from Maryland and, finally, with the arrival of federal marines during the night of October 17. Under the command of Colonel Robert E. Lee, the marines assaulted the engine house in the morning, successfully breaking through, killing three raiders and wounding Brown. In the end, ten raiders were killed in battle along with an undetermined number of slave allies, while five raiders escaped—including Brown's son Owen and black enlistee Osborne Anderson from Canada. Ultimately six were hanged following the execution of their leader.[107]

* * *

In their haste to narrate the story of the Harper's Ferry raid, historians have often moved far too quickly over the several months of Brown's residence in the region, lending the impression that he did little more than write letters and shuttle back-and-forth from Chambersburg, Pennsylvania, his secondary base of operations. To the contrary, Brown probably made a number of trips, moving "from place to place at a fantastic rate," making observations, contacts, and investigations in anticipation of the raid. Indeed, this may be the most mysterious period of his career as an anti-slavery leader, especially because it entails interaction with free blacks, possible contact with enslaved people, and other appearances in the region—all of which suggest that his surveillance and strategy went beyond what has usually been credited by historians. Just as the ostensible Isaac Smith's alleged business interests in mining served as a pretense for receiving heavy freight loads of weapons, his alleged business movements also provided an excellent excuse to move about the greater area in preparing for the establishment of his guerilla program. The hackneyed notion that he simply assumed that the slaves would join him without making prior contact is really quite presumptuous, even illogical considering Brown's unwavering tendency to seek out blacks on their own turf. To presume that he did nothing but set up shop and wait for the hour to strike is self-serving to his critics, especially those who suppose the raid was little more than a quixotic adventure doomed to failure.

While there are stories of Brown's movements in the South that clearly are fictive, other accounts exist that seem far more substantial and worthy of note. For instance, there is good evidence that Brown made a hasty tour through western Virginia in Clarksburg and the Monogahela Valley in July-August 1859. Apparently what drew him in that direction was the case of Charlotte Harris, a free woman married to an enslaved man. Harris had secretly planned to lead a large number of slaves into the North with the assistance of another free woman from Pennsylvania. When the plan was betrayed, Harris was arrested and then taken into custody by her husband's owner, who then attempted to persuade Harris to enslave herself to him. When a local judge took an interest in the case and sued out a writ of habeus corpus for Harris's release, a trial date was set for the circuit court on August 1. Brown may have read about the Harris case in the newspapers, for soon he appeared in the county posing as a cattle buyer. Anonymously retaining a defense lawyer for Harris at his own expense, he attended the court hearing as a spectator. When a prominent citizen in attendance grew curious about the mysterious bearded man seated in court, he asked another attender, a sketch artist, to make a portrait of him. "He tries to look like a rock but is as restless as a squirrel," noted the curious onlooker. "No doubt an abolitionist, every hair of him, and he has a big crop of it." Local leaders likely found the bearded stranger more than curious, especially if they had learned that he had paid for Harris's legal defense. Brown would have been drawn to the Harris case like a moth to a flame, for it had all the elements of interest to his own plans. Western Virginia was never a strongly pro-slavery region (something that President Lincoln exploited during the Civil War by making it into the state of West Virginia) and there would be good reason for him to expect to find black and white supporters in the Monongahela Valley. In particular, the Harris case showed another local attempt on the part of blacks to liberate themselves, and this probably drew Brown's interest as a possible source of support, or as a base of operations when his operation began to unfold. Finally, he may have been interested in Harris and her free black contact from Pennsylvania, Malvina Nixon, as possible recruiters for his own operation.

Whatever the case, residents of Clarksburg later recognized the similarity between the mysterious visitor and newspaper sketches of Brown that were published after the failure of the Harper's Ferry raid. Brown likely made another recorded stop while in the Clarksburg area, this time posing as a Mason, in order to request financial assistance from the local lodge. Once more, local Masons recognized Brown's newspaper sketches after the raid as highly resembling the man to whom they had given twenty dollars several months earlier. Certainly Brown, an ex-Mason, was well aware of the order's ways and rhetoric and could easily have convinced a Mason of his fraternal need. Such a pretense was frankly unethical according to Brown's Christian convictions, but if he was the man who begged money in the name of the worthy brotherhood, it may be that he felt it was a fitting form of reparations for local white leaders to reimburse him for the cost of defending an anti-slavery activist. In Kansas and Missouri he had thought nothing of taking the material and livestock of slave masters in the name of repaying stolen labor. Given Brown's disdain for the lodge, especially pro-slavery Masons, he may have derived double pleasure at the outcome. These curious episodes in western Virginia show that John Brown's antennae were quite receptive to regional developments that might weigh in the favor of his movement, and that the months prior to the Harper's Ferry raid were undoubtedly marked by any number of clandestine movements in a variety of directions. While one would not expect to find written records of Brown's efforts to contact or even interact with enslaved people, the context of his movements and associations in the vicinity suggest that there is a hidden layer of activity and preparation prior to the raid that traditional scholarship has overlooked.[108]

In reconsidering the Harper's Ferry raid itself, one should understand the intensely political nature of the record that has defined Brown and his failed venture within the ruling narrative of history. It was not until the 1970s that Jean Libby and Barrie Stavis made critical observations about the prevailing tendency of white scholars to accept the testimony of slave holders and white Virginians uncritically, as well as to overlook that of Brown's followers, especially his black followers.[109] In fact, the first "official" historians of the raid were the slave holders themselves, who had a real interest in diminishing Brown's impact on the enslaved community by portraying the supposed impotency of his efforts to attract the slaves to his side. Following the well-publicized version of the slave master was the official state record produced by the federal government in 1860, a bipartisan congressional report overseen and shaped by the majority Democratic pro-slavery leadership. This so-called Mason Report contains a fascinating collection of testimonies and transcriptions of many important documents, making it a highly valuable resource for students of the raid, yet it is hardly an objective framework for studying Brown's efforts. Indeed, the Mason Report is essentially a pro-slavery production with a minority contribution mainly intent on denying the culpability or involvement of anti-slavery Republicans in the Harper's Ferry raid. As the rhetoric of Republican leaders shows, by 1860 it was a foregone conclusion among them that the raid was sheer folly, outrageous and ill-contrived as much as it was illegal in its goal of undermining the property rights of slave owners. While Brown emerged as a northern hero for the Civil War generation, this was only a temporary reprieve in the broader reckoning of United States history. With the demise of Reconstruction and the rise of a generation that held little or no regard for either John Brown or black people, it was ultimately the discourse of the South as well as antagonistic northern writers that shaped Brown's historical image as either a frenzied brigand or a delusional fanatic. By the turn of the 20th century, the line that separated his friends and enemies was virtually identical to the color line. Even the supposed "friendly" white liberal biographer Oswald Garrison Villard, writing fifty years after Brown's execution, dismissed both the black eyewitness and scholarly understanding of the raid.[110]

While a growing number of grassroots and independent scholars no longer embrace the "official" account of the raid, it is still presumed by many that the assault on Harper's Ferry was half-baked and founded upon flagrant misjudgment and delusion. It has also been assumed that the raid's failure negates Brown's ability, rationale, and the overall premise of his strategy. Often too there is the insistence that he intended a violent uprising or insurrection. Along with these mistaken ideas concerning the raid, the accepted narrative has established a false standard concerning the alleged lack of support by the enslaved community. Likewise, it is erroneously presumed that either the enslaved community was not informed in advance of the raid or that the slaves simply refused to cooperate for lack of confidence or familiarity. Yet these roaring assumptions are but paper lions when challenged by the evidence as well as recognition of the political prejudice underlying what Hannah Geffert calls the "conventional histories" of the raid.[111]

Whether or not they were sympathetic toward Brown, most northerners believed that the Harper's Ferry raid was preposterous as a military objective. Given the fact that few people in the North understood Brown's intentions, the idea that he would attack a government armory in the South with a small number of men made the whole affair seem a dismissible act of marginal extremism. Jacob Collamer, a Republican senator from Vermont, thus concluded in the Mason Report that Brown had exploited the sentiments of some young Kansas veterans, bringing forth the "atrocity" at Harper's Ferry. Collamer also embraced the notion of "the entire disinclination of the slaves to insurrection, or to receive aid for that purpose" and assured the South that another such outbreak was even beyond "the most distant probability." Much to the dismay of the Republicans, however, the South had quite a different view. Even though northerners had accepted their claim that blacks were indifferent to Brown's liberation movement, southern leaders tended to view the raid as a real expression of the northern anti-slavery consensus. As Virginia's Governor Henry Wise demonstrated in his determination to hang John Brown, southerners assumed that the raid "was not the insignificant thing which it appeared to be before the public." Indeed, Republicans were deeply concerned over the determination shown by Virginia's Senator James Mason and the other pro-slavery committee members to root out and destroy the widespread northern conspiracy which they believed to be behind the Harper's Ferry raid.

Neither side was correct. Fearing the escalation of civil strife, the Republican party sought to assuage the South by accepting its claim that Brown's conspiracy was not only immoral but also impotent in the face of slave loyalty. While most northern whites were hardly inclined to plot liberation movements in the South, it was an error on the part of the Republicans to overlook the ripening difficulties faced by slave holders. From the mid-1850s there had been a marked increase in unrest among enslaved people in the South, probably sparked by incidents in the Kansas territory. Slave masters from Virginia to Texas were well aware that insurrection often stood just outside the door. Rather than attributing these uprisings to the oppressive grip of slavery itself, Republican leaders sought to placate southern interests, at least enough to preserve the Union. In contrast, southern leaders upheld the self-serving myth of slave loyalty and blamed any occurrence of unrest and rebellion upon the agitation of northern abolitionists. While broadcasting the supposed loyalty of the slave, the slave master and his allies actually lived in anxiety about the possibility of explosive insurrections and rebellions. They likewise knew full well that enslaved people were quite capable of revolt without being incited by northern abolitionists, just as they knew that the slave community was extremely sensitive to the rumor and rumination of revolt across regions. Whites and free blacks got their news from the telegraph and the press, but the enslaved had the "underground wire," a startlingly effective means of communication that carried news over many miles like electricity along a human wire of souls and whispers. "There was a mysterious connection between the Negroes of all parts of the South, which made the [Harper's Ferry raid] feasible," abolitionist Passmore Williamson later wrote. "By some system of secret communication, any matter looking to the freedom of the slaves was spread amongst them in some effectual way, and it was this that Mr. Brown depended on to make the scheme a success." Contrary to Republican rhetoric, as long as slavery endured and civil war was avoided, more liberation efforts likely would have occurred because the enslaved themselves would have continued to revolt, with or without white northern support. In contrast, the South might pretend that slaves were essentially loyal and content, but their armed militia and untiring vigilance suggests that they knew otherwise. In either case, North and South, the claim that enslaved people did not know or care about John Brown's efforts is ludicrous if one discerns slavery from the standpoint of the slave instead of the propaganda of the slave holding elites, their political representatives, and northerners who acquiesced to them for political reasons.[112]

Contrary to many narratives, John Brown's intentions at Harper's Ferry were both reasonable and sufficiently developed, failing only in execution. While he was invariably reticent about his plans, or given to selectively divulging his intentions in order to protect his strategy or authority (thus he did not readily reveal his intention of seizing the government armory to his men), the assault on Harper's Ferry was an idea that he had been considering for some time. It is likely that Brown had begun to contemplate seizing the armory as far back as the late 1840s when he was operating the wool commission business in Springfield, Massachusetts. In this respect the significance of Springfield is undoubtable since it was the site of the only government armory in the North, the only other federal armory being located in Harper's Ferry. Brown probably toured the Springfield armory, which was virtually in plain sight from his home on Hastings (now Franklin) Street. Given his interests, he could easily acquaint himself with the details of its function, just as he later made a number of incognito visits in the summer of 1859 to observe its sister operation in Virginia. No doubt this interest in the government's two armories was an aspect of his broader analysis of southern maneuvering within the antebellum federal government. In his last meeting with William Phillips in Kansas, Brown told the young writer that for years he had been observing southern interests at work in manipulating military, navy, and armaments in providing for the possibility of secession. Though the journalist later acknowledged the prophetic nature of Brown's words, he balked at this analysis in 1859, particularly the old man's insistence that the country was "on the eve of one of the greatest wars in history" which—if won by the South—would mark "an end of all aspirations for human freedom." In light of Brown's careful study of the federal government's operations and the fact that Harper's Ferry was the only armory in the South, it is no surprise that the quiet Virginia town was the primary target rather than other points in the domain of slavery. If the testimony of associate George Gill is trustworthy, Brown even raised the idea of seizing the armory during the Chatham convention in May 1858. While John Jr. later said that he was surprised by his father's decision to attack Harper's Ferry, this only suggests the old man's reticence, perhaps because Junior had chosen not to join his father in the field. Yet even he recalled that his father had "expressly stated that the first blow would be struck at some place in Virginia or Maryland," apparently a veiled reference to Harper's Ferry.

Brown's hesitance to declare his intentions about attacking Harper's Ferry makes sense when we consider that doing so upgraded the risk and penalty attached to the mission. While Brown was ready to accept the supreme penalty for his actions, he clearly differed from others with respect to the risk involved in invading the town and armory. While the prevailing assumption was that a government site would be extremely difficult to assault, Brown evidently knew that neither armory was well-guarded and both were under negligible civilian supervision. In fact Brown's assessment was afterward justified by Alfred Barbour, superintendent of the Harper's Ferry armory, who admitted that actually it would have taken "corps of soldiers" to prevent "old Brown's temporary success here." Given the element of nocturnal surprise, as Barbour insinuates, the Harper's Ferry invasion might have proven a brilliant stroke had Brown paid greater heed to the fleeting nature of his advantage and moved out of town without delay.

After his defeat by federal forces, Brown was cross-examined by Governor Henry Wise of Virginia, who attempted to belittle the old man as being foolish for having dared to attack Harper's Ferry with only a small force of men. Rarely outdone in a contest of words, Wise was nevertheless flabbergasted by Brown's retort: "Why Governor, I did take it and hold it the better part of two days." Like the governor, many writers have long since diminished Brown for having dared to attack Harper's Ferry with so small a force of men. Yet they have also missed the point that considering that it took nearly two days, and finally the assistance of federal marines, to defeat the raiders, the idea of the invasion itself hardly seems unreasonable. If executed with lightning speed and undistracted determination, Brown and his men would have faced no adequate counter-attack and certainly no formidable pursuit force. They, along with their initial black recruits, might easily have slipped into the mountains, dissolved into small, scattered bands of plantation raiders and embarked upon the most elusive and demoralizing campaign against slavery in the history of the United States.[113]

Just as Brown's failure at Harper's Ferry neither discredits his sanity nor the rationality of his plan, it is also not the case that he plotted an *insurrection*, though many historians likewise follow the rhetoric of slave masters in viewing his intentions as such. To be sure, his denial of plotting an insurrection meant little to southerners, who viewed any liberation effort as fundamentally hostile and murderous. However it was a point of strategic and ethical concern to Brown that differentiation be made between his intentions and those typically associated with slave uprisings. After his arrest, Brown told Clement Vallindigham, a pro-slavery Ohio congressman, that he neither expected nor wished for a "general uprising of the slaves" but intended "to gather them up from time to time, and set them free." He reiterated the same differentiation in his statement at trial on November 2, 1859, when he told the Court: "I never did intend murder, or treason, or the destruction of property, or to excite or incite slaves to rebellion, or to make insurrection." Three weeks later, Brown wrote to the special prosecutor emphasizing that "it was my object to place the slaves in a condition to defend their liberties, if they would, without any bloodshed, but not that I intended to run them out of the slave States." According to Owen Brown, one of the surviving raiders, his father "feared that this method might lead to the use of firearms occasionally, but he hoped to avoid serious bloodshed."[114]

Like his southern captors, Brown was well aware of the Nat Turner revolt of 1831, when a small army of enslaved men hacked and bludgeoned their way through a Virginia community, even killing infants and children. While Brown sympathized with the Turner movement, he clearly devised an alternative model of rebellion where the enslaved would flee, incite others to flight, and resort to violence only in defense of their operations. Far from the terrorist notion so prominent among contemporary writing, Brown abhorred the idea of making war on civilians and even more dreaded the possibility that his movement might lapse into a blood-letting insurrection. "I may perhaps feel no more love of the business than they do," Brown wrote in 1857 about his sons' decision to evade further fighting and violence on behalf of the anti-slavery cause. "[S]till I think there may be possibly in their day that which is more to be dreaded, if such things *do not now exist*." In other words, he felt that a minimalist approach to violence in opposition to slavery was far better than allowing the course of events to run to the extremes of civil war. In fact, Brown was prescient, for his sons lived to see the horrible bloodletting that he feared would occur if slavery went unchecked. When he failed to circumvent the tragedy and faced the gallows for his effort, Brown's last written statement thus declared that he had intended to undermine slavery "without verry [sic] much bloodshed." Recognizing his real agenda, Jean Libby, one of foremost authorities on the Harper's Ferry raid, knowingly asks: "Had John Brown designed another way? Was his method, always called 'violence,' actually a planned nonviolent revolution?" While "nonviolent revolution" may be an overstatement, her grasp of Brown's intentions are sound. Contrary to all that is presumed about him in so many historical narratives, the hope underlying the raid at Harper's Ferry was to drain slavery of its economic vitality, not terrorize and kill slave masters. "Do not, therefore, take the life of any one, if you can possibly avoid it," Brown told his raiders prior to attacking Harper's Ferry, "but if it is necessary to take life in order to save your own, then make sure work of it."[115]

In order to undercut the possibility of his movement becoming unhinged and deleterious, Brown's first measure was the *Provisional Constitution*, based on the assumption that the rule of law must guide any liberation effort in order to safeguard both the oppressed and the oppressor from immoral abuse and crimes of war. Second, he sought to retain black leaders like Douglass and Harriet Tubman, who would act as effective agents in organizing and guiding the liberated, and restraining possible outbursts of lawlessness. "Come with me, Douglass," Brown told the orator in Chambersburg, "I will defend you with my life. I want you for a special purpose. When I strike the bees will begin to swarm, and I shall want you to help hive them." Of course Douglass and other established black leaders demurred and refrained. Although Tubman—now acknowledged as the "Moses" of her people—was enthusiastically favorable toward Brown and initially supported his recruitment efforts in 1858, even she did not follow through for reasons that remain unclear. It has long been held that sickness alone kept her from joining him in 1859, though a recent biographer suggests that Tubman may have feigned illness rather than "endure Brown's disapproval." Perhaps she was likewise influenced by the sympathetic opposition of Frederick Douglass and others who thought it best not to risk their freedom on Brown's uncertain plan—particularly after word got around that he intended to attack Harper's Ferry. Some have presumed that Brown was a paternalist who did not appoint blacks as officers because he believed a liberation movement could not succeed without white leadership. However Osborne Anderson, one of the black raiders, made it clear that Brown "did offer the captaincy, and other military positions, to colored men equally with others," but their lack of acquaintance with military tactics "was the invariable excuse." Anderson himself declined Brown's offer of a command position. Others have concluded that despite Brown's egalitarian convictions, he was fundamentally conflicted within by a fear of black people—a phobia that blacks allegedly interpreted as a kind of futility. But this clever argument is premised on the flawed notion that he was typical of the mainstream white abolitionists. To the contrary, Brown never manifested the "conflicting strands" of humanitarian idealism and Negrophobia that frequently characterized white abolitionism, including some of the "Secret Six."[116]

In August 1861, when the Union army followed John Brown's footsteps to Harper's Ferry, Lieutenant Robert Morris Copeland was among those serving with the Massachusetts 2nd Regiment, which was supervising the federal occupation under General Nathaniel Banks. Copeland was from a prosperous Boston family, a Harvard graduate, a landscape and planning professional, and author of the popular antebellum book, *Country Life*. He was also on the vanguard of abolitionists calling for the enlistment of black fighters in the Union army, and actually preceded his more famous associate and neighbor, Robert Gould Shaw, in advocating the inclusion of African Americans (Shaw was in the Massachusetts 2nd Regiment before assuming command of the now famous black Massachusetts 54th Regiment). As Copeland recalled eight years later, it was during this occupation that he met a black fugitive named Antony Hunter, who had fled from slavery in nearby Shepherdstown, seeking sanctuary in the northern camp. As was the custom of many Union officers, Copeland took Hunter as his personal aid, and the young man proved a valuable servant and enthusiastic supporter, albeit one who feared reprisal should he be returned to slavery. Given Copeland's abolitionist interests, it was not long before he raised the subject of John Brown's raid, asking the fugitive what he knew about it. To his surprise, Hunter flatly contradicted the official record, particularly with respect to the involvement of enslaved blacks in the raid. According to the fugitive, he himself had been selected as a lieutenant for Shepherdstown blacks who answered Brown's call. Copeland used racially caricatured language in reporting the black man's words, an unfortunate tendency among white writers in the 19th century, including abolitionists. Yet the content of his testimony is clear: Hunter estimated that hundreds of blacks had been enlisted by Brown and his men, many of them slaves who had been "hired out" to whites outside of the immediate vicinity. Furthermore, the notion that the slaves did not care for Brown or choose to help him was only the propaganda of whites, although actually more "hired out" slaves returned to Jefferson County to join Brown's movement than normally returned on weekends and holidays. Copeland was naturally put off by Hunter's claim, especially since so many black recruits would have been evident in town and would surely have made a significant difference in the outcome of the raid. However the fugitive slave explained that the original plan determined by Brown and agreed upon by local blacks was that they would meet in the mountains instead of returning to work on Monday. There they would wait for a signal to rendezvous with the raiders after they had left the town. However when they arrived, they found that Brown and his men were still down in Harper's Ferry, and now the town was exploding in combat. Worse, they quickly learned that blacks as well as whites had been killed, no doubt also hearing that Brown's men had killed the baggage master Haywood Shepherd, a free black man. Paralyzed by the fear of being "cheated" by whites, Hunter said, the assembling black volunteers looked on without certainty, now having to decide whether or not to expose themselves in the midst of this conflict. Knowing that their capture would mean either death or being sold farther south, the slave recruits chose to wait and see what happened. With the final marine assault and the capture of Brown and his surviving raiders, the slaves had no recourse but to withdraw quietly and return to their places of labor. According to Antony Hunter, neither the slaves nor Brown and his men would ever admit the extent of their contact, although the fugitive was sure that many more blacks would have joined the effort had its leader moved according to plan. Indeed, the number of blacks joining him would have swelled to a militant army in two days, Hunter concluded, "an' dey'd hab fought fur him till all was killed, ef dey could hab beliebed in de white men bein' true." As for Brown himself, "dar warn't many such men as Mr. Brown; he was de saviour an' redeemer ob de cullud people, an' mos' ob dem beliebe he was Jesus Christ come back ter sabe us."

The testimony of Antony Hunter obviously flies in the face of the conventional record of the raid, especially in his claim that hundreds—perhaps nearly one thousand—enslaved people were actually gathering in the mountains near Harper's Ferry on October 17, 1859, awaiting Brown and his men. Given the prevalence of the slave master's version of the raid, one might suspect that Copeland simply fabricated this story out of sympathy for Brown's cause. However, it does not follow that even an abolitionist would have done so because of his political views or his admiration for John Brown. During the years of the Civil War and Reconstruction, Brown was immensely popular in the North, posthumously admired by whites and blacks even though it was commonly accepted that he had failed to gain significant support from slaves. Indeed, those who uplifted Brown the most had no concern for whether he had ever really been a strategic threat to slavery, since they saw his efforts at Harper's Ferry as an episode of hopeless self-sacrifice. To the Civil War generation, it was John Brown's death as a martyr that was the central theme of his triumph, and there was no real interest in justifying his strategy. The assumption that he had failed to draw slaves to his side was so preponderant among the anti-slavery generation of the mid-to-late 19th century that even Brown's unknowing family members apparently accepted it as fact. "He misjudged the negroes as well as the soldiers of the standing army," daughter Anne Brown wrote, quite erroneously, in later years. "He expected they would recognize and receive him as the 'Moses.'"[117]

Furthermore, Robert Morris Copeland's military record affirms the basis of his account since his presence at Harper's Ferry as a lieutenant in the Massachusetts 2nd Regiment in August 1861 is verified. Even more, his narrative is strengthened by the fact that Antony Hunter was a real person, appearing in the 1870 census as a thirty-year-old farm laborer living in the Shepherdstown vicinity. Indeed the black man identified as Anthony Hunter in the census completely fits the profile of the Antony Hunter portrayed by Copeland—his age, illiteracy, laborer status, and birth in [West] Virginia all attest to the integrity of the story. Finally, Copeland's Antony Hunter claimed that his slave mistress was from the leading Shepherd family, although her exact identity is not clear. Historian Hannah Geffert notes that Shepherdstown was a small farming village settled by Pennsylvanians; the census and slave schedules for 1860 show several Shepherd families, most of whom were slave owners. Interestingly, Shepherdstown was bordered on both sides by communities of enslaved and free blacks known as Little Philadelphia and Angel Hill, which would have been logical sites of interest to Brown and his men and likely where he made contact with Hunter and other Shepherdstown blacks prior to the raid.[118]

The testimony of Antony Hunter further affirms what historians like Jean Libby and Hannah Geffert have shown by closely studying the black communities of Jefferson County and the testimony of John Brown's black Canadian enlistee, Osborne Anderson. These scholars have shown that even apart from the revelatory testimony of Hunter, there is pregnant evidence of extensive black involvement in the raid, even excluding the many slaves who came close to joining Brown but withdrew. Geffert says that in the initial phase of the raid, from twenty-five to fifty black men were armed, including those who came "after hearing of the raid from 'underground wires.'" Considering that most slaves were scattered in the rural areas of the county and the ratio of whites to blacks was two to one, the active presence of this many enslaved men in town is quite meaningful. "Eyewitness accounts tell of considerable local black activity," Geffert continues, "'Negroes' in the early hours of the fight in and around 'John Brown's Fort' [the engine house] and slaves with spears in their hands near the engine-house. One of Brown's hostages said Harper's Ferry 'looked like war—Negroes armed with pikes, and sentinels with muskets all around.'" Geffert writes further that at least fourteen black men assisted Brown's raiders on the Maryland side by protecting weapons and guarding prisoners, and also by transporting arms from the Kennedy farm to a school house designated as a rendezvous point. Others acted as messengers to further spread the word among the enslaved. Finally, she concludes by pointing out that the neighboring hillside was congested with frightened white people, but that "armed Africans were seen in some numbers." Unlike traditional historians, Geffert speaks for those who question the slave master's version, instead seeing that "in fact [Brown] did manage to accomplish some of what he had set out to do. He had identified and made common cause with active black abolitionists and had found a location for his raid where the attack would have a significant impact on the institution of slavery."[119]

After having done extensive field research in the oral history of the black community of Jefferson County, likewise scouring archives and newspaper sources and carefully scrutinizing every extant contemporary testimony concerning the raid, historian Jean Libby similarly concluded that the official record cannot be taken as fact. Indeed her narrative is rife with evidence of an overarching presence of blacks within and surrounding Harper's Ferry at the time of the raid, the facts of which have long been overlooked because of the political agenda of slave owners and the presuppositions of historians, most of whom have never closely studied the details and testimonies surrounding the incident. She admits that trying to come to absolute certainty about the number of blacks who fought and died at Harper's Ferry is difficult, yet a thorough reckoning of the evidence and testimony of eyewitnesses shows that many more people were part of the raid, and that Brown's effort, although failing, invoked passionate responses from local blacks afterward. In fact, both Libby and Geffert agree that in the aftermath of the raid, black zeal and sympathy for Brown and his cause resulted in a wave of subversive reactions, from the damaging and destruction of slave holders' and jurors' property to an unprecedented increase in runaways.[120]

Apart from her careful discovery of long overlooked black participants throughout the story of the raid, Libby's greatest contribution has been to make a serious study of Osborne Anderson's worthy narrative, *A Voice from Harper's Ferry* (1861), the only primary sketch of Brown and the raid written by one of the participating raiders, who was also the only African American expatriate who joined the effort from Canada. Despite the fact that Anderson wrote as an honest eyewitness, white historians and scholars have usually diminished or altogether ignored his account in favor of the testimony of slave holders. While many recent historians have simply overlooked Anderson's testimony without offering a worthy explanation, they seem to have followed the pattern first established in 1910 by biographer Oswald Villard, who dismissed the black raider's version altogether. According to Villard, a "monstrous discrepancy" in Anderson's account discredited his narrative because he claimed to have seen the engine house assaulted and Brown captured by the marines before he escaped on Monday, October 17, although the final assault did not take place until Tuesday morning, October 18. But Libby shows that it was Villard who erred by failing to study the events of the raid in detail. Had he done so, the biographer would have realized that Anderson indeed saw the movement of armed troops across the Potomac on Monday afternoon, followed by a uniformed deployment and a "charge upon the engine house with the ladder." However Libby shows that the armed troops in uniform that Anderson saw were not the federal marines, but the Jefferson Guards, a militia organization from nearby Charles Town. Similarly, the ramming of the engine house door observed from a distance was an effort by a group of brave railroad men, who made a nearly successful attempt on Monday at around three o'clock in the afternoon, at the time that Anderson was fleeing. Notwithstanding his error in confusing the earlier assault with the final marine assault (which he could only have learned about after making good his escape), the overall testimony of Osborne Anderson is vindicated by Libby.[121] Considering the fact that he was an associate and eyewitness of John Brown in both Canada and at Harper's Ferry, as well as the only raider to have written a basically reliable and richly detailed account of the raid, only oversight and human prejudice can explain why *A Voice from Harper's Ferry* has repeatedly been slighted by historians. Indeed, without a careful study of Anderson's narrative, no analysis of the raid and its incidents can stand respectably as sound historical work—especially regarding the involvement and activities of local blacks and the nature of Brown's failure.

8. John Brown—for the Record

Osborne Anderson was clearly offended by the prominent version of the raid put forth by slave masters and further exaggerated by the political cartoonist for *Harper's Weekly*, David Hunter Strother (known as Porte Crayon), which characterized blacks as fearful, ineffectual, and unsupportive of John Brown's efforts. As Libby observes, Strother's cartoons "greatly influenced history toward the slaveholders' viewpoint by his caricatures of fearful slaves and a mad John Brown—more insidiously memorable than a thousand words." Strother was a pro-Union southerner but was clearly a racist. In one *Harper's* article, he spoke of blacks as "half-monkey," and in another article portrayed one of Brown's heroic black raiders as a thief loaded down with the treasures of slave masters he had killed. In his political cartoons, he shows a presumptuous Brown being put off by cowardly slaves, and the only warlike black portrayed by Strother is a loyal matron ready to fight for her master. To the contrary, Anderson contended, blacks fought bravely alongside the Harper's Ferry raiders while captive slave masters cowered in fear and wept for their lives—so much so that they distracted and detained John Brown. "The Virginians may well conceal their losses . . . for their boasted bravery was well tested that day, and in no way to their advantage," Anderson wrote. According to the raider, another aspect of southern misrepresentation was the "studied attempt to enforce the belief that the slaves were cowardly, and that they were really more in favor of Virginia masters and slavery, than of their freedom."[122]

As an eyewitness, Anderson gave details of the enthusiastic response of enslaved people to the raiders, with the exception of one freedman who refused to participate on the night of the raid. Indeed his only criticism of blacks concerned certain freedmen in the South who had proven to be unreliable. As for the slaves, he wrote, even John Brown was "surprised and pleased" when so many actually volunteered to join him in the fighting at Harper's Ferry—apparently assuming that they would more readily have joined him in the mountains after exiting town. The fact that many slaves boldly volunteered to fight alongside his men in Harper's Ferry was a point that "agreeably disappointed" Brown, "for he did not expect one out of ten to be willing to fight."[123] Essentially agreeing with the testimony of Antony Hunter, Osborne Anderson concluded:

> That hundreds of slaves were ready, and would have joined in the work, had Captain Brown's sympathies not been aroused in favor of the families of his prisoners, and that a very different result would have been seen, in consequence, there is no question. There was abundant opportunity for him and the party to leave a place in which they held entire sway and possession, before the arrival of the troops.[124]

Anderson verifies what Brown and his men clearly knew, that many slaves were eagerly awaiting his exit from Harper's Ferry and movement toward the mountains, and that his plan might very well have succeeded had he not delayed in town. He likewise shows that Brown was apparently stymied by the pitiable responses of the whites, particularly the slave holders who blubbered, moaned, and wept "cowardly tears."

In the face of horrified, fearful spectators and prisoners, Brown's apparent puzzlement shows that he was not emotionally prepared for their reaction. He had long preached that "slaveholders will never give up their slaves peaceably. They will never give them up until they feel the big stick over their heads." Had the slave holders around Harper's Ferry cursed and fought like tigers, perhaps he would have found it easier to expedite his plans. But these were a different class of people from the thugs and terrorist collaborators he had known in Kansas. Instead he came face-to-face with quaint, helpless, sobbing men, and their pathetic reactions disarmed him. This is precisely the side of John Brown that historians have failed to recognize in their determination to portray him as a cold-hearted "Old Testament" warrior and terrorist. The longer he remained in Harper's Ferry, the more he succumbed to his "New Testament" sensibilities, which got the best of him to the point that he became fixated on placating and comforting his prisoners. This was most evident in the fact that instead of rallying slaves and free blacks, he began to discuss possible terms of release with his prisoners, doubtless assuring them that his intentions were markedly different from that of an insurrectionist. When some prisoners "wanted to go home to see their families, as if for the last time," Brown went so far as to grant them the privilege to do so, sending them home with an armed escort and then bringing them back in the same manner. This peculiar sensitivity toward the enemy was hardly the manner of a terrorist, and it was this kind of concern for the feelings of his foes that ultimately undermined his own efforts. "Hold on a little longer, boys, until I get matters arranged with the prisoners," Brown told his worried raiders as he temporized over the victory within his reach. Indeed, Osborne Anderson and his fellow raiders were put off by their leader's "tardiness" in departing from town. As precious moments of opportunity slipped away, they feared that Brown's behavior was "an omen of evil." Anderson recognized that this vivid concern for the enemy "was no part of the original plan to hold on to the Ferry, or to parley with prisoners; but by so doing, time was afforded to carry the news of its capture to several points, and forces were thrown into the place, which surrounded us."[125] In retrospect, he gently if not adoringly chided Brown's greatest shortcoming at Harper's Ferry:

> . . . and could our brave old Captain have steeled his heart against the entreaties of his captives, or shut up the fountain of his sympathies against their families—could he, for the moment, have forgotten them, in the selfish thought of his own friends and kindred, or, by adhering to the original plan, have left the place, and thus looked forward to the prospective freedom of the slave—hundreds ready and waiting would have been armed before twenty-four hours had elapsed.[126]

Few if any have criticized John Brown for his reckless compassion, or attributed his failure at Harper's Ferry to a worried devotion to the Golden Rule. Yet it was neither inept planning nor a lack of strategic support that proved his downfall at Harper's Ferry, but rather the same deep-rooted sympathy that had always driven him to the side of the downcast. Thinking that he could somehow balance the enemies' peace with the success of his mission, he was caught in a trap of his own making, but not the "perfect steel trap" that Frederick Douglass had predicted two months before. John Brown had done his homework well and easily captured the defenseless town and armory, and could just as easily have walked away had he not delayed. It was his own heartfelt blunder that allowed him to fall into the hands of the Old Dominion.

Not long after his defeat and capture, Brown thus gave an interview to the *Spirit of Jefferson*, published in nearby Charles Town. According to the reporter's summary

> Capt. Brown requested us to state that he and his party positively deny any intention to commit murder, to shoot at, or injure in any way, persons who were not fighting against them. And further, that it was a feeling of humanity that betrayed him into an error which caused the failure of his plans. This

error was in permitting the train of cars to pass, and delaying with his prisoners. For this he is blameable in a military point of view as the leader of the
expedition.[127]

As he awaited his appointment with the gallows in the waning days
of 1859, John Brown could not help but replay the raid and the error of
his judgments in mind. "It is solely my own fault, in a military point of
view, that we met with our disaster," he wrote to a Quaker admirer on
November 1. "I mean that I mingled with our prisoners and so far sympathized with them and their families that I neglected my duty in other
respects" [Document 17]. How could he fully explain to anyone, especially his self-denying wife, that the project for which they had prayed
and planned for so many years had come to such a tragic failure? "Full
particulars relating to our disaster; I can not now give: & may never give
probably," he wrote to Mary on November 10. "I am dayly [*sic*] & hourly
striving to gather up what little I may from the wreck" [Document 18].
What was he "gathering up" in the labors of his mind and heart? Always
given to looking for hope in the most dire circumstances, Brown was
now weighing his error and loss against the new opportunity to redeem
himself on the gallows. Yet the fact of his misjudgment haunted him. "I
have been a good deal disappointed as it regards myself in not keeping
up to my own plans," he wrote to an elderly acquaintance on November
15; "but I now feel entirely reconciled to that, even, for God's plan was
infinitely better, no doubt, or I should have kept to my own." In hind-
sight he could see that he had been "induced to act very *contrary* to my
better judgment." Now he could only reconcile failure as he had done at
other times of bitter disappointment, by reminding himself of the sovereignty of God and his own belief that the purpose of the divine might
yet overrule the purpose of man [Document 19]. "I failed," he told one
of his guards, "but it is only delay, for as certain as the sun shines, the
negroes will soon be set free."[128]

Finally, one week before his hanging, Brown responded to the letter
of his relative Heman Humphrey of Massachusetts, in order to clarify
some aspects of the raid. "But I will here state that I know it to be wholly
my own fault as a leader that caused our disaster," he wrote on November 25 [Document 20]. "Of this you have no proper means of judging,
not being on the ground, or a practical soldier."

> I will only add, that it was in yielding to my feelings of humanity (if I ever
> exercised such a feeling), in leaving my proper place and mingling with my
> prisoners to quiet their fears, that occasioned our being caught. I firmly
> believe that God reigns, and that he overrules all things in the best possible

manner; and in that view of the subject I try to be in some degree reconciled to my own weaknesses and follies . . . . The impression that we intended a general insurrection is equally untrue.[129]

There was little else that John Brown could do now but write letters, pray, and tie up the loose ends of his affairs while awaiting his appointment with the hangman. Throughout his final weeks, he received scores of letters and responded to many of them. There would also be tender epistles to his wife and children, the preparation of a last will and testament, and even an attempt to lessen the possibility of vendetta against the enslaved in the aftermath of the raid. "Regarding my intentions respecting the slaves *we took* about the Ferry," he wrote gratuitously to Prosecutor Andrew Hunter, ". . . it was my object to place the slaves in a condition to defend their liberties, if they would, without any bloodshed, but not that I intended to run them out of the slave States." Of course, he had not *taken* slaves, the notion of which was purely a southern fantasy. For the record, Brown himself was now contributing something to the myth of the raid by telling the Special Prosecutor that he had taken slaves against their wills. His plans dashed, now hope rested only in the gallows and the "rebound" of his own sacrifice, as Osborne Anderson finally put it.[130] By appearing to admit that the slaves had joined him by force, Brown wanted to assuage the fears of Virginians, evidently hoping to undercut a possible white backlash, the kind of which had been known to have taken place following black uprisings. Why should the slave suffer any further because of his errors? Off the record, however, Brown knew how close he had come to realizing his plans, and that even his errors of judgment could not hinder the coming year of jubilee. "He did not expect to destroy slavery at once by a general uprising," his son Owen said many years later.

> [H]e sought to harass it, cripple it; in short to so make slavery unprofitable that it would be abandoned. He failed at the beginning by staying too long at Harper's Ferry. And yet he did not fail. That event, his death, aroused the nation. Men were compelled to face the issue. And so by his sacrifice he hastened the emancipation of the slaves.[131]

As far as the support of the slaves was concerned, John Brown had neither doubt nor disappointment. "No, I knew, of course, that the Negroes would rally to my standard," he told a sympathetic jailer. "If I had only got the thing fairly started, you Virginians would have seen sights that would have opened your eyes!"[132]

9. John Brown's Body Revisited

After they hanged him, his body was cut down and dumped into a crude pine coffin. The doctors who presided at the gallows were not satisfied that he was dead, even though he had hung, swaying in the breeze, for half an hour after the trap door had swung out. Adjourning for an afternoon repast, the doctors made their final inspection later in the day, officially declaring that their unrepentant enemy was dead. To underscore their contempt, they left the noose around his neck. Mary Brown somberly collected her husband's remains, entrusting the coffin to some abolitionists who, like her, had risked their own safety to enter the indignant South on behalf of the most controversial anti-slavery figure of the hour.

In February 1860, barely three months after Brown's execution, presidential hopeful Abraham Lincoln told an audience at the Cooper Union in New York City that the late abolitionist was a brooding, delusional fanatic whose unwarranted invasion of Virginia merited the harshest penalty. Brown deserved to be hanged, Lincoln declared before an audience of 1,500 New Yorkers. As for slavery, he concluded, "we can yet afford to leave it alone where it is."[133] He made quite a stir with his Cooper Union speech, and many think it was a turning point in his quest for the presidency. Yet it was by distancing himself from Harper's Ferry and black liberation that Lincoln secured an election victory. On that snowy night in Manhattan, it was quite apparent that John Brown's body was a burden to the Republicans, who believed the ending of slavery was a matter best set aside for the sake of the Union. Brown had forcefully disagreed, insisting that the plight of oppressed millions should be the first order of business for democracy. To the dismay of the Republicans, however, the South presumed that the attitude of the North was typified by the militant Brown instead of the moderate Lincoln. Thus Lincoln had tried to unload John Brown's body in New York City, figuratively speaking—a point that has a special resonance only because the real body had actually been unloaded there about twelve weeks before his speech.

Shipped north by train from Harper's Ferry to Philadelphia, Pennsylvania, on December 2, 1859, Brown's remains were accompanied by his widow and James Miller McKim, a prominent abolitionist from the city of brotherly love. Mary needed to rest among friends over night, but the excitement and controversy surrounding Brown's body prompted the mayor to insist that his coffin not remain in town. The mayor claimed that he had the grieving widow's best interests in mind since the uproar might interrupt her mourning, but he was far more concerned that the excitement might lead to rioting in the city. The *New York Tribune* thus reported that "he preemptorily insisted that another stopping place should be selected." There had already been an uproar in Philadelphia on the day of the execution, when pro-Brown meetings were interrupted by anti-Brown protestors. Recognizing that large numbers of Brown's supporters, particularly from the black community, would turn out to welcome his remains in the city, the mayor and police chief feared a reactionary "outbreak" from southern medical students and laborers employed by southern-owned companies. To avoid an explosion, they sent out a well-guarded but empty hearse as a decoy, while Brown's coffin was placed in a furniture car and taken to the wharf on Walnut Street, where it was shipped northward.[134]

After being rejected at Philadelphia, the guardians of John Brown's body turned elsewhere. The abolitionist and poet, Theodore Tilton, only twenty-four-years-old at the time, was thus appointed to escort Brown's pitiful remains farther northward. Wanting to avert both notoriety and controversy, Tilton had the casket secretly placed on board a steamboat bound for New York City. Arriving near the Battery on Saturday evening December 3, Tilton and his associates used the night hours to their advantage. Leaving the body on board, he hurried over to Brooklyn, to the home of Jacob Hopper, a Quaker abolitionist and undertaker at 18 Court Street. When Tilton asked him if he could "take charge of an old man's body" over in New York, Hopper surmised that it was the body of John Brown. He probably knew that Tilton, an abolitionist, had hosted Mary Brown at his Brooklyn home during her recent trip down to Virginia to see her husband for the last time. The body was in a crude box, Tilton explained, and prominent abolitionists had insisted that it be properly prepared and placed in a more suitable coffin before being shipped home to Brown's family in North Elba, New York. Tilton was emphatic: he wanted the whole matter done secretly, without letting the press learn anything. Hopper grasped his hand, promising to care for matters accordingly.

To avoid undo attention, Hopper rented a private room at the offices of McGraw & Taylor, undertakers and coffin manufacturers, at 163 Bowery Street, and brought the body there sometime before midnight. When he opened the pine box, he found that Brown had been contemptuously thrown inside, his body contorted in the position in which it had fallen, wearing its noose like a necktie. The face had begun to darken and his clothes still held the slashes and cuts of a marine bayonet since Brown had been obligated to wear the same outfit from the raid in October until his execution in December. After being washed and prepared, John Brown's body was left to chill on ice. On early Sunday morning, Tilton came over from Brooklyn to view the embellished remains. He was pleased to find the body dressed in a good suit and resting in a "simple but elegant" walnut coffin. "I shall never forget the face of the sleeper," Tilton said in an interview many years later in Paris, "for he did not seem dead."

Tilton did not mention it, but John Brown's last visit did not remain a secret to New Yorkers. When Hopper brought in the body, the only other person who knew about it was proprietor Thomas Taylor. But the next day, Taylor had to attend to business and told his brother about Brown's lifeless presence in the shop. The brother soon told the assistant undertakers and then some of his friends, and by Sunday afternoon, scores and perhaps hundreds of New Yorkers were stopping into McGraw & Taylor, many of them claiming to be shopping for coffins but all of them whispering excitedly about John Brown's body. By Sunday evening, six police officers were stationed near the shop to ward off the pressing crowds. The incident was so exciting that Louisa Williamson, one of Taylor's employees, afterward wrote to her brother in Long Island that some of the most "illustrious guests—the very biggest bugs" of the city had filed in to view the body. In the shop, the workers had given away Brown's Virginia necktie by the inch and had even removed the screws from the crude pine coffin for souvenirs. They would undoubtedly have taken the battle-torn clothing too, except that undertaker Hopper demanded to keep them for himself—a vestige of John Brown that he cherished the rest of his life.[135] When asked to wash the dead man's suit, Williamson at least got a chance to go through his pockets, delightedly finding a rifle cap. Afterward she went into see John

Brown for herself, finding him "as serene as if asleep," the ice having returned a lifelike blush to his face. She had never seen "a finer looking man of his age, after such a death too." In the end, Hopper provided Tilton with an itemized bill but refused to accept a penny, and with emotion welling up in his voice, declared that he wished "to testify his respect for the old man's splendid courage." It had cost a total of $45 to prepare John Brown's body for history, including the $8 charge for his icy repose in Manhattan.[136]

According to the famous diarist George Templeton Strong, nine-tenths of New York City's population in 1859 were quite opposed to John Brown's raid and were equally vociferous in opposing the outpouring of northern sympathy in newspapers and rallies resulting from his execution. Like many northern whites in the antebellum period, Strong was nevertheless disgusted by the demands and threats of the Southern slave states and had grown weary of "seeing the North on its knees . . . begging the South not to commit the treason and violence it is forever threatening." Even though he disapproved of the tributes to Brown in the *New York Tribune*, Strong could not help but see the impact that the abolitionist had made on people throughout the free states. "His simplicity and consistency, the absence of fuss, parade and bravado, the strength and clearness of his letters, all indicate a depth of conviction that one does not expect in an Abolitionist," he wrote the week after Brown's execution in Virginia. "Slavery has received no such blow in my time as his strangulation." Yet Strong and other conservative northerners could not escape the forces in the wind that had changed the swaying of John Brown's body on a Southern gallows into something of a national pendulum—as if marking the months, days, and hours that remained before the whole nation exploded into civil war. Soldiers dressed in blue would soon be singing John Brown's anthem as they marched into battle and a troubled President Lincoln would finally be forced to follow Brown's example by arming black warriors. But it would take years before Lincoln was ready to do so.

"We all esteem him here in reality a good man but mistaken, or misguided," wrote Louisa Williamson the funeral parlor employee, "or he would never have done that last deed when he did, where he did, or in the manner he did." To this white woman, Brown "must have known, if he were not monomania on the subject[,] that he would be sure to fail." However different Williamson the laborer was from Strong the socialite, they both shared the same belief that Brown was a misguided fanatic, despite their awkward admiration and sympathy for him as well.

Unlike Williamson, however, Strong did not care to view Brown's body even though his friend George Anthon could barely contain himself about the prospect of seeing the dead abolitionist. Anthon had stopped by just before tea that Sunday afternoon, announcing to his friend that old John Brown was in the city, laid out at McGraw & Taylor's shop. It just so happened, Anthon told him, that Charley Carpenter, sexton of St. Mark's Church in the Bowery, had assisted the undertaker in placing the old man on ice and was going to get him inside to see the most celebrated corpse in the North. The following Sunday, a delighted Anthon stopped in once more, this time showing off a lock of Brown's hair and a small section of the hanging rope. Strong found the whole thing quite funny, privately mocking in his diary that his friend Anthon had acquired "relics" of "S[aint] Giovanni Bruno." But the joke was on George Templeton Strong. He not only missed the opportunity to see John Brown's body before it was transformed into a cultural mantra, but along with Lincoln and the Republicans, he mistakenly assumed that Brown would be forgotten by the dawn of the 20th century. To the contrary, even as his body was shipped northward to its final resting place in New York's Adirondacks, a perennial contest over the meaning of his life and death in the collective memory of the nation was only beginning.

ENGLISH BULLS.

THE subscriber has two fine English Bulls, of two and three years old, one of which he offers for sale at thirty dollars cash in hand, or thirty three dollars on a credit of 8 months.

The stock of said Bulls may be seen with the subscriber and in the neighborhood.

JOHN BROWN.

Richmond, Crawford co. May 18, 1831.

John Brown, then resident in Crawford County, Pennsylvania, placed this advertisement in the *Crawford Messenger* in May 1831 for the sale of "two fine English Bulls." Brown was resident of Crawford County, near Meadville, Pennsylvania, from 1826-1835. *Courtesy of Crawford County Historical Society, Meadville, Pa.*

Brown probably appropriated his famous *nom de guerre*, "Isaac Smith," from a businessman of the same name whose umbrella manufacturing company had offices in New York City and Boston, and who advertised frequently in the *Springfield Republican* (Mass.), such as in this ad from July 20, 1849.

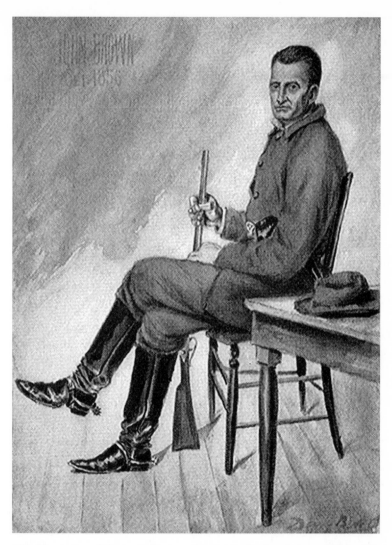

This illustration of Brown in Kansas appeared in the frontispiece of Richard J. Hinton's favorable biography, *John Brown and His Men* (1894). According to documentarian Jean Libby, it was rendered by artist Daniel Beard from an actual daguerreotype of Brown that was made in the free state town of Lawrence in September 1856 by John Bowles, an abolitionist.

This stylized, heroic sketch of Brown first appeared in a 19th century history of Springfield, Massachusetts, portraying the abolitionist's efforts in opposition to the Fugitive Slave Law of 1850. Unfortunately the artist erred in portraying Brown with a beard, although he did not grow his famous disguise until the late 1850s.

An unidentified artist made this sketch of a wounded John Brown after his defeat and capture at Harper's Ferry, in *Frank Leslie's Illustrated Newspaper*, Octorber 29, 1859. The editor erroneously referred to "bullet holes in his forehead" but according to Brown, he received only sword and bayonet wounds.

This reasonably authentic illustration of John Brown in Iowa during the winter of 1858-59 shows him riding a mule—perhaps his mule "Dolly," which he later had in Maryland just prior to the Harper's Ferry raid in 1859. *Weekly Gazette* (Davenport, Iowa), November 21, 1877.

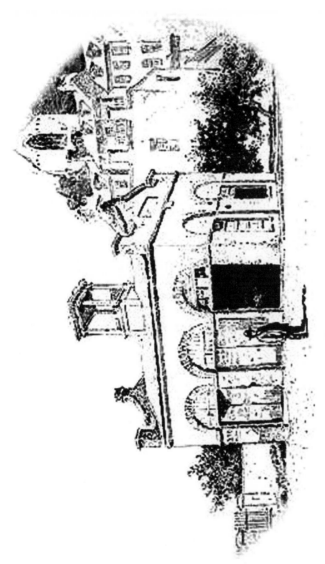

An unidentified sketch of "John Brown's Fort," where the abolitionist and some of his men made their last stand at Harper's Ferry in October 1859. At the time of the raid the structure served as the fire engine house (with adjoining guard house) of the federal armory. The structure still stands but not without a peculiar history of having been relocated, dissembled, reassembled, and displayed. It is now situated a short distance from its original site in town.

This sketch, from Leila Amos Pendleton's *A Narrative of the Negro* (1912), shows Brown and his men fighting inside the Harper's Ferry engine house, with son Oliver lying dead and son Watson mortally wounded, in his father's arms.

An unidentified artist made this sketch of Brown ascending the scaffold on December 2, 1859. *Frank Leslie's Illustrated Newspaper*, December 17, 1859.

An unidentified artist sketched family and guests surrounding Brown's coffin prior to burial on December 8, 1859. According to the late Edwin Cotter, the tall man at the left near the head of the coffin is abolitionist Wendell Phillips, who performed Brown's eulogy; the black man is Brown's friend and neighbor, Lyman Epps, and the little girl next to him is undoubtedly Brown's five-year-old daughter, Ellen; standing next to her at the center are J. Miller McKim, the Philadelphia abolitionist who hosted Mary Brown and escorted her to Virginia to see her husband alive for the last time, and the widow herself. *The New York Illustrated News*, December 24, 1859.

APPENDIX-A

Key to Source Abbreviations

AVHF   Osborne P. Anderson, *A Voice From Harper's Ferry*. Boston: self-published, 1861.

BS-CG   Correspondence of Boyd Stutler to Clarence Gee, microfilm edition in the Hudson Library and Historical Society, Hudson, Ohio.

BBS   Boyd B. Stutler John Brown Collection, on-line archive of the West Virginia Division of Culture and History, Charleston, West Virginia.

BBS-MIC   John Brown Collection of Boyd B. Stutler, microfilm edition in the Ohio Historical Society, Columbus, Ohio.

CCHS   Crawford County Historical Society, Meadville Public Library, Meadville, Pennsylvania.

CHFI   *U.S. Congress, Senate Select Commission on the Harper's Ferry Invasion*. Washington, D.C.: 36th Congress, 1860.

GEE   Clarence S. Gee's John Brown Collection in the Hudson Library and Historical Society, Hudson, Ohio.

GLC   Gilder Lehrman Collection at New York Historical Society, New York City, New York.

JB2   John Brown Junior Collection in the Ohio Historical Society, Columbus, Ohio.

JBR   Louis Ruchames, editor. *A John Brown Reader*. New York: Abelard-Schuman, 1959.

KSHS   John Brown Collection of the Kansas State Historical Society, Topeka, Kansas.

LLJB   Franklin B. Sanborn, *The Life and Letters of John Brown, Liberator of Kansas, and Martyr of Virginia*. Boston, 1885; rpt. New York: Negro Universities Press, 1969.

NYHS   New York Historical Society, New York City, New York.

OGV   John Brown Papers of Oswald Garrison Villard, Rare Book and Manuscript Collection of Columbia University Library, New York City, New York.

OHS   Ohio Historical Society, Columbus, Ohio.

RWL   John Brown Collection, Robert Woodruff Library, Atlanta University, Atlanta, Georgia.

APPENDIX-B

Documents: Selected Letters of John Brown

A Note on John Brown's Writing and the Style of Transcription Employed

Wherever possible I have followed original manuscripts in making my own transcriptions, although in a number of cases these documents were available only as secondary transcriptions and are overly edited to the point of obscuring Brown's style as a writer. The abolitionist's handwriting, like his spelling, is peculiar though predictable and happily quite readable. Sometimes his spelling reflects the British style (e.g., labour), indicative of his orientation toward what he called an "English education." Yet due to scant, interrupted schooling, his writing is often fraught with misspellings too. Preferring to sustain the flavor of the original letters available to me, I have thus chosen not to correct his spelling errors or mark them with the conventional editorial device ("sic"). Similarly, I have preserved Brown's use of punctuation as much as possible. Minimal editorial comments or emendations are inserted in italics within brackets ([*italics*]) to distinguish them from the original document text. I have also imposed certain conventions throughout transcriptions made from original documents:

1. While Brown commonly indented only the first line of a letter, I have initiated new paragraphs when he left additional spaces at the end of a sentence. All indented paragraphs follow the standard five-character indentation even though his practice was highly irregular.

2. Original line breaks are not maintained for reasons of expedience in publishing. Rather than follow Brown's use of the hyphen due to line breaks (he often hyphenated both parts of a word), I have transcribed the word in its entirety, except if a hyphenated word spans a page break.

3. In keeping with Brown's style, place lines and dates are kept together but are aligned to the left margin for uniformity. Where Brown has occasionally provided an incorrect date, the correct (or approximate) date is placed within brackets followed by an editor's note (May 8, 185[6]). Marginalia is placed at the end of the document on its own line and indicated by double up and double down arrows (↑↑marginalia↓↓) and followed by an editorial comment. Salutations are aligned to the left margin with one blank line between the date and the salutation. Closings are aligned to the right margin with one blank line between the

last line of the body of the text and the closing. Brown's signature is aligned to the right margin on the line following the closing. Where his signature was cut away from the original manuscript, it appears in italics within brackets ([*John Brown*]). Postscripts appear like normal paragraph text with one blank line between the signature line and the postscript.

4. Capitalization is maintained as it appears in the original text. When it was unclear whether Brown used the upper or lower case of a letter, it is transcribed according to modern usage.

5. Superscript interlineations (commonly used by Brown) have been brought down to the line at the place of insertion.

6. Cancelled words or passages are written in strikeout type (~~cancelled~~).

7. The word "and" is almost never used by Brown in writing since he preferred to use an ampersand (&), and so the latter is used throughout the text, except where "and" has been reinserted by editors in secondary transcriptions.

8. Underlining is frequent in Brown's letters, and underlined text is placed in italics whether or not he employed single or double underlines.

9. Abbreviations with superscripted letters and numbers, also common in Brown's letters, are brought down to the line (for example, "FebY 1ST" is rendered "Feby 1st).

Document 1

John Brown, Red Rock, Iowa, to Henry L. Stearns, Medford, Massachusetts, July 15-Aug. 8, 1857, and an appended letter from John Brown to George L. Stearns, Aug. 8, 1857. 6 pp., from a photographic image in the Clarence S. Gee Papers, Hudson Library and Historical Society, Hudson, Ohio.

In the summer of 1857, Brown wrote an autobiographical sketch for Henry L. Stearns, the adolescent son of George L. Stearns, one of his so-called "Secret Six" supporters and certainly his most generous financial supporter. Brown visited the Stearns family in Medford, Massachusetts, in January and March 1857, and during the latter visit received a small monetary gift from the younger Stearns, who also asked Brown to write something about his youth. He did not comply with the request immediately and had to be nudged the following month in a letter by the elder Stearns, in which he also enclosed another small cash gift from his son as a further reminder. Brown worked on the sketch over a period of weeks, from July 15 through August 8, 1857, when he finally appended a letter to the elder Stearns. In 1957, the Reverend Clarence Gee was able to locate the owner and subsequently obtained a copy of the original. Unfortunately, the whereabouts of the original document are no longer known.[1]

* * *

Page 1st

Red Rock, Iowa, 15,th July, 1857.

Mr Henry L Stearns   My Dear Young Friend

I have not forgotten my promise to write you; but my constant care, & anxiety have obliged me put it off a long time. I do not flatter myself that I *can* write anything that will very much interest you; but have concluded to send you a short story of a certain boy of my acquaintance: & for convenience & shortness of name, I will call him John. This story will be mainly a naration of follies & errors; which it is to be hoped *you may avoid.* but there is one thing connected with it, which will be calculated to encourage any young person to persevereing effort: & that is the degree of success *in accomplishing his objects* which to a great extent marked the course of this boy throughout my entire acquaintance with him; notwithstanding his moderate capacity; & still more moderate acquirements. John was born May 9th 1800, at Torrington. Litchfield Co. Connecticut of poor but respectable parents: a decandant on the side of his Father of one of the company of the Mayflower who landed at Plymouth 1620. His Mother was decended from a man who came at an early period to New England from Amsterdam, in Holland. Both his Fathers & his Mothers Fathers served in the war of the revolution: His Fathers Father; died in a barn at New York while in the service, in 1776. I cannot tell you of any thing in the first Four years of Johns life worth mentioning save that at that *early age* he was tempted by Three Large Brass Pins belonging to a girl who lived in the family & *stole them.* In this he was detected by his Mother; & after having a full day to think of the wrong: received from her a thorough whipping. When he was Five years old his Father moved to Ohio; then a wilderness filled with wild beasts, & Indians. During the long journey which was performed in part or mostly with an *Ox team;* he was called on by turns to assist a boy Five years older (who had been adopted by his Father & Mother) & learned to think he could accomplish *smart things* in driving the Cows; & riding the horses. Sometimes he met with Rattle Snakes which were very large; & which some of the company generally managed to Kill. After getting to Ohio in 1805 he was for some time rather afraid of the Indians, & of their Rifles; but this soon wore off: & he used to hang about them quite as much as was consistent with good manners; & learned a trifle of their talk. His Father learned to dress Deer skins

Page 2d

& at 6 years old John was installed a young Buck Skin. He was perhaps rather observing as he ever after remembered the entire process of Deer Skin *dressing;* so that he could at any time dress his own leather such as Squirel. Raccoon, Cat, Wolf, or Dog Skins: & also learned to make Whip Lashes: which brought him some change at times; & was of considerable service in many ways. At Six years old John began to be quite a rambler in the wild new country finding birds, & Squirels, & sometimes a wild Turkeys nest. But about this period he was placed in the School of *adversity:* which my young friend was a most necessary part of his early training. You may *laugh* when you come to read about it; but these were *sore trials* to John: whose earthly treasures were very *few, & small.* These were the beginning of a severe but *much needed course* of discipline which he afterward was to pass through; & which it is to be hoped has learned him before this time that the Heavenly Father sees it best to take all the little things out of his hands which he has ever placed in them. When John was in his Sixth year a poor *Indian boy* gave him a Yellow Marble the first he had ever seen. This he thought a great deal of; & kept it a good while: but at last *he lost it* beyound recovery. *It took years to heal the wound;* & I *think* he cried at times about it. About Five months after this he caught a young Squirel tearing off his tail in doing it & getting severely bitten at the same time himself. He however held on *to the little bob* tail *Squirrel*; & finally got him perfectly tamed, so that he almost idolized his pet. *This too he lost*; by its wandering away or by getting killed: & for a year or Two John was *in mourning*; & looking at all the Squirrels he could see to try & discover Bob tail, *if possible.*

I must not neglect to tell you of a verry *bad & foolish* habbit to which John was some what addicted. I mean *telling lies*; generally to screen himself from blame: or from punishment. He could not well endure to be reproached; & I now think had be been oftener encouraged to be entirely frank; by making *frankness a kind of atonement* for some of his faults; he would not have been so often guilty of this fault; nor have been obliged to struggle *so long* in after life with *so mean* a habit. John was *never quarrelsome*: but was *excessively* fond of the *hardest & roughest* kind of plays; & could never get enough [*of*] them. Indeed when for a short time he was sometimes sent to School the opportunity it afforded to wrestle, & Snow ball, & run, & jump, & knock off old seedy Wool hats; offered to him almost the only compensation for the confinement; & restraints of school. I need not tell you that with such a feeling & but little chance of going to school at all: he did not become much of a schollar. He would always choose to stay at home, & work hard, rather than be sent to school; & during the warm season might generally be seen *bare footed*, & bare *headed*: with Buckskin Breeches suspened often with one leather strap over his shoulder but sometimes with Two.

To be sent off through the wilderness alone to very considerable distances was particularly his delight; & in this he was often indulged so that by the time he was Twelve years old he was sent off more than a Hundred Miles with companies of cattle; & he would have thought his character much injured had he been obliged to be helped in any such job. This was a boyish kind of feeling but characteristic however. At Eight years old John was left a Motherless boy which loss was complete & permanent for notwithstanding his Father again married to a sensible, inteligent, & on many accounts a very

Page 3d

estimable woman: *yet he never addopted her in feeling*: but continued to pine after his own Mother for years. This opperated very unfavourably uppon him; as he was both naturally fond of females; & withall extremely diffident; & deprived him of a suitable conne[c]ting link between the different sexes; the want of which might under some circumstance have proved his ruin.

When the war broke out *with England*: his Father soon commenced furnishing the troops with beef cattle, the collecting & driving of which afforded him some opportunity for the chase (on foot) of wild Steers, & other cattle through the woods. During this war he had some chance to form his own boyish judgment of *men & measures*: & to become somwhat familiarly acquainted with some who have figured before the country since that time. The effect of what he saw during the war was to so far disgust him with Military affairs that he would neither train, *or drill*; but paid fines; & got along like a Quaker untill his age finally had cleared him of Military duty. During the war with England a circumstance occurred that in the end made him a most *determined Abolitionist*, & led him to declare, or Swear: Eternal war with Slavery. He was staying for [*a*] short time with a very gentlemanly land lord since a United States Marshall who held a slave boy near his own age very active, inteligent, & good feeling; & to whom John was under considerable obligation for numerous little acts of kindness. *The Master* made a great pet of John: brought him to table with his first company; & friends; called their attention to every little smart thing he *said, or did*: & to the fact of his being more than a hundred Miles from home with a company of cattle alone: while the *negro boy* (who was fully if not more than his equal) was badly clothed, poorly fed; *& lodged in cold weather*. & beaten before his ey[*e*]s with Iron Shovels or any other thing that came first to hand. This brought John to reflect on the wretched; hopeless condition, of *Fatherless & Motherless* slave *children*: for such children have neither Fathers or Mothers; to protect, & provide for them. He sometimes would raise the question: *is God their Father?*

At the age of Ten years an old friend induced him to read a little history; & offered him the free use of a good library; by; which he acquired some taste for reading: which formed the principle part of his early education: & divested him in a great measure from bad company. He by this means grew to be very fond of the company, & conversation of

Page 4th

old & inteligent persons. He never attempted to dance in his life; nor did he ever learn to know *one* of a pack of *Cards*, from *another*. He learned nothing of Grammer; nor did he get at school so much knowledge of comm[*on*] Arithmetic as the Four ground rules. This will give you some general idea of the first Fifteen years of his life: during which time he became very strong & large of his age & ambitious to perform the full labour of a man; at almost any kind of hard work. By reading the lives of great, wise, & good men their sayings, & writings; he grew to a dislike of vain & frivolous conversation, & persons; & was often greatly obliged by the kind manner in which older, & more inteligent persons treated him at their houses; & in conversation: which was a great relief on account of his extreme bashfulness. He very early in life became ambitious to excel in doing any thing he undertook to perform. This kind of feeling I would recommend to all young persons both *male & female*: as it will certainly tend to secure admission to the company of the more inteligent; & better portion of every community. By all means endeavour to excel in some laudable pursuit. I had like to have forgotten to tell you of one of Johns missfortunes which set rather hard on him while a young boy. He had by some means *perhaps* by gift of his Father become the owner of a little Ewe Lamb which did finely till it was about Two Thirds grown; & then sickened & died. This brought another protracted *mourning season*: not that he felt the pecuniary loss so hevily: for that was never his disposition: but so strong & earnest were his atachments.

John had been taught from earliest childhood to "fear God & Keep his commandments"; & though quite skeptical, he had always by turns felt much serious doubt as to his future well being, & about this time became to some extent a convert to Christianity & ever after a firm believer in the divine authenticity of the Bible. With this book he became very familiar: & possessed a most unu[*su*]al memory of it[*s*] entire contents. Now some of the things I have been *telling of*, were just such as I would recommend to you: & I would like to know that you had selected those out; & adopted them as part of your own plan of life, & I wish you to have *some deffinite plan*. Many seem to have none: & others never stick to any that do have form. This was not the case with John. He followed up with *tenacity* whatever he set about so long as it answered his general purpose: & hence he rarely failed in some good degree to effect the things he undertook. This was so much the case that he *habitually expected to succeed* in his undertakings. With this feeling *should be coupled*; the conciousness that our plans are right in themselves. During the period I have named John had acquired a kind of ownership to certain animals of some little value but as he had come to understand that the *title of minors* might be a little imperfect; he had recourse to various means in order to secure a more *independent, & perfect*, right of property.

One of those means was to exchange with his Father for some thing of far less value. Another was by trading with other persons for some thing his Father had never owned. Older persons have sometimes found difficulty with *titles*. From Fifteen to Twenty years old, he spent most of his time working at the Tannery & Curriers trade keeping Bachelors hall; & he officiateing as Cook; & for most of the time as

Page 5th

foreman of the establishment under his Father. During this period he found much trouble with some of the bad habits I have mentioned & with some that I have not told you of; his concience urging him forward with great power in this matter: but his close attention to *business*; & success in its management: together with the way he got along with a company of men, & boys; made him quite a favorite with the serious & more inteligent portion of older persons. This was so much the case; & secured for him so many little notices from those he esteemed; that his vanity was very much fed by it: & he came forward to man hood quite full of self conceit; & self confident: notwithstanding his *extreme* bashfulness. A younger brother used sometimes to remind him of this: & to repeat to him *this expression* which you may somewhere find; "A King against whom there is no rising up." The habit so early formed of being obeyed rendered him in after life too much disposed to speak in an imperious or dictating way. From Fifteen years & upward he felt a good deal of anxiety to learn; but could only read, & studdy a little: both for want of time; & on account of inflamation of the eyes. He however managed by the help of books to make himself tolerably well acquainted with common Arithmetic; & Surveying: which he practiced more or less after he was Twenty years old. At a little past Twenty years led by his own inclination *&* *prompted also* by his Father he married a *remarkably plain*: but neat industrious, & economical girl; of excellent character; earnest piety; & good practical common sence; about one year younger than himself. This woman by her mild, frank, & *more than all else*. by her very consistent conduct; acquired; & ever while she lived maintained a most powerful; & good influence over him. Her plain but kind admonitions generally had the right effect; without arousing his haughty obstinate temper.

John began early in life to discover a great liking to fine Cattle, Horses, Sheep; & Swine: & as soon as circumstances would enable him he began to be a practical *Shepherd*: *it being* a calling for which *in early life* he had a kind of *enthusiastic longing*. together with the idea that as a business it bid fair to afford him the means of carrying out his greatest or principle object.

I have now given you a kind of general idea of the early life of this boy; & if I believed it would be worth the trouble: or afford much interest to any good feeling person: I might be tempted to
Page 6th
tell you something of his course in after life; or manhood. I do not say that I *will do it*. You will discover that in using up my *half* sheets to *save paper*, I have written Two pages, so that one does not follow the other as it should. I have no time to write it over: & but for unavoidable hindrances in travelling I can har[d]ly say when I should have written what I have.

With an honest desire for your best good I subscribe myself
Your Friend
J Brown

PS I had like to have forgotten to acknowledge your contribution in aid of the cause in which I ser[v]e. God Allmighty *bless you*, my Son.
JB

Tabor, Iowa, 8th Aug. 1857
George L Stearns Esqr
Boston Mass
My Dear Sir

In consequence of ill health & other hindrances too numerous; & unpleasant to write about; the least of which has *not been* the lack of sufficient means for freight bills; & other expences I have never as yet returned to Kansas. This has been unavoidable unless I returned without securing the principal object for which I came back from the territory; & I am now waiting for teams & means to come from there to enable me to go on.* I obtained Two teams and Waggons as I talked of at a cost of $786 but was obliged to hire a teamster; & to drive one team myself. This unexpected increase of labour together with being much of the time quite unwell; & depressed with disappointments, & delays: has prevented my writing sooner. Indeed I had pretty much determined not to write again till I should do it from Kansas. *I will tell* you some of my disappointments. I was flattered with the expectation of getting $1,000. from Hartford City & also $1000. from New Haven. From Hartford I did get about $260, & a little over in some repair of arms. From New Haven I got $25, at any rate that is all I can get any advice of. Gerrit Smith supplied me with $350. or I could not have reached this place. He also loaned me $110. to pay to the Thompsons who were disappointed *of getting their* money for the farm I had agreed for; & got possession of for use. I have been continually hearing from them that I *have not fulfilled*; & that I told them I should not leave the country till the thing was completed. This has exceedingly mortifyed me.

I could tell you much more had I room, & time. *Have not given up*. Will write more when I get to Kansas.

Your Friend
John Brown

↑↑*Have here & at Nebraska City Five full loads.↓↓ [*This statement is written vertically along the lower left side of the letter.*]

Document 2

John Brown, Randolph Township, Pennsylvania, to Frederick Brown, Hudson, Ohio, Nov. 21, 1834. Edited transcription by Franklin B. Sanborn in *LLJB*, pages 40–41. The original document is privately owned.

John Brown lived in northwestern Pennsylvania from 1826–1835, a period of enterprise, reputation, and burgeoning success. Given his conservative orientation and his demanding work and family concerns, it is unlikely that he had little more than intermittent involvement in underground railroad efforts, though he was strongly convicted about the anti-slavery movement and was already interested in matters pertaining to the black community. As this letter to his younger brother Frederick (1807–77) shows, their recent visit and discussion had stirred him to thinking about doing more on behalf of black people. If not pro-black, Crawford County in the 1830s was at least a safe and secure area for African Americans, and had a good share of anti-slavery sentiment among the white population as well as a small but economically stable black community. Indeed, Brown preferred the general attitude of whites in the Meadville area to those back in Hudson, which yet reflected the "conflicting interests and feelings" of the racist colonization movement. This letter reflects Brown's youthful Christian conservatism, as well as the inclination of sentiments and convictions that would eventually culminate in more radical ventures. Unfortunately, Sanborn's manner of editing and transcription significantly muted the original style of the document.

* * *

Randolph, Nov. 21, 1834.

Dear Brother,

As I have had only one letter from Hudson since you left here, and that some weeks since, I begin to get uneasy and apprehensive that all is not well. I had satisfied my mind about it for some time, in expectation of seeing father here, but I begin to give that up for the present. Since you left me I have been trying to devise some means whereby I might do something in a practical way for my poor fellow-men who are in bondage, and having fully consulted the feelings of my wife and my three boys, we have agreed to get at least one negro boy or youth, and bring him up as we do our own,—viz., give him a good English education, learn him what we can about the history of the world, about business, about general subjects, and, above all, try to teach him the fear of God. We think of three ways to obtain one: First, to try to get some Christian slave-holder to release one to us. Second, to get a free one if no one will let us have one that is a slave. Third, if that does not succeed, we have all agreed to submit to considerable privation in order to buy one. This we are now using means in order to effect, in the confident expectation that God is about to bring them all out of the house of bondage.

I will just mention that when this subject was first introduced, Jason had gone to bed; but no sooner did he hear the thing hinted, than his warm heart kindled, and he turned out to have a part in the discussion of a subject of such exceeding interest. I have for years been trying to devise some way to get a school a-going here for blacks, and I think that on many accounts it would be a most favorable location. Children here would have no intercourse with vicious people of their own kind, nor with openly vicious persons of any kind. There would be no powerful opposition influence against such a thing; and should there be any, I believe the settlement might be so effected in future as to have almost the whole influence of the place in favor of such a school. Write me how you would like to join me, and try to get on from Hudson and thereabouts some first rate abolitionist families with you. I do honestly believe that our united exertions alone might soon, with the good hand of our God upon us, effect it all.

This has been with me a favorite theme of reflection for years. I think that a place which might be in some measure settled with a view to such an object would be much more favorable to such an undertaking than would any such place as Hudson, with all its conflicting interests and feelings; and I do think such advantages ought to be afforded the young blacks, whether they are all to be immediately set free or not. Perhaps we might, under God, in that way do more towards breaking their yoke effectually than in any other. If the young blacks of our country could once become enlightened, it would most assuredly operate on slavery like firing powder confined in rock, and all slaveholders know it well. Witness their heaven-daring laws against teaching blacks. If once the Christians in the free States would set to work in earnest in teaching the blacks, the people of the slaveholding States would find themselves constitutionally driven to set about the work of emancipation immediately. The laws of this State are now such that the inhabitants of any township may raise by a tax in aid of the State school-fund any amount of money they may choose by a vote, for the purpose of common schools, which any child may have access to by application. If you will join me in this undertaking, I will make with you any arrangement of our temporal concerns that shall be fair. Our health is good, and our prospects about business rather brightening.

Affectionately yours,
John Brown

Document 3

John Brown, Franklin Mills, Ohio, to H. J. Huidekoper, Meadville, Crawford County, Pa., July 5, 1838. 1 p., addressed on verso. Courtesy of Special Collections, Pelletier Library, Allegheny College.

Harm Jan Huidekoper (1776–1854) is a prominent business and religious fig-ure in northwestern Pennsylvania history. A native of the Netherlands, Huidekoper emigrated to the United States in 1796 and launched a prosperous Pennsylvania career as an officer of the Holland Land Company, and then the Pennsylvania Population Company (PPC), based in Philadelphia. He was also an outspoken advocate and benefactor of the Unitarian movement, and his business and theological dealings created controversy. As an agent, Huidekoper succeeded in undermining a movement of settlers in northwestern Pennsylvania whom the PPC considered squatters, though perhaps their claims to the land were morally if not legally superior. After the PPC pulled out of northwestern Pennsylvania, Huidekoper made a major purchase of their holdings in 1836, making him the foremost land owner in the region; he likewise owned flocks and businesses.

The extent of Brown's dealings with Huidekoper is not clear, though he probably enjoyed little more than a cordial business relationship. Brown was hardly sympathetic to Huidekoper's unorthodox theology, and there is reasonably good evidence that in the 1820s he was more than sympathetic toward the settlers in their struggle against the PPC. However at least Huidekoper and Brown shared a common anti-slavery sentiment, and in the 1830s the latter was hardly a political dynamo. As an otherwise conservative, upwardly mobile figure, Brown probably set aside whatever reservations he privately held for Huidekoper's views, instead choosing to work cooperatively with the tycoon wherever possible. Documentary evidence suggests that Brown acted as his agent in at least one business transaction five years before this letter was written.

The specific nature of this letter is unclear, but seems to pertain to an overdue payment on a loan from Huidekoper, probably made at the onset of land speculations dating from his return to Ohio in 1836. There is a tinge of patronizing in Brown's tone, and considering Huidekoper's stature, this is understandable. However the letter is genuine enough, and furthermore shows that the Panic of 1837 had not devastated the economies of the western states and that businessmen in Ohio and elsewhere were yet optimistic. It would take the Crisis of 1839 to dash their hopes.

* * *

Franklin 5th July 1838
H J Huidekoper Esqr
Dr Sr

I intended to go to Meadville about the Middle of May last, in order to see to my affairs, & collect and pay over what money I could, but have been prevented as yet on account of sickness in my family. I hope to be able to come out in a few days now, & shall, as quick as I can feel in any measure content to be absent from home. I feel truly mortifyed at the great use I have made of your patience & good will, & I can assure you I feel no disposition to put you off an hour because you are so kind. During the first year after my return to this country I made money rather too fast, but since the change in the times I have not suffered much in that way, but am just about holding where I was two years ago. We in this country feel now in hope that another year will effectually relieve us.

Respectfully your friend
John Brown

Document 4

John Brown, Franklin Mills, Ohio, to George Kellogg, Vernon, Connecticut, Sept., 20, 1839. 1 p., addressed on verso. Charles Aldrich Autograph Collection, State Historical Society of Iowa, Des Moines.

Brown's correspondent, George Kellogg, was an agent of the New England Company, which advanced $2800 to Brown for a business transaction on their behalf.[2] The New England Company was a religious organization chartered in the colonial era for the purpose of bringing the Christian religion to Native Americans in the United States and Canada, and later for missions in the Caribbean. Its business investments were thus conducted to produce revenue for the support of missionaries and other activities of the organization. This is undoubtedly what Brown means when he refers to the Company's "holy and greatly suffering cause." In an attempt to resolve his own personal financial issues, Brown unfortunately appropriated the Company's money with the intention of replacing it with money he assumed he could borrow. When he found that he could not secure these funds, Brown finally had to admit his error and place his meager estate on assignment so that the New England Company could sue for reparations. A letter of explanation from Brown dated August 27, 1839[3] describes his initial anxiety and hopes of being able to redress his abuse. However this letter was written afterward, in response to an apparently gracious letter from Kellogg, and is published here for the first time. It further highlights Brown's circumstances, including the sincerity that effectively persuaded the lenience of those whom he had wronged.

* * *

Franklin Mills 20th September 1839
George Kellogg Esqr
Dear Sir

Your kind letter of the 12th Inst I have just read and I feel grateful to learn that you have feelings of tenderness towards one that has abused (I do not say with a fraudulent intent) your confidence, injured your business, and what is worse than all, wounded a holy and greatly suffering cause. I think I can cordially join you in hopeing that a merciful God will give me wisdom, firmness, propper sence of duty, and ability to render speedily to all their due. That I ever had a fraudulent or trickish design, I utterly deny, but that I in my distress to meet punctually my engagements, foolishly, and wickedly, presumed, relying on the engagements of others, is a sorrowful truth to me, & to my much injured friends. The assignment of my property has been made to a trustee who thereby becomes an officer of the Court for the settlement of my business, and who has since I wrote you before made a contract the balance in one year from date. The name of the trustee is George B Depeyster is one of the former associate judges of our Court, is empowered either to sell at private sale, or to put any or all my lands and other property under the Hammer as he may deem propper. He resides in this place and the assignment is a matter of record in the recorders office of the County. I wish you to present a claim of sufficient amount abundantly to cover interest, and every species of damage, and disappointment, and should you so receive it as to feel in the end that your claim was to[o] large, I will trust it to your own judgment of what may be right. I would not wrong you or any one, and I feel confident that ample justice can be rendered to all. I will do as you requested with the Box of Cloths and forward a propper receipt for them, and also forward your wool Bags, or do with them as you may hereafter direct.

[*Signature line missing from original.*]

Document 5

John Brown, Springfield, Massachusetts, to Mary Brown, Akron, Ohio, Mar. 7, 1846, mistakenly dated "1844." 2 pp., addressed on verso. MS 01-0016, Boyd B. Stutler Collection, West Virginia State Archives.

This personal letter from Brown to his wife was undoubtedly misdated by Brown as 1844, but was almost certainly written in 1846, after he relocated to Massachusetts to set up a wool commission operation. His family joined him later that year, and this letter clearly reflects the pining and sentimentality of a family man parted from his loved ones for an extended time. It is an honest letter, Brown making himself vulnerable to his wife and family by owning up to his business and domestic shortcomings, and praising his wife as his "better half." The letter shows that Mary Brown had to contend with discipline issues in her husband's absence, and the "large boys" reference is probably to Brown's son Frederick (Mary's stepson), a troubled sixteen-year-old, as well as their own sprouting, mischievous boys, Watson and Salmon, ages eleven and ten, respectively. Other affectionate references are made to "Little Chick," baby Amelia, nine-months-old, and "strange" Anne, who was a little more than two-years-old. (Amelia died in a tragic household accident later that year.) The letter reveals the closeness of the family as well as Brown's growing regret over his harsh disciplinary practices as a younger parent.

* * *

Springfield Mass 7th March 184[6]
My Dear Mary
 It is once more Sabbath evening, & nothing so much accords with my feelings as to spend a portion of it converseing with the

partner of my own choice, & the sharer of my poverty, trials, discredit, & sore afflictions; as well as of what of comfort, & seeming prosperity has fallen to my lot; for quite a number of years. I would you should realise that notwithstanding I am absent in boddy I am verry much of the time present in spirit. I do not forget the firm attachment of her who has remained my fast, & faithful affectionate friend, when others said of me (now that he lieth he shall rise up no more.) When I reflect on these things together with the verry considerabl[e] difference in our age, as well as all the follies, & faults with which I am justly chargeable, I really admire at your constancy; & really feel notwithstanding I sometimes chide you severely that you ar[e] *really* my better half. I now feel encouraged to believe that my absence will not be verry long. After being so much away, it seems as if I knew pretty well how to appreciate the quiet of home. There is a peculiar music in the word which a half years absence in a distant country would enable you to understand. Millions there are who have no such thing to lay claim to. I feel considerable regret by turns that I have lived so many years, & have in reality done

Page 2d

so verry little to increase the amount of human hapiness. I often regret that my manner is no more kind & affectionate to those I really love, & esteem; but I trust my friends will overlook my harsh rough ways when I cease to be in their way; as an occasion of pain, & unhapiness. In immagination I often see you in your room with Little Chick; & that strange Anna. You must say to her that Father means to come before long, & Kiss someboddy. I will close for this time by saying that it is my growing resolution to endeavour to promote my *own* hapiness by doing what I can to render those around me more so. If the large boys do wrong call them alone into your room, & expostulate with them kindly, & see if you cannot reach them by a kind but powerful appeal to their honor. I do not claim that such a theory accords verry much with my *practice; I frankly confess it does not*; but I want *your face* to shine even if my own should be dark, & cloudy. You can let the family read this letter, & perhaps you may not feel it a great burden to answer it & let me hear all about how you get along.

Affectionately Yours
John Brown

Document 6

John Brown, Akron, Ohio, to A. B. Allen, editor, Feb. 15, 1846, in *American Agriculturalist* [New York] (Apr. 1846): 18–19. Excerpt from published text.

By the mid-1840s, John Brown was a nationally known expert in sheep and wool, but was particularly known by the wool-growing farmers of Ohio, Pennsylvania, and western Virginia whose interests he primarily represented. This letter was written just before Brown moved to Springfield, Massachusetts in the spring of 1846, to open a wool commission house representing the interests of sheep farmers who otherwise were at the mercy of the more sophisticated manufacturers of New England. The excerpted segments of this lengthy letter provide insight into Brown's breadth of experience and insights into the concerns of wool growers. In this case he is addressing a prominent debate among farmers regarding the superiority of sheep breeds. Brown's argument is that it is the quality of cultivation that is important, not the elevation of one breed over another. All breeds, Brown contends, would decline in quality if not properly cultivated. The original copy of this letter is no longer extant, and the distinctive and peculiar features of his writing have obviously been edited. However this is undoubtedly an authentic and heretofore unpublished letter of John Brown.

* * *

(Excerpt)

After so long a time, I will in some measure fulfill my engagement about writing you in regard to sheep and wool growing. My intention is, and has ever been, to get up a flock that would combine as much as possible the following traits: First, a strong constitution; a heavy fleece of *real wool*, of the very best quality that the world can boast; and a just form. It has been a favorite theory with me, that by judicious selection and good breeding, all this might be effected, and I have for years spared neither time, nor expense, nor travel, to bring it about: and if I have in any good measure effected my object, it has been by selecting according to my best judgment, disregarding entirely all names of breeds, and names of men as breeders, except so far as to examine their flocks carefully, or specimens of them, as they have been exhibited at the shows, or their different lots of wool at numerous manufacturing establishments . . . .

Some of the best flocks I have ever found in the country (after going over much of it time after time, beginning with Vermont and New Hampshire, and ending with Virginia), are a mixture of Saxony and Merino, where the breeding has been upward, as I call it (for want of a better expression); that is, where the advantage as to quality is on the side of the buck. The getting of really fine sheep in any part of the world is, I believe, the fruit of uncommon pains, nice discrimination, great perseverance, and incessant care; but it will cost nothing to reduce the quality of any breed, but to let it alone. It costs a considerable sum to raise the last stone on some of the monuments in our own country, and some skill, but a very ordinary man for a trifle would get them down . . . . Such is the downward tendency of almost everything we have to do with. If this view is correct of breeding downward, then all that the ewes exceed the bucks will be nearly or quite lost. If it is best for us in the United States to grow fine wool at all, we ought to be less fickle in our course. European breeders are wonderfully steady and persevering, and whole districts unite as to a particular standard. Witness the Devon cattle, the Southdown sheep, the Berkshire pigs, &c., &c.

John Brown
of the firm of Perkins & Brown.

Document 7

John Brown, Burgettstown, Pa., to John Brown, Jr. and Wealthy Brown, New York City, Apr. 12, 1850. The signature line is based on Sanborn's transcription of the original, which was made before the signature line was cut away (see *LLJB*, 74). MIC 50 Papers of John Brown, Jr. [microform]; Ohio Historical Society.

This document demonstrates that despite the failure of P&B, Brown did not bear the brunt of its loss, nor was he devastated as many historians have supposed. After closing the commission house, Perkins enthusiastically sought to sustain their collaboration, mainly because his herds, flock, and farm in Akron had so prospered under Brown's management. As this letter indicates, Perkins wanted a permanent arrangement, whereby their joint enterprise would become an estate that both men could leave to their heirs. Had Perkins not subsequently lost money in other investments apart from Brown, their partnership might have continued toward long-term profit. As the letter also suggests, John Jr. and his wife Wealthy were residing in New York City at this time, as the younger Brown was employed by the firm of Orson Fowler and Samuel Wells, which specialized in phrenology, a new "scientific" method of studying human behavior. Based on the specious notion that human intellect, ability, and personality could be measured according to the shape of the skull, Fowler & Wells provided lecturers, publications, and skull-readings. John Brown himself embraced this alleged science with optimism, further admiring Fowler for his firm abolitionist views. Having had his own skull analyzed by Fowler, he was quite familiar with the firm's office at 131 Nassau Street in Manhattan.

*   *   *

Burgettstown Pa 12th April 1850
Dear Son John & Wife
When at New York on my way home I called at Mssr Fowler &
Wells office, but you were absent. Mr Perkins has made me a visit
here, & left for home yesterday. All well in Essex when I left. All
well at Akron when he left, one week since. Our meeting together
was one of the most cordial, & pleasant I ever experienced. He
met a full history of our difficulties, *& probable lapses* without a
frown on his countenance or one sylable of reflection, but on the
contrary with words of comfort, & encouragement. He is wholly
averse to any seperation of our business or interests, & gave me
the fullest assurance of his undiminishe[d] confidence & personal
regard. He expressed a strong desire to have our flock of sheep
remain undivided to become the joint possession of our families
when we have gone off the stage. Such a meeting I had not dared
to expect, & I most heartily wish each of my family could have
shared in the comfort of it. Mr Perkins has in this whole business
from first to last set an example worthy of a Philosopher, or of a
Christian. I am meeting with a good deal of trouble from those to
whom we have over-advanced but feel nerved to have any difficulty
while God continues me such a partner. Expect to be in New York
within 3 or 4 week[s.]

[Your affectionate father John Brown]

Document 8

John Brown, Springfield, Massachusetts, to Mary Brown, North Elba, New York,
Nov. 28, 1850. Clarence Gee's transcription from a copy of the original, in Gee
Papers, Hudson Library and Historical Society, Hudson, Ohio. This transciption
has been somewhat edited of Brown's writing style.

A somewhat sentimental letter, this was undoubtedly written after Sunday
church attendance, which was Brown's custom when parted from his family.
Brown specifically mentions having attended a Thanksgiving service, undoubtedly at the Zion Methodist Church, Springfield's leading black congregation.
He alludes to preparations for an obligatory move back to the Perkins estate in
Akron, Ohio, and the necessity of economizing with farm supplies during the
long Adirondack winter. "Massasoit of Springfield" refers to a famous restaurant
within a hotel of the same name, considered "first among the foremost" by the

Springfield *Republican* in Brown's time. The phrase, "trust in God and keep their powder dry" is a favorite quote from Brown's hero, the Puritan warrior Oliver Cromwell. The phrase, "there's mercy in every place, and mercy, encouraging thought" is an excerpt from the last stanza of William Cowper's poem, "The Solitude of Alexander Selkirk" (1782). Selkirk was a lonely castaway and the son of a tanner, so it is evident that Brown identified with him somewhat. Owen, Brown's third son (then twenty-six-years old), is also mentioned.

* * *

Springfield Mass 28th Nov 1850
Dear Wife;

As I can not yet say how soon I can return, or what the prospect is of our moving at all this winter, I write to let you hear from me, as you said. I have been well, and have effected a sale of our wool at about 60 cents per lb. Since leaving home I have thought that under all the circumstances of doubt attending the time of our removal; and the possibility that we may not remove at all that I had perhaps encouraged the boys to feed out the potatoes too freely. I now wish them to stop when they have fed out the small ones, as, should any thing prevent our moving longer than we had expected, or prevent it entirely I do not wish to be obliged to buy. When the small potatoes are fed out, the boys can mess the cows that give milk with clean vats. I want to have them very careful to have no hay or straw wasted, but I would have them use enough straw for bedding the cattle to keep them from lying in the mire. I heard from Ohio a few days since; all were there well. It now seems that the fugitive slave law was to be the means of making more abolitionists than all the lectures we have had for years. It really looks as if God had his hand in this wickedness also. I of course keep encouraging my friends "to trust in God and keep their powder dry." I did so today at thanksgiving meeting publicly. I may get ready to get home the middle of next month, but am wholly in the dark about it yet; do not mean that idleness shall prevent me. While here, and at almost all places where I stop, I am treated with all kindness and attention, but it all does not make home. I feel lonely and restless, no matter how neat and comfortable my room and bed, nor how richly loaded may be the table; they have very few charms for me. Away from home, I can look back to our log cabin at the centre of Richfield with a supper of Porridge and Johnny cake as to a place of far more interest to me than the Massasoit of Springfield. But, "there's mercy in every place, and mercy, encouraging thought." I shall endeavor when I come home to bring the things that Owen and others of the family stood in need of. I told Mr. Cutting of Westport he might have either of the yearling heifers for thirty dollars. I want Owen to get the largest bull in order, if he can do it by any means. May God in very deed bless and keep all my family is the continued prayer of

Your affectionate husband
John Brown

[*P.S.*] Will any of them write me here? I should think they might afford to, some one of them.

Document 9

John Brown, Springfield, Massachusetts, to Mary Brown, North Elba, New York, Jan. 17, 1851, from *LLJB*, 107 and 132. Besides editing out Brown's style, Sanborn also divided this document into two separate portions in the book.

In early 1851, Brown traveled down to Springfield from his home in New York State with the express purpose of coming to the aid of his black friends, whose crisis was heightening in the shadows of the Fugitive Slave Law, especially after a black man named Henry Long was seized in New York City, quickly being tried and deported to the South. The seizure sent a wave of trauma throughout the African American community, and Brown's descriptions are first hand descriptions of this tragic episode. His statement about "advising them how to act" pertains to his attempt to organize a self-defense and resistance group, and the writing of a document for that organization (see Document 10). Besides the reference to his older son Owen, Brown mentions boys and girls, these being the children from his second marriage, to Mary: Watson, age 16; Salmon, age 15; Oliver, age 12; Anne, age 8; and Sarah, age 5.

* * *

Springfield, Mass., Jan. 17, 1851
Dear Wife
. . . Since the sending off to slavery of Long from New York, I have improved my leisure hours quite busily with colored people here, in advising them how to act, and in giving them all the encouragement in my power. They very much need encouragement and advice; and some of them are so alarmed that they tell me they cannot sleep on account of either themselves or their

wives and children. I can only say I think I have been enabled to do something to revive their broken spirits. I want all my family to imagine themselves in the same dreadful condition. My only spare time being taken up (often till late hours at night) in the way I speak of, has prevented me from the gloomy homesick feelings which had before so much oppressed me; not that I forgot my family at all . . . .

. . . . I wrote Owen last week that if he had not the means on hand to buy a little sugar, to write Mr. Cutting, of Westport, to send out some. I conclude you have got your belt before this. I could not manage to send the slates for the boys, as I intended, so they must be provided for some other way . . . . Say to the little girls that I will run home the first chance I get; but I want to have them learn to be a little more still. May God in his infinite mercy bless and keep you all is the unceasing prayer of

Your affectionate husband,
John Brown

Document 10

Unfortunately the original copy of Brown's first document of political organization has been misplaced and possibly lost to history. In 1870, William Wells
Brown published a reminiscence of his visit to Springfield in the days of the Fugitive Slave Law, including a transcript of Brown's document.[4] In 1883, Franklin
Sanborn published the next reliable transcription in *LLJB*, 123–27. Both writers
apparently had access to the original document, although only Sanborn furnished
the complete text.[5] An extended excerpt is published here.

In January 1851, Brown and his black associates in Springfield formed an organization called The United States League of Gileadites, drawing from a biblical account of some brave Israelite warriors [Judges 7:3; 20:8]. No doubt the decision to form the Gileadite organization was a response to the state-sanctioned kidnaping of Henry Long (see Document 9) and others taken under the new Fugitive Slave Law. Given that Brown referred to it as a "branch" suggests he hoped to establish a nationwide movement with affiliate organizations in other cities. He probably also hoped to broaden the agenda of the Gileadites to include offensive measures in the South. More than one source states that Brown also furnished members with weapons, although there is no record of any skirmish or counter-assault by the Gileadites against slave-hunters. The document is uniquely Brown's brainchild, not only reflecting his religious devotion and belief in armed resistance, but in his constructive criticism of free blacks and his strong devotion to the flag of the United States. However militant, this is a document of radical reform, not revolution. The original document was signed by forty-four people, but Sanborn recorded only twenty-seven of the signatures on the document.

* * *

(Excerpt)

WORDS OF ADVICE.
Branch of the United States League of Gileadites. Adopted January 15th, 1851, as *written and recommended by John Brown.*

UNION IS STRENGTH

Nothing so charms the American people as personal bravery. The trial for life of one bold and to some extent successful man, for defending his rights in good earnest, would arouse more sympathy throughout the nation than the accumulated wrongs and sufferings of more than three millions of our submissive colored population. We need not mention the Greeks struggling against the oppressive Turks, the Poles against Russia, nor the Hungarians against Austria and Russian combined to prove this. *No jury can be found in the Northern Sates that would convict a man for defending his rights to the last extremity. This is well understood by Southern congressmen, who insisted that the right of trial by jury should not be granted to the fugitive.* Colored people have more fast friends amongst the whites than they suppose, and would have ten times the number they now have were they but half as much in earnest to secure their dearest rights as they are to ape the follies and extravagances of their white neighbors, and to indulge in idle show, in ease, and in luxury. Just think of the money expended by individuals in your behalf in the past twenty years. Think of the number who have been mobbed and imprisoned on your account. Have any of you seen the Branded Hand? Do you remember the names of Lovejoy and Torrey?[6] Should one of your number be arrested, you must collect together as quickly as possible, so as to outnumber your adversaries who are taking an active part against you. Let no able-bodied man appear on the ground unequipped or with his weapons exposed to view; let that be understood beforehand. Your plans must be known only to yourself, and with the understanding that all traitors must die, wherever caught and proven to be guilty. "Whosoever is fearful or afraid, let him return and depart early from Mount Gilead." Judges, vii. chap., 8 verse; Deut., xx. chap, 8 verse. Give all cowards an opportunity to show it on condition of holding their peace. *Do not delay one moment after you are ready; you will lose all your resolution if you do. Let the first blow be the signal for all to engage, and when engaged do not do your work by halves; but make clean work with your enemies, and be sure you meddle not with any others.* By going about your business quietly, you will get the job disposed of before the number that an uproar would bring together can collect; and you will have the advantage of those who come out against you, for they will be wholly unprepared with either equipments or matured plans—all with them will be confusion and terror. Your enemies will be slow to attack you after you have once done up the work nicely; and, if they should, they will have to encounter your white friends as well as you, for you may safely calculate on a division of the whites, and may by that means get to an honorable parley.

Be firm, determined, and cool; but let it be understood that you are not to be driven to desperation without making it an awful dear job to others as well as to you. Give them to know distinctly that those who live in wooden houses should not throw fire, and that you are just as able to suffer as your white neighbor. *After effecting a rescue, if you are assailed go into the houses of your most prominent and influential white friends with your wives, and that will effectually fasten; upon them the suspicion of being connected with you, and will compel them to make a common cause, with you, whether they would otherwise live up to their profession or not. This would leave them no choice in the matter.* Some would, doubtless, prove themselves true of their own choice; others would flinch. That would be taking them at their own words. You may make a tumult in the court-room where a trial is going on, by burning gun powder freely in paper packages, if you cannot think of any better way to create a momentary alarm, and might possibly give one or more of your enemies a hoist. But in such case the prisoner will need to take the hint at once and bestir himself; and so should his friends improve the opportunity for a general rush.

A lasso might possibly be applied to a slave-catcher for once with good effect. Hold on to your weapons, and never be persuaded to leave them, part with them, or have them far away from you. *Stand by one another, and by your friends, while a drop of blood remains; and be hanged, if you must; but tell no tales out of school. Make no confession.*

Union is strength. Without some well-digested arrangements nothing to any good purpose is likely to be done, let the demand be never so great. Witness the case of Hamlet and Long in New York, when there was no well-defined plan of operations or suitable preparation beforehand. The desired end may be effectually secured by the means proposed; namely, the enjoyment of our inalienable rights.

AGREEMENT

As citizens of the United States of America, trusting in a Just and Merciful God, whose spirit and all-powerful aid, we humbly implore, *we will ever be true to the Flag of our beloved Country, always acting under it.* We whose names are hereunto affixed do constitute ourselves a Branch of the United States League of Gileadites. That we will provide ourselves at once with suitable implements, and will aid those who do not possess the means, if any such are disposed to join us. We invite every colored person whose heart is engaged for the performance of our business, whether male or female, old or young. The duty of the aged, infirm, and young members of the League shall be to give instant notice to all members in case of an attack upon any of our people.

We agree to have no officers except a Treasurer and Secretary *pro tem.*, until after some trial of courage and talent of able bodied members shall enable us to elect officers from those who shall have rendered the most important services. Nothing but wisdom and undaunted courage, efficiency, and general good conduct shall in any way influence us in electing our officers.

Document 11

John Brown, Osawatomie, Kansas Territory, Jan. 19, 1856, to Owen Brown, Hudson, Ohio. Oswald Garrison Villard—John Brown Collection, Rare Book and Manuscript Library, Columbia University. Based on a 1909 transcription from the original by Villard assistant, Katherine Mayo. Mayo did not record the location of this document and it has since disappeared. There was a verso inscription in the hand of Owen Brown, who apparently forwarded the letter to others in the family, perhaps to his granddaughter Ruth Thompson Brown in North Elba, New York.

Although Brown had been optimistic about the success of the free state cause in the Kansas territory fro the time of his arrival in October 1855, it soon became clear that pro-slavery politicians, officials, and terrorists were not going to permit the process of the ballot to function according to the will of the free state majority. Having narrowly survived an attack by pro-slavery forces in December 1855, free state settlers were keeping an eye on further intrusions into the territory by Missouri-based terrorists, known at the time as "border ruffians," and other Southerners working for the pro-slavery cause. Brown visited Westport, Missouri on New Year's Day 1856 to purchase supplies and found things quiet; as this letter suggests, however, free state settlers felt that peace was quite tentative, and were looking forward to the election of the free state legislature in February.

This short letter to father Owen Brown in Ohio gives some detail as to the difficulties of living on the Kansas prairie in the dead of winter, including frostbite and sickness. More interesting are Brown's revealing evaluation of the presence of "a great many" free state Southern settlers, whom he considered only "half right" because they opposed slavery but advocated racist exclusion of blacks. "They probably out number the real Anti-Slavery men here," he concludes, referring to a minority of pro-black settlers such as the Browns themselves. The Browns were thus a minority within the free state presence in Kansas.

* * *

Osawatomie Kansas Territory 19th Jany 1856
Dear Father

I have but little to write that will interest either yourself, or any other Ohio friends: & yet I cannot allow myself to neglect writing I am much pressed for time; & I hope you will show my Letters to as many of the friends as may care to see them or as you *conveniently* can: & I also hope they will accept them as written to themselves. It is impossible under my circumstances to write One half my friends. It will be Three Weeks on the 12th inst since we have had such constant hard freezing that the Snow has not softened so as not to blow into drifts. During all this time Jason, Fredk, Salmon, & Oliver, have all had their toes more or less frozen: Jason so as to lame him some; & the Cows their Teats; & some of the Cattle the ends of their Noses frozen. All the friends here have to appearance recovered from the Ague, for which we should be very thankful. Mr Adairs folks are very comfortably situated. They have received the $20 you sent by me; Some time since. John is nominated as a member of the Free State Legislature; & will most likely be elected (on the 15th) when the Election comes off. We have just heard that all are well at North Elba; & they acknowledge with gratitude the money you sent them. Since the Kansas invasion we have but little stir here; & we get no News from the States of any account however hungry we may be for news. We have in the Territory a great many Southern men who are as yet but half right in regard to Slavery; & go for Negro, & Mullatto exclusion. Some of them are very earnest Free State men. We are glad to have them begin to get right. They probably out number the real Anti-Slavery men here. I am sorry for the extreme leanness of my letter: but can do no better now.

Your Affectionate Son
John Brown

[*verso*]
Jan 23d 56
Dear Children, all well nothing new, very cold give God thanks for
mercies

O Brown

Document 12

John Brown, Osawatomie, Kansas Territory, to T. W. Carter, Massachusetts Arms
Company, Chicopee Falls, Massachusetts, Feb. 20, 1856, from a photographic
image of the original letter in the Springfield *Republican*, Apr. 30, 1941.

By early February 1856, free state settlers in Kansas were expecting an
onslaught of pro-slavery terrorists and thugs from Missouri; however, as Brown
noted in a letter to his wife on February 6, they also expected the coming winter snows to delay these invasions. In the mean time, however, Brown and other
free state settlers were even more concerned about the presence of the U.S. military already in the territory, ostensibly under orders to force intruders from
Indian lands. Free state people considered their presence "of a most suspicious
character," as he put it in a letter to Congressmen Joshua Giddings on February
20.[7] Concerned that free state men might end up having to fight against their
own government soldiers, Brown thus appealed to Giddings to intervene on
their behalf. On the same day, however, he wrote a letter to T. W. Carter, an
agent of the Massachusetts Arms Company, who had already supplied Brown
with weapons. As this letter illustrates, Brown was bracing for a renewed offensive from pro-slavery militants in the spring and reasonably feared that the pro-
slavery administration of President Franklin Pierce would use federal troops to
further oppose the legitimate efforts of the majority free state settlers. However
distasteful the thought of opposing the army of his own nation, Brown's interest
in obtaining carbines for the free state side reflects his commitment to opposing
the "bogus" laws of the fraudulently elected pro-slavery territorial government,
and his greater objective to oppose slavery by any means necessary.

* * *

Osawatomie, Kansas Territory, 20th Feby 1856
T W Carter Esqr Agt
Chicopee Falls Mass
Dear Sir
　　Your kind favour of the 5th Jany was received a few days since;
mentioning receipt of Draft, & offering a further supply of arms. I
would again immediately take the responsibility of ordering
another lot: but I am not of this moment prepared to say how I

would *dare* to have them directed. The other lot I came on with myself; bringing with them other Arms contributed by the friends of Freedom in Mass & other parts. I cannot just now name any one who is coming on; suitable to take charge of them. Gen Pomeroy[8] went East lately; but I do not now know where a letter would find him. I now think I shall immediately make a *further; & more earnest* appeal to the lovers of Freedom in New England for the means of procuring Arms; & Amunition for the maintainance of that cause in Kansas; as I think the Crisis *has not yet come.* I firmly believe that the Administration intends to drive the people here to an abject submission; or to fight the Government troops (now in the Territory ostensibly to remove intruders from certain Indian lands.) Bow in submission to the vilest tyrany or be guilty of what *will be called* Treason; will I believe be the next, & only alternative for the Free State men of Kansas. O God must this thing be? Must the people here Shoot down the poor Soldiers with whom they have no quarrel? Can you not through your extensive acquaintance aid me in this work; if you can be satisfied that I am *trust worthy.* I am well known by many at Springfield. I very much want a lot of the Carbines as soon as I can see any *way clear* to pay for them; & then to get them through Safe. Please write me the lowest terms at wholesale for just such Carbines as you furnish the Government. I may write you further within [a] few days

Very Respectfully Your Friend
John Brown

Document 13

John Brown, "Near Browns Station," Kansas Territory, to Mary Brown, North Elba, N.Y., June 24, 1856, 4 pp. John Brown Papers, Abraham Lincoln Presidential Library, Springfield, Ill. This letter was written entirely in pencil and over the years the original has been smudged in places quite badly, especially the last page. Fortunately, Sanborn made an earlier transcription from the original (*LLJB*, 236–41), and the now obscured portions in the original are supplied from his version in brackets without italics.

After leading the party that killed five pro-slavery collaborators in their vicinity on May 24, 1856, Brown was thereafter a wanted man by authorities in the Kansas territory as well as by pro-slavery thugs, whose self-assured campaign of terrorism and conquest was suddenly undercut by the Browns' ruthless strike at Pottawatomie Creek. After the killings, Brown and his men were forced to take to the field, and continued to operate while evading capture by pro-slavery men, finally defeating them in battle on June 2, although their victory was undermined when they were met by federal troops. Though sympathetic to the free state cause, the commander forced Brown and his men to release their pro-slavery prisoners and then disband. Brown describes these and other events of May-June 1856, noting that he wished for it to be recopied in ink and distributed among abolitionists, especially the influential Gerrit Smith.

* * *

Near *Browns Station, K T, 24th June, 1856*
   * There are but very few who wish real facts about these matters to go out.
Dear Wife & Children every One
   It is now about Five Weeks since I have seen a line from North Elba or had any chance of writing you. During that period we here have passed through an almost constant series of very trying events. We were called to go to the relief of Lawrence May 22 & every man (Eight in all) except Orson turned out; he staying with the women & Children & to take care of the cattle. John was Captain of a Company to which Jason belonged the other Six were a little Co[mpany] by ourselves. On our way to Lawrence we learned that it had been alredy destroyed, & we encamped with Johns Co[mpany] over Night. Next day our little Co[mpany] left, & during the day we stopped & searched Three men. Lawrence was destroyed in this way; their leading men had (as I think) decided in a very cowardly maner not to resist any process having any Government official to serve it, notwithstanding the process might be wholly a Bogus affair. The consequence was that a Man called a U S Marshall came on with a horde of ruffians which he called his posse & after aresting a few persons turned the ruffians loose on the defenceless people. They robed the inhabitants of their money & other property, & even women of their ornaments, & burned considerable of the town. On the 2d day & Evening after we left Johns men we encountered quite a number of pro Slavery men & took quite a number prisoner. Our prisoners we let go; but we kept some Four or Five Hordes. We were immediately after this accused of murdering Five men at Potawatomie; & great efforts have since been made by the Missourians & their ruffian allies to capture us. Johns company soon afterwards disbanded, & also the Osawatomie men. June 26 * Jason is set at liberty & we have hopes for John. Jason started to go & place himself under the protection of the government troops; but on his way he was taken prisoner by the

Bogus men & is yet a prisoner I suppose. John tryed to hide for several days but from feelings of the ungrateful conduct of those

Page 2d

who had ought to have stood by him excessive fatigue, anxiety, & constant loss of of sleep; became quite insane, & in that situation gave up or as we are told was betrayed at Osawatomie into the hands of the Bogus men. We do not know all the truth about this affair. He has since we are told been kept in Irons & brought to a trial before a bogus Court the result of which we have not yet learned. We have great anxiety both for him & Jason; & numerous other prisoners with the men (who have all the while had the government troops to sustain them). We can only commend them to God. The cowardly mean conduct of Osawatomie & vicinity did not save them for the rufians came on them made numerous prisoners fired their buildings & robbed them. After this a picked party of the Bogus men went to Browns Station burned Johns & Jasons houses, & their contents to Ashes in which burning we have all suffered more or less. Orson & boy have been prisoners but were soon set at liberty.[9] They are well & have not been seriously injured. Owen & I have just come here for the first time to look at the ruins. All looks desolate & forsaken; the grass & weeds fast covering up the signs that these places were lately the abodes of quiet families. After burning the houses this self same party of picked men some Forty in number set out as they supposed, (& as was the fact) on the track of my little company boasting with awful profanity that they would have our scalps. They howev[er] passed the place where we were hid, & robbed a little Town some Four or Five miles beyound [our] camp [in the] timber. I had omitted to say that some murders had been committed at the time Lawrence was sacked. On learning that this party were in pursuit of us my little Co[mpany] now increased to 10 in all started after them in company of a Capt Shore with Eighteen men he included. June 1st We were all mounted as we traveled. We did not meet them on that day but took Five prisoners Four of whom were of their scouts & well armed. We were out all Night but could find nothing of them untill about Six Oclock next Morning when we prepared to attack them at once; on foot leaveing Fredk & one of Capt Shores men to guard the Horses. As I was much older that Capt Shore the principle direction of the fight devolved on me. We got to within about a mile of their camp before being discovered by their scouts; & then moved

Page 3d

at a brisk pace, Capt Shore & men forming our left, & my Co[*mpany*] the right. When at about Sixty rods of the enemy Capt Shores men halted by mistake in a very exposed situation & continued the fire both *his* men & the enemy being armed with Sharps Rifles. My Co[*mpany*] had no long shooters. We my Co[*mpany*]) did not fire a gun untill we joined the rear of a bank about Fifteen to Twenty Rods to the right of the enemy, where we commenced, & soon compelled them to hide in a ravine. Capt Shore after getting one man wounded & exhausting his amunition came with part of his men to the right of my position much discouraged. The balance of his men including the one wounded had left the ground. Five of Capt Shores men came boldly down & Joined my Co[*mpany*] & all but one more wounded helped to maintain the fight untill it was over. I was obliged to give my consent that he should go after more help when all his men left but Eight Four of whom I persuaded to remain in a secure position, & then busied one of them in shooting the Horses & Mules of the enemy which served for a show of fight. After the fireing had continued for some Two to Three hours Capt Pate with 23 men (Two badly wounded) laid down their arms to Nine men myself included. Four of Capt Shores men & Four of [*my own.*] One of my men (Henry Thomson) was badly wounded & after continueing his fire for an Hour after was obliged to quit the ground. Three others of my Co[*mpany*] (but not of my family) had gone off. Salmon was dreadfully wounded by accident soon after the fight but both he & henry are fast recovering. A day or Two after the fight Col Sumner of the U.S. army came suddenly uppon us while fortifying our camp & guarding our prisoners (which by the way it had been agreed mutually should be exchanged for as many Free State men John & Jason included) and compelled us to let go our prisoners without being exchanged & to give them up their horses & arms. They did not go more than Two or 3 Miles before they began to rob & injure Free State people. We consider this as in good keeping with the cruel & unjust course of the administration & its tools throughout this whole Kansas difficulty. Col Sumner also compeled us to disband & we being only a handful were obliged to submit. Since then we have like David of old had our dwelling with the serpents of the Rocks, & wild beasts

Page 4th

of the wilderness being obliged to hide away from our enemies. We are not disheartened though nearly destitute of food; Clothing, & money. God who has not given us over to the will of our enemies but has moreover delivered them into our hand; will we humbly trust still ~~still~~ keep & deliver us. We feel assured that he who sees not as men see does not lay the guilt of innocent blood to our charge. I ought to have said that Capt Shore & his men stood their ground nobly in their unfortunate but mistaken position during the early part of the fight. I ought to say further that a Capt Abbot being some miles distant with a company came forward promptly to sustain us but could not march till the fight was over. After the fight numerous Free State men who would not be got out before were on hand & some of them I am ashamed to add were very busy not only with the plunder of our enemies, but with our private [effects,] leaveing [us while guarding our prisoners and providing] in regard to them much poorer [than before the battle.] If under God [this letter reaches] you so that it can be read I wish it at once carefully copied in Ink & a coppy of it sent to Gerrit Smith. I know of no other way to get these facts, & our situation before the world, nor when I can write again. Owen has the Ague today. Our camp is some Miles off. Have heard that letters are in for some of us but have not seen them. Do continue writing. We heard that last Mail brought only Three letters & all those for pro Slavery men. It is said that both the Lawrence, & Osawatomie men when ruffians came on them either hid or gave up their arms, & that their leading men counceled to take such course. May God bless & keep you all.

Your affectionate Husband & Father
John Brown

P S Ellen, & Wealthy are staying at Osawatomie The above is a true accont of the first regular battle fought between Free State & pro Slavery men in Kansas. May God still gird our Loins & hold our right hands, & to him may we give the glory. JB I ought in justice to say that *after* the Sacking & burning of several towns the government troops appeared for their protection & drove off some of the enemy.

Document 14

John Brown, Albany, New York, to George L. Stearns, Boston, Mass., Apr. 28, 1857. Based on a transcription from the original by Villard assistant, Katherine Mayo. Oswald Garrison Villard—John Brown Collection, Rare Book and Manuscript Library, Columbia University.

In his efforts to raise support for the Kansas struggle in 1857, Brown began to build a network of anti-slavery associates, especially in New England, some of whom would become close supporters and allies. This is another letter to George L. Stearns [Document 1], including a reference to the Reverend Theodore Parker, both of whom became members of Brown's "Secret Six," illustrating Brown's determined quest for money and weapons for the cause of Kansas. He refers to weapons produced by two different gun manufacturers in New England, interestingly mentioning that he had purchased revolvers from the Massachusetts Arms Company that were similar to the more popular Colt revolvers, but apparently were less expensive. The Colt weapon was extremely popular during the 1850s and launched a new market for revolvers at the time.[10]

* * *

Albany, N Y, 28th April, 1857
George L. Stearns Esqr
Boston Mass
My Dear Sir

The Worcester Gun Factory cannot supply me with Revolvers in *time*, but the Mass. Arms Co; (whose Revolvers I have used; & which are much the same as Colts) offer to let me have what I need being 200 for $1300, Thirteen Hundred Dollars. This they have given me in a written memorandum from Col. T. W. Carter; their Agent at Chicopee Falls: saying they *mean it to be* a donation *in part from them*; if the purchase is made. This is by far the best offer I have got. They should be each supplied with Powder Flaske, Ram Rod, Moulds, Screw driver; & an Extra Spring. The last is not mentioned in the memorandum, but Col Carter had some time ago told me he would supply them; & I have no doubt he will. He did *not want* the thing to be made public. Now if Rev. T Parker, & other good people of Boston, would make up that amount. I might *at least be well armed*. Please write Watson Brown, Elizabethtown, Essex Co, NY, Care of David Judd Esqr.[11] My best wishes to yourself and Family.

Very Respectfully Your Friend
John Brown

Document 15

John Brown (with postscript by Frederick Douglass), Rochester, N.Y., to Mary Brown and Ruth Brown Thompson, North Elba, N.Y., Jan. 30, 1858, from *LLJB*, 440–41. Transcriptions and copies of this letter are found in a number of collections, although the original is privately owned.

In 1858 Brown had appropriated the name of Ohioan Nelson Hawkins and grown a beard. Wanted for his activities in Missouri and Kansas, he traveled cautiously and kept a low profile, including a quiet retreat in the home of abolitionist Frederick Douglass. As this letter shows, Brown expressed sentimental feelings for his younger children while also seeking to recruit some of his older sons and his son-in-law, Henry Thompson, who had fought alongside him in Kansas.

* * *

Rochester N Y, 30th Jany, 1858,
My Dear Wife & Children every one

I am (*praised be God*) once more in [*New*] York State. Whether I shall be permitted to visit you or not this Winter or Spring I cannot now say; but it is some relief of mind to feel that I am again so near you *Possibly*; if I cannot go *to see you*; that I may be able to devise some way for some *one, or more* of you to meet ~~meet~~ me somewhere. The anxiety I feel to see my *Wife*; & children once more; I *am* unable to describe. I want exceedingly to see my big Baby; & "Mums Baby": & to see how that little company of Sheep look about this time.[12] The *cries* of my poor *sorrow stricken despairing children* whoose "*tears on their cheeks*" are ever in my Eye; & whose *sighs* are *ever* in my Ears, may however prevent my enjoying the happiness I so much desire But *courage Courage Courage* the great work of my *life* * (: the unseen Hand that "girded me; & who has *indeed* holden *my right* hand; may hold it still *though* I have not known Him"; at all *as I ought*;) *I may yet see it accomplished; (*God helping*;) & be permitted to return, *& rest*; at Evening." O my Daughter Ruth could any plan be devised whereby you could let Henry go "*to School*" (as you expressed it in your letter to him while in Kansas;) I would rather *now* have *him* "for another term"; than to have a Hundred average schollars. I have a *particular & very important*; (*but not dangerous*) place *for him to fill*; in the "school"; & I know of *no man living*; so well adapted to fill it. I am quite confident some way can be devised; so that *you; & your children* could be *with* him; & be quite happy *even*; & safe but "*God forbid*" me to flatter you into trouble. *I did not do it before.*

Page 2d

My dear child *could you* face *such music*: *if on a full explanation Henry* could *be satisfyed* that his family *might be safe*? I *would make* a similar enquiry of my own dear *Wife*; but I have kept her tumbling "here & there"; over a stormy & tempestus sea for so many years that I cannot *ask* her such a question. The *natural ingenuity* of Salmon: in connection with some experience *he,* & *Oliver* have both had; would point him out as the next best man I could now select; but I am dumb in his case; as *also* in the case of Watson, & all my other sons. Jasons qualifications are *some of them* like Henrys also. I want to hear from you all if possible before I leave this neighborhood. Do *not* noise it about; that I am in these parts; & direct to N Hawkins; Care of Fredk Douglas Esqr Rochester NY. I want to hear how you all are supplied with Winter clothing, Boots, &c. God bless you all

Your Affectionate Husband & Father

[postscript by Frederick Douglass:]

My dear Friends:

Your brave husband and father is now my guest-and has been since Thursday of this week. Gladly indeed we hailed him, and joyfully we entertain him. It does not seem safe—or desirable for him to come to you just now—though he could most gladly do so. I shall retain him here as long as he desires to remain and would be glad for you to meet him here. I remember with pleasure the pleasant moments spent under your roof [*vertically along the left fold*]— and take ~~know~~ no small satisfaction in the thoughts of your Friendship. [*vertically along right fold*] I shall be truly glad to see either of you or both of you at my house at any time during Capt Brown's stay-Fred. Douglass.

Document 16

> [John Brown], Chicago, Illinois, to Frederick Douglass, Rochester, New York, June 22, 1858, 1 p., from Gen. Mss. [Misc.], Manuscripts Division, Department of Rare Books and Special Collections, Princeton University Library. Published with permission of the Princeton University Library.

After traveling east and stopping into visit his family in the Adirondacks, he visited the home of Frederick Douglass in Rochester, New York, sometime between June 2–20, 1858. En route to Kansas, Brown stopped in Cleveland, Ohio, then Chicago, Illinois, where he wrote this letter while staying at the Richmond House hotel.

Certainly this document expands our appreciation of Brown's rapport with Douglass as well as his admiration of Harriet Tubman. In this letter, like another one written to John Brown Jr. more than two months before,[13] he employs manly references, a laudatory form that was even acceptable to female abolitionists at the time. According to one interview made in the early 20th century, the undaunted Tubman "bundled up feather bed, broad-axe, mother, father—all, and landed them in Canada."[14] Having brought her parents to a new country, she badly needed funds for their new homestead too, and so hoped to appear with Douglass—the most famous black man in the nation—in his public appearance in order to raise support from generous abolitionists. Brown knew this was a big favor, since allowing Tubman to join Douglass on the road would detract from his own intake of needed funds. He thus expresses the hope that Douglass could somehow make up for the loss despite the inconvenience.

The letter itself was written on the hotel's stationary, the original featuring a woodcut engraving of the Richmond House (Brown having written in "22d June" into the printed heading). After misspelling Douglass's first and last names, he mentions having met Tubman in Canada West, and notes that someone had already given $25 to the cause. However he was hesitant to give the name in full, referring to the donor only by initials, which subsequently were scratched out. Most likely, the initials were "GS," for Gerrit Smith, the renowned and wealthy abolitionist of Peterboro, New York. Brown probably did not scratch out the initials; it is more likely that Douglass did so subsequently—possibly after the Harper's Ferry raid, for fear that his friend Smith might be further jeopardized by evidence of association with Brown. We may suppose that Douglass responded favorably in some way to his friend's request for help on behalf of Tubman. Certainly he was amused by Brown's closing signature, which appears to be a dryly humorous allusion to the one-hundred-dollar request; but it may have also been a double *entendre*, the meaning of which has now been lost to history. Regardless, the humor and good feeling between the two friends is much evident in this short letter, and its sentimental value may in part explain why Douglass preserved it for posterity.

* * *

Richmond House,
Chicago, 22d June 1858
Fredrick Douglas Esqr
Dear Sir

When at your place I forgot in my haste to say a word in behalf of my friend Hariet Tubman of St Catharines C.W. She wants to raise $100. towards furnishing a home for herself; & her aged Father; & Mother. I know of no one better deserving assi[s]tance; G S[?] has given her $25. to start the thing with. She spoke of asking you to let her travel with you a little, when you should be out from home. Could you not manage to *make* as ~~as~~ much as you

would *loose* by her presence? Any thing you *can do* for Gen Tubman
the *man of deeds* will be fully apreciated by your
    Sincere Friend Old Hundred

Document 17

John Brown to "E.B.," Nov. 1, 1859, in James Redpath, *The Public Life of Capt. John Brown* (Boston: Thayer and Eldridge, 1860), 348–49.

After the failure of the Harper's Ferry raid and his imprisonment in Virginia, Brown received many letters and replied to a good number of them. One such correspondent was a Quaker woman from Newport, Rhode Island, who wrote to him on Oct. 27, 1859, before his conviction and sentencing had taken place. Known only by her initials, "E.B." wrote a warmly supportive letter, although making clear her religious disapproval of Brown's use of "carnal" weapons.[15] Despite this ideological difference, E.B.'s words to Brown were largely laudatory, especially her prediction that "Posterity will do thee justice" as a kind of Moses figure, far more worthy that George Washington, who merely fought for freedom from an "unjust tax." While Brown had had contact with Rhode Islanders in the 1840s during his days as a specialist in sheep and wool, it appears he was unfamiliar with "E.B., yet felt compelled by her letter to respond with great warmth. In so doing, he provided insight into his regrets, personal spirituality, and concerns for his family. Like Sanborn's later transcriptions, Redpath provides a fairly sanitized version, with little of the character of Brown's handwriting remaining. Given Brown's style, the date line, which reads, "November 1, 1859," more likely read, "1st Nov. 1859."

* * *

Charlestown, Jefferson Co., Va., November 1, 1859.
My dear Friend, E.B. of R.I.:
    Your most cheering letter of 27th of October is received, and may the Lord reward you a thousand fold for the kind feeling you express towards me; but more especially for your fidelity to the "poor that cry, and those that have no help." For this I am a prisoner in bonds. It is solely my own fault, in a military point of view, that we met with our disaster—I mean that I mingled with our prisoners, and so far sympathized with them and their families, that I neglected by duty *in other respects.* But God's will, not mine, be done.
    You know that Christ once armed Peter.[16] So also in my case; I think he put a sword into my hand, and there continued it, so long as he saw best, and then kindly took it from me. I mean when I first went to Kansas. I wish you could know with what cheerfulness I am

now wielding the "sword of the Spirit" on the right hand and on the left.[17] I bless God that it proves "mighty to the pulling down of strongholds" [2 Corinthians 10:4]. I always loved my Quaker friends, and I commend to their kind regard my poor, bereaved, widowed wife, and my daughters and daughters-in-law, whose husbands fell at my side. One is a mother, and the other likely to become so soon.[18] They, as well as my own sorrow-stricken daughter, are left very poor, and have much greater need of sympathy than I, who, through Infinite Grace and the kindness of strangers, am "joyful in all my tribulations" [2 Corinthians 7:4].

Dear sister, write them at North Elba, Essex Co., N.Y., to comfort their sad hearts. Direct to Mary A. Brown, wife of John Brown. There is also another, a widow, wife of Thompson, who fell with my poor boys in the affair at Harper's Ferry, at the same place.[19]

I do not feel conscious of guilt in taking up arms; and had it been in behalf of the rich and powerful, the intelligent, the great,—as men count greatness,—of those who form enactments to suit themselves and corrupt others, or some of their friends, that I interfered, suffered, sacrificed, and fell, it would have been doing very well. But enough of this.

These light afflictions, which endure for a moment, shall work out for me *a far more exceeding and eternal weight of glory* [2 Corinthians 4:7]. I would be very grateful for another letter from you. My wounds are healing. *Farewell.* God will surely attend to his own cause in the best possible way and time, and he will not forget the work of his own hands.

Your friend,
John Brown

Document 18

John Brown, Charlestown, Virginia, to Mary Brown, Philadelphia, Pa., Nov. 10, 1859, from a typewritten transcript, Oswald Garrison Villard —John Brown Collection, Rare Book and Manuscript Library, Columbia University.

* * *

Charlestown Jefferson Co. Va. 10th Nov. 1859
My Dear devoted Wife

I have just learned from Mr Hoyt[20] of Boston that he saw you with dear kind friends in Philadelphia on your return trip you had so far made in the expectation of again seeing me in this world of "sin & sorrow."[21] I need not tell you that I had a great desire to see you again: but that many strong objections exist in my mind against it. I have before alluded to them in what I have said in my other letters (which I hope you will soon get) & will not now repeat them; as it is exceedingly laborious for me to write at all. I am under renewed obligation to you my ever faithful & beloved wife, for heeding what may be my last but earnest request. I have before given you a very brief statement of the fall of our dear sons; & other friends. Full particulars relating to our disaster; I can not now give: & may never give *probably*. I am greatly comforted by learning of the kindness already shown you; & allow me *humbly* to repeat the language of a far greater man & better sinner than I. "I have been young; & now am old: yet have I not seen the righteous forsaken nor his seed begging bread" [*Psalm 37:25*]. I will here say that the sacrifises *you*; & I, have been called to make in behalf of the *cause we love* the *cause of God; & of humanity*: do not seem to me as at all too great. I have been *whiped* as the saying *is*; but am sure I can recover all the lost capital occasioned by that disaster; by only hanging a few moments by the neck; & I feel quite determined to make the utmost possible out of a defeat. I am dayly & hourly striving to gather up what little I may from the wreck. I mean to write you as *much & as often* as I have Strength (or may be permitted to write.)

"Be of good cheer:" in the world we must have tribulation: "'but the *cords* that have bound *you* as well as I; to earth: have been many of them severed already. Let us with sincere gratitude receive all that "our Father in Heaven" may send us; for "he doeth all thing well." *You* must kiss our dear children and grandchildren for me. May the "God of my fathers" be the God, & father of all—"To him be everlasting praise."[22] "Although the fig tree shall not blossom: neither shall fruit be in the vines: the labor of the olive shall fail, and the fields shall yield no meat: the flock shall be cut off from the fold, and there shall be no herd in the stalls: yet *I will rejoice* in the Lord, I will joy in the God of my salvation" [*Habakkuk 3:17–18*]. I want dear Ruth; *or Anne*, to send copies (when they can) to their deeply afflicted brothers, of all I write. I cannot muster strength to write them all. If after Virginia has applied the finishing stroke to the picture already made of me (in order to "*establish Justice*") you can afford to meet the expence & trouble of coming on here to gather up the bones of our beloved sons,[23] & of your husband; and the people here will suffer you to do so; I should be entirely willing. I have just received a most welcome letter from a dear old friend of my youth; Rev. H. L. Vail of Litchfield Connecticut.[24] Will you get some kind friend to copy this letter to you & send him very plain as all the acknowledgment I have *now* the strength to make him; & the other kind friends he mentions. I cannot write my friends as I would do; if I had strength. Will you answer to Jeremiah in the same way *for the present* a letter I have received from him?[25] Write me wont you? God bless you all

Your affectionate Husband
John Brown

Document 19

John Brown to H. L. Vaill, Nov. 15, 1859. Transcription from the original document in *JBR*, 135–36.

Herman L. Vaill was a Congregational clergyman and educator who served as an assistant schoolmaster at the Morris Academy, in Litchfield County, Connecticut, when a teenage John Brown came east to prepare for the ministry. Since many young men like Brown lacked sufficient schooling, these preparatory academies were prerequisites to the more rigorous college and seminary training that followed. In 1816, John Brown came from Ohio, along with his younger brother Salmon (1802–33) and neighbor Orson Oviatt, to study under the auspices of Vaill and the headmaster, the Reverend William R. Weeks. Due to personal and financial difficulties, the Browns returned to Ohio without completing their educational program, although Salmon went on to study and practice law. In 1818, Vaill was also an instructor at the Foreign Mission School at Cornwall, Connecticut, in the same county, which provided education to Native Americans and Asian immigrants.[26] After the Harper's Ferry raid, a 65-year-old Vaill wrote to Brown in jail on Nov. 9, 1859, briefly rehearsing their past association and offering words of comfort. This appreciative response not only reflects Brown's spirituality and serenity though awaiting the death sentence but reveals the developing warm relations between himself and his jailer, John Avis.

* * *

Charlestown, Jefferson Co. Va., 15th Nov. 1859.
Rev H L Vaill
My Dear stedfast Friend
Your most kind & most welcome letter of the 8th inst reached me in due time, *I am very grateful* for all the good feeling you express & also for the kind counsels you give together-with your prayers in my behalf. Allow me here to say that notwithstanding "my soul is amongst lions," still I believe that "God in very deed is

with me." You will not therefore feel surprised when I tell you that I am "joyful in all my tribulations": that I do not feel condemned of Him whose judgment is just; nor of my own conscience. Nor do I feel degraded by may imprisonment, my chains or prospect of the Gallows. I have not only been (*though utterly unworthy*) permit-ted ["]to suffer affliction with God's people," but have also had *a great many rare* opportunities for "preaching *righteousness* in the great congregation."[27] I trust it will not all be lost. *The jailor* (in whose charge I am) *& his family; & assistants* have all been most kind: & notwithstanding he is was one of the bravest of all who *fought me*: he is *now* being abused for his humanity. So far as my observation goes; *none but brave* men: are likely to be *humane*; to a fallen foe. "Cowards *prove* their *courage* by their *ferocity*." It may be done in that way with but little risk. I wish I could write you about a few only of the interesting times, I here experience with different classes of men; *clergymen* among others. Christ the great Captain of *liberty*; as well as of salvation; & who began his mission, as foretold of him; by proclaiming it, *saw fit* to take from me a sword of steel after I had carried it for a time but he has put another in my hand: ("The sword of the Spirit;") & I pray God to make me a faithful sol-dier wherever he may send me, not less on the scaffold, then when surrounded by my warmest sympathizers. My dear old friend I do assure you I have not forgotten our last meeting nor our retro-spective look over the route by which God had then led us; & I bless his name that he has again enabled me to hear your words of cheering; & comfort, at a time when I at least am on the "brink of Jordan." See Bunyan's Pilgrim. God in Infinite mercy grant us *soon* another meeting on the opposite shore. I have often passed under the rod of him whom I *call my* Father; & certainly no son ever needed it oftener; & yet I have enjoyed much of life, as I was enabled to discover the secret of this; somewhat early. It has been in making the prosperity, & the happiness of others *my own*: so that really I have had a great deal of prosperity. I am very prosperous still; & looking forward to a time when "peace on Earth & good will to *men* shall every where prevail."[28] I have no murmuring thoughts or *envyous* feelings to fret my mind. "I'll praise my *maker* with my *breath*."[29] I am *an unworthy* nephew of Deacon John;[30] & I loved him much; & in view of the many choice friends *I have had* here: I am led the more earnestly to pray; "gather *not* my soul with the *unright-eous*." Your assurance of the earnest sympathy of the friends in my native land is very greatful to my feelings; & allow me to say a word of comfort to them. As I believe most firmly that God reigns; I cannot believe that any thing I have *done suffered or may yet suffer will be lost*; to the *cause of God or of humanity*: & before I began my work at Harpers Ferry; I left assured that in the *worst event*; it would certainly PAY. I often expressed that belief; & I can now see no possible cause to alter my mind. I am not as yet in the *maine* at all disappointed. I have been *a good deal* disappointed as it regards *myself* in not keeping up to *my own plans*; but I now feel entirely reconciled to that even: for Gods plan, was Infinitely better; *no doubt*; or I should have kept to my own. Had Samson kept to his *determination* of not telling Delilah wherein his great strength lay; he would probably have never overturned the house. I did not tell Delilah; but I was induced to act very *contrary* to my *better judgment*; & I have lost my two noble boys; *& other friends, if not my two eyes.*

But "Gods will *not mine* be done." I feel a comfortable hope that like the *erring servant* of whom I have just been writing *even I* may (through Infinite mercy in Christ Jesus) yet *"die in faith."* As to both the time, & manner of my death: I have but very little trouble on that score; *& am able* to be (as you exhort) "of good cheer." I send through you my best wishes to Mrs. Woodruff & her son George;[31] & to all dear friends. May the God of the *poor and oppressed*; be the God & Saveior of you all.

Farewell till we *"meet again."*

Your friend in truth
John Brown

Document 20

John Brown to Heman Humphrey, November 25, 1859, *LLJB*, 603–05.

Among the relatives who wrote to Brown in jail were his cousins, Luther and Heman Humphrey, whose letters (dated Nov. 12 and 20, respectively) reached him in time for him to write in response.[32] Brown's relation to the renowned Humphrey family was based on the side of his maternal grandmother, Ruth Humphrey. While both cousins were anti-slavery men and wrote to support Brown, Heman Humphrey was evidently more sympathetic to his efforts.

* * *

Charlestown, Jefferson County, Va., Nov. 25, 1859.
Rev. Heman Humphrey, D.D.
My Dear and Honored Kinsman,
Your very sorrowful, kind, and faithful letter of the 20th instant is now before me. I accept it with all kindness. I have honestly

endeavored to profit by the faithful advice it contains. Indeed, such advice could never come amiss. You will allow me to say that I deeply sympathize with you and all my sorrowing friends in their grief and terrible mortification. I feel ten times more afflicted on their account than on account of my own circumstances. But I must say that I am neither conscious of being "infatuated" nor "mad." You will doubtless agree with me in this, that neither imprisonment, irons, nor the gallows falling to one's lot are of themselves evidence of either guilt, "infatuation, or madness."

I discover that you labor under a mistaken impression as to some important facts, which my peculiar circumstances will in all probability prevent the possibility of my removing; and I do not propose to take up any argument to prove that any motion or act of my life is right. But I will here state that I know it to be wholly my own fault as a leader that caused our disaster. Of this you have no proper means of judging, not being on the ground, or a practical soldier. I will only add, that it was in yielding to my feelings of humanity (if I ever exercised such a feeling), in leaving my proper place and mingling with my prisoners to quiet their fears, that occasioned our being caught. I firmly believe that God reigns, and that he overrules all things in the best possible manner; and in that view of the subject I try to be in some degree reconciled to my own weaknesses and follies even.

If you were here on the spot, and could be with me by day and by night, and know the facts and how my time is spent here, I think you would find much to reconcile your own mind to the ignominious death I am about to suffer, and to mitigate your sorrow. I am, to say the least, quite cheerful. "He shall begin to deliver Israel out of the hand of the Philistines." This was said of a poor erring servant many years ago; and for many years I have felt a strong impression that God had given me powers and faculties, unworthy as I was, that he intended to use for a similar purpose.[33] This most unmerited honor He has seen fit to bestow; and whether, like the same poor frail man to whom I allude, my death may not be of vastly more value than my life is, I think quite beyond all human foresight. I really have strong hopes that notwithstanding all my many sins, I too may yet die "in faith."

If you do not believe I had a murderous intention (while I *know* I had not), why grieve so terribly on my account? The scaffold has but few terrors for me. God has often covered my head in the day of battle, and granted me many times deliverances that were almost so miraculous that I can scarce realize their truth; and now, when it seems quite certain that he intends to use me in a different way, shall I not most cheerfully go? I may be deceived, but I humbly trust that he will not forsake me "till I have showed his favor to this generation and his strength to every one that is to come." Your letter is most faithfully and kindly written, and I mean to profit by it. I am certainly quite grateful for it. I feel that a great responsibility rests upon me as regards the lives of those who have fallen and may yet fall. I must in that view cast myself on the care of Him "whose mercy endureth forever." If the cause in which I engaged in any possible degree approximated to be "infinitely better" than the one which Saul of Tarsus undertook,[34] I have no reason to be ashamed of it; and indeed I cannot now, after more than a month for reflection, find in my heart (before God in whose presence I expect to stand within another week) any cause for shame.

I got a long and most kind letter from your pure-hearted brother Luther, to which I replied at some length. The statement that seems to be going around in the newspapers that I told Governor Wise that I came on here to seek revenge for the wrongs of either myself or my family, is utterly false. I never intended to convey such an idea, and I bless God that I am able even now to say that I have never yet harbored such a feeling. See testimony of witnesses who were with me while I had one son lying dead by my side, and another mortally wounded and dying on my other side. I do not believe that Governor Wise so understood, and I think he ought to correct that impression. The impression that we intended a general insurrection is equally untrue.

Now, my much beloved and much respected kinsman, farewell. May the God of our fathers save and abundantly bless you and yours!

John Brown

END NOTES

1. W.E.B. DuBois, *John Brown* (Philadelphia, Pa.: George W. Jacobs & Company, 1909; rpt. New York: International Publishers, 1962), 383, 395.

Chapter 1: The Man and His Times, pp 3–15

2. This discussion of John Brown's youth and Christian abolitionist upbringing follows my expanded discussion in *"Fire from the Midst of You"* (chapters 2, 4, and 5); also see Gerald W. McFarland, *A Scattered People: An American Family Moves West* (New York: Pantheon Books, 1985).
3. Chester G. Hearn, *Companions in Conspiracy: John Brown & Gerrit Smith* (Gettysburg, Pa.: Thomas Publications, 1996), 1.
4. *Memoir of Stonewall Jackson by His Widow, Mary Anna Jackson* (Louisville: The Prentice Press, 1895), 64.
5. See Neil Postman, *Amusing Ourselves to Death: Public Discourse in the Age of Show Business* (New York: Penguin, 1985).
6. Agricola, "The Model Farmer," *Ohio Cultivator* (Dec. 15, 1845), 187.
7. Nell Irvin Painter, *Sojourner Truth: A Life, a Symbol* (New York: W. W. Norton, 1997), 8.
8. See the extensive series of articles under the special issue entitled, "Complicity: How Connecticut Chained Itself to Slavery," *The Sunday Magazine of the Hartford Courant* [Hartford, Conn.] (Sept., 29, 2002).
9. See Frederick Douglass's speech, Jan. 12, 1851, in *The Life and Writings of Frederick Douglass, Vol. 5*, edited by Philip Foner (New York: International Publishers, 1975), 170–72 and 525, n. 10.
10. Andrew E. Murray, *Presbyterians and the Negro—A History* (Philadephia, Pa.: Presbyterian Historical Society,1966), 90–91.
11. Owen Brown wrote two autobiographical pieces, a shorter one in 1841, and then an extended one around 1850. Clarence Gee located these documents and made thorough transcriptions, found in GEE; F. B. Sanborn published his edited version of Owen's writings in *LLJB*, 4–11; also see "Owen Brown on Intemperance" (ca. 1850), transcription from the original by Clarence Gee, in Owen Brown folder, Gray Box 5, GEE.
12. Leon F. Litwack, *North of Slavery: The Negro in the Free States, 1790–1860* (Chicago: University of Chicago Press, 1961), 20–24, and Henry Mayer, *All On Fire: William Lloyd Garrison and the Abolition of Slavery* (New York: St. Martin's Griffin, 1998), 541–43.
13. Guinean Sam is recalled in Owen Brown's 1850 autobiographical sketch. See note 11 above.

14. In the 1950s, Clarence Gee located a photocopy of the original autobiographical sketch by John Brown, written to Henry L. Stearns, July 15, 1857. The original has long since vanished—hopefully only into a private collection. The photocopy of Brown's autobiographical sketch, which includes a letter to Henry's father, George L. Stearns, dated Aug. 8, 1857, is in Box 31, GEE.

15. In 1857, when Brown was traveling in New England to raise funds for his war on slavery, he hid himself from U.S. marshals in the home of Judge Thomas Russell of Boston. Holed up, Brown nevertheless enjoyed the wide-eyed attention of Russell's twenty-three-year-old wife, Nellie, who was impressed by his stories, weapons, and prairie machismo. See Katherine Mayo's notes from a speech by Mrs. [Nellie] Russell on Jan. 11, 1908, in Judge Thomas Russell folder, Box 15, OGV. The substance of this speech is reiterated in Katherine Mayo, "Brown in Hiding and in Jail," *New York Post* (Oct. 23, 1909), supplement section, 1, 3.

16. Katherine Mayo's interview with Sarah Brown, Saratoga, Calif., Sept. 16 and 20, 1908, in Sarah Brown folder, Box 6, OGV; Reminiscence of Mrs. [Nellie] Russell, Jan. 11, 1908.

17. Reminiscence of Mrs. [Nellie] Russell; Brown's "badger" story from an anonymous clipping in the Franklin B. Sanborn Scrapbook, Reel 5, BBS-MIC; Reminiscence of James Foreman, an employee and friend of John Brown, in letter to James Redpath, Dec. 28, 1859, *JBR*, 167. Emendation of "jocuse."

18. The real Nelson Hawkins appears in a warmly picturesque letter from John Brown Jr., Akron, Ohio, to Ruth Brown Thompson, North Elba, N.Y., Feb. 23, 1851, p. 2, 4463.05, in GLC. According to the 1850 census, Nelson Hawkins was born about 1828 and would have been about 23-years old in 1851, when the Browns resettled on the Perkins estate in Akron, Ohio. See the census for Portage, District 140, Summit County, Ohio, Oct. 15, 1850, p. 433. There are nine recorded "Nelson Hawkins" letters from John Brown in 1857, seven of which are written to John Jr., one to wife Mary Brown, and one each to abolitionist associates Augustus Wattles and Franklin Sanborn.

19. James G. Blunt's undated, handwritten narrative, Reel 2, John Brown Papers of the Kansas State Historical Society on microfilm.

20. There are two accounts of this incident, the first being from Anne Brown Adams, one of John and Mary Brown's children. The other is reiterated in two articles by Daniel Hadley, who unfortunately cannot be fully trusted with respect to some statements concerning Brown's later life. Nevertheless, see Katherine Mayo's interview with Anne Brown Adams, Oct. 2–3, 1908, in JB Anecdotes folder, Box 3, OGV; Daniel Hadley, "John Brown," *Kansas Magazine* [Topeka] (July 1873), 93–95; idem, "Reminiscences of Old John Brown," *McClure's Magazine* [New York] (Jan. 1898), 278–82.

21. Gary, "Old John Brown; An Interesting Interview with His Younger Brother," *Cleveland Leader* (ca. Jan. 1884), in John Brown clipping file, NYHS; "John Brown," *The Circular* [Oneida, N.Y.] (Nov. 10, 1859), 166.

Chapter 2: The Real Story of Businessman Brown, pp 16–27

22. Allen C. Guelzo, "Terrorist Or Madman? A Review of *John Brown: The Legend Revisited*, by Merrill D. Peterson," *The Claremont Review of Books* (Fall 2003), an

on-line publication. Retrieved from <http://www.claremont.org/writings/crb/fall2003/guelzo.html> on Feb. 23, 2005.

23. I have argued for Brown's unique egalitarian orientation in *"Fire from the Midst of You."* David S. Reynolds has subsequently made much use of this theme in his *John Brown, Abolitionist* (New York: Alfred A. Knopf, 2005).

24. Mark O'Keefe, "Maybe the Puritans Weren't Puritanical," *Star-Ledger* [Newark, N.J.] (Jan. 5, 2003), Sec. 2, 5.

25. See John Hammond Barrett, *The Secularization of Christian Schools: A Case Study of Western Reserve College and Academy* (MA Thesis, Trinity Episcopal School for Ministry, Ambridge, Pa., 2002), 56. Another study says the Hudson observatory was the third in the nation. See Amy Ackerburg-Hastings, "Elias Loomis: 1811–1889," on the website of Bowling Green University's Department of Mathematics and Statistics. Retrieved from <http://www.bgsu.edu/departments/math/ Ohio-section/bicen/loomis.html> on July 4, 2005.

26. Brown conducted personal experiments in treatments and published a perfected medicinal cure for sheep suffering from infestation of "grub" worms. See John Brown to M. B. Bateman (ed.), in "Remedy for Rots or Grubs, in the heads of Sheep," *Ohio Cultivator* [Columbus] (Apr. 15, 1846), 59–60.

27. Peter F. Drucker, "Beyond the Information Revolution," *The Atlantic Monthly* (Oct. 1999): 50; see the definitive article by Jean Libby, "The John Brown Daguerreotypes: A Leader Uses His Likeness for Remembrance and Promotion," *The Daguerreian Annual 2002–2003* (Pittsburgh, Pa.: The Daguerreian Society, 2004): 31–50.

28. "John Brown," in *Shotgun's Home of the American Civil War*, a website. Retrieved from <http://www.civilwarhome.com/johnbrownbio.htm> on June 27, 2005; Edward J. Renehan, Jr., *The Secret Six: The True Tale of the Men Who Conspired with John Brown* (Columbia, S.C.: University of South Carolina Press, 1997), 63.

29. A helpful website that addresses the inspirational myth of Lincoln's failures and the historical facts of his public career is "The Glurge of Springfield," *Urban Legends Reference Pages*, a website. Retrieved from <http://www.snopes.com/glurge/lincoln.htm> on June 28, 2005.

30. See interview with E. O. Randall, grandson of Brown's associate Heman Oviatt, Dec. 26, 1908, in JB Prior to 1859; Ohio Interviews folder, Box 5, OGV; excerpt from letter of Marvin Kent to David Utter, Nov. 29, 1883, in letter of Boyd Stutler to Clarence Gee, Sept., 28, 1952, Gray Box 6, GEE; See remarks of E.C. Leonard, *LLJB*, 64–65.

31. Boyd B. Stutler to Louis Filler, July 29, 1958, pp. 1–2, RP04–0205, BBS.

32. In 1858, Brown wrote to Franklin B. Sanborn, passingly referring to his *"earlier life,"* when he "felt for a number of years . . . a steady, strong desire to *die*." Brown was undoubtedly referring to the hard years, probably including the death of his first wife in 1832, but especially the difficulties and losses of the 1830s and 1840s. See John Brown to Franklin B. Sanborn, Feb. 24, 1858, Box 3, Folder 3, JB2. An excellent photographic copy of this letter is also found in *LLJB*, flyleaf at pages 444–45.

33. Referring to himself in the third person, Brown wrote: "From Fifteen years & upward he felt a good deal of anxiety to learn; but could only read, & studdy [sic] a little: both for want of time; & on account of inflamation [sic] of the eyes." See Document 1. According to Brown family history, young John went to New England to do college preparatory study, after which he planned to enter Amherst College to prepare for the

ministry. "But he was attacked with inflammation of the eyes, which soon became so serious that the was obliged to give up study and go back to Hudson." See Katherine Mayo's undated interview [ca. 1909] notes with "Miss Thompson" [probably John Brown's granddaughter Mary, daughter of Henry Thompson and his daughter Ruth Brown Thompson], in JB in Hudson, Franklin, and Kent folder, Box 4, OGV; One of Brown's close Pennsylvania associates recalled that John's pre-ministerial studies were interrupted by "eye problems." See James Foreman to James Redpath, Dec. 28, 1859 (transcript), Reel 2, BBS-MIC; Obviously it is impossible to diagnose Brown's condition with certainty.

34. Interview with Amelia Blakeslee Hobart, Dec. 1908, in JB Prior to 1859; Ohio Interviews folder, Box 5, OGV; Boyd Stutler to Stephen B. Oates, June 6, 1968, RP09–0106, and Stutler to Oates, June 15, 1968, RP09–0106, BBS.

35. "I left Ohio in 1826, and settled in western Pennsylvania." See transcription of interview with the *Baltimore American and Commercial Advertiser*, Oct. 24, 1859, based on excerpts of an interview conducted by the *Spirit of Jefferson* [Charlestown, Va.], in JB First Days in Charlestown Jail folder, Box 4, OGV.

36. While hardly a complete picture, Brown's business and personal life can be appreciated in some detail within the scope of his letters to Seth Thompson, forty-seven of which have survived and are now held in RWL; Boyd Stutler, *John Brown*, an unpublished, incomplete manuscript, in GEE, 31–32; and Anne W. Stewart, "John Brown: From the Record; The Crawford County Years: 1827–1835; The Young Family Man," *The Journal of Erie Studies* 32:2 [Erie, Pa.] (Fall 2002): 47; Reynolds, *John Brown, Abolitionist*, 45.

37. Beside Anne Stewart's essay, two other works remain essential in this regard: Boyd B. Stutler, "John Brown Postmaster," *The American Philatelist* Vol. 66: No. 6 (Mar. 1953): 443–49; and Ernest C. Miller, *John Brown: Pennsylvania Citizen* (Warren, Pa.: The Penn State Press, 1952).

38. Stutler, *John Brown*, 31–33; Stewart, "John Brown: From the Record," 62; also see my discussion on Brown's Pennsylvania years in *"Fire from the Midst of You,"* 71–95. However my treatment of Brown's church affiliations stands to be corrected. The Brown settlement was too far for comfortable travel to any of the existing Congregational churches in Crawford County. The best guide in this respect is Stewart's article, pages 56–59.

39. Stutler, *John Brown*, 33; Interview with Alfred Hawkes [younger associate of Brown while in Pennsylvania], Jan. 2, 1909, in JB in Pennsylvania folder, Box 4, OGV. Emphasis in the original.

40. Stewart, "John Brown: From the Record," 47 and 54.

41. "Democratic Ticket . . . Auditor John Brown," *Crawford Messenger* [Meadville, Pa.] (Aug. 29, 1834), CCHS clipping files. This was the Democratic-Republican Party, whose followers favored either the Whigs or the Jacksonian Democrats. When Brown declined the nomination (due to "circumstances of a domestic nature"), he referred to the nominating party as the "Whig Convention," which suggests that the Democrats who nominated him were not Jacksonians. Certainly, Brown was not supportive of Jackson. Stewart, "John Brown: From the Record," 68.

42. Marvin Kent later wrote: "The tannery . . . was just completed when I rented the same from my father for my own business. This put John Brown out of a job and led

him to take a construction contract on the line of the P&O Canal from Kent to Akron. During this period, he traded many hundreds of dollars with my family." Quoted in a letter from Dudley Weaver to Boyd B. Stutler, Aug. 12, 1952, RP05–0042, BBS; "John Brown, of Harper's Ferry," [*Kent* (Ohio) *Courier*], [Sept., 7(14?)], 1906, Box 4, OGV.

43. "Wildcat" originated in the early 1800s, referring to free banks established in remote locations where wild animals still abounded. In the absence of a national bank after 1832, western building projects were often funded by these "wildcat" banks amidst an uneven and unstable economy, and were thus associated with the term. See Gerald P. Dwyer, Jr., "Wildcat Banking, Banking Panics, and Free Banking in the United States," *Economic Review* [Federal Bank of Atlanta, Ga.] (Dec. 1996): 1.

44. Brown bought 200-acres when he went to Crawford County and then purchased 200-acres more in 1829. By 1830, he sold 100-acres, and one year later, he had sold all but 100-acres. Stewart, "John Brown: From the Record," 59–60, and 75, n. 47.

45. "John Brown Had Faith in Kent, O," *Plain Dealer* [Cleveland, Ohio] (July 6, 1926), in Boyd Stutler's Scrapbook 9, Reel 7, BBS-MIC; Mary Land, "John Brown's Ohio Environment," *Ohio Archaeological and Historical Quarterly* (Jan. 1948):33; J.B. Holm, "John Brown Was Resident of Kent; 100th Anniversary of Harper's Ferry Is Today," *Record-Courier* [Ravenna-Kent, Ohio] (Oct. 16, 1959), 9; Dudley Weaver to Boyd B. Stutler, Aug. 12, 1952, RP05–0042, BBS.

46. John Brown to H. J. Huidekoper, July 5, 1838, in the John Brown Collection of Pelletier Library, Allegheny College, Meadville, Pa.

47. Oswald G. Villard, *John Brown: A Biography 1800–1859* (Garden City, N.Y.: Doubleday, Doran & Company, Inc., 1910, 1929), 36–37; Holm, "John Brown Was Resident of Kent," 9; John Brown to Seth Thompson, Dec. 13, 1838, Box 1, Folder 63, RWL. The mill venture is found in Brown to Thompson, Oct. 7, 1839, Box 1, Folder 66, RWL; Brown to Thompson, May 28, 1839, Box 1, Folder 64, RWL; Brown to Thompson, July 10, 1839, Box 1, Folder 65.

48. Boyd Stutler to Clarence Gee, Jan. 19, 1953, 2, BS-CG; DeCaro, *"Fire from the Midst of You,"* 98–120; John Brown to Seth Thompson, July 21, 1840, Box 1, Folder 68, RWL.

49. Author's interview with Thomas L. Vince, archivist/historian of The Western Reserve Academy, Hudson, Ohio, Mar. 16, 2000.

50. Author's interview with Larry Lawrence, founder and chairman of the John Brown Society, New York, New York, June 7, 2005; Karen Flamme, "1995 National Report: A Brief History of Our Nation's Paper Money," *Federal Reserve Bank of San Francisco*, an on-line source. Retrieved from <http://www.frbsf.org/publications/federalreserve/annual/1995/ history.html#A5> on June 22, 2005.

51. Stephen Oates simplistically writes that the Panic of 1837 "shook the national economy" and "brought all of Brown's castles crashing down on him." He likewise errs in saying that Brown "should have expected the worst" in the 1830s because President Jackson's refusal to renew the Bank of the United States had left the national economy "extremely unstable." Lacking a fuller explanation of the downturns of the 1830s, Oates imputes greater blame to Brown than he deserves. It is interesting, too, that Oates relied heavily on John Brown Jr.'s testimony, yet too easily rejects Brown's claim that he was largely undone by dealing in credit. Cf. Stephen B. Oates, *To Purge This*

Land With Blood: A Biography of John Brown (New York: Harper Torchbooks, 1970), 36–37; and *LLJB*, 87–88.

52. John J. Wallis, "What Caused the Crisis of 1839?" Historical Paper 133 (Cambridge, Mass.: National Bureau of Economic Research, Apr. 2001), 10; Brown to Thompson, Dec. 13, 1838.

53. Mary Land, "John Brown's Ohio Environment," *Ohio Archaeological and Historical Quarterly* (Jan. 1948): 33; "John Brown: Citizen of Kent," *The Kent Historical Society Home Page* (Kent, Ohio), an on-line resource. Retrieved from <http://www.geocities.com/Heartland/ Park/9580/ brown.html> on July 16, 2005; "John Brown Had Faith in Kent, O"; John Brown to Mary Brown, Mar. 7, 184[6], MS01–0016, BBS. Quotation marks and punctuation are not in the original. Brown quotes from the biblical Psalm 41:7–8 (Authorized or King James Version): "All that hate me whisper together against me: against me do they devise my hurt. 'An evil disease,' say they, 'cleaveth fast unto him: and now that he lieth he shall rise up no more'"; also see DeCaro, *"Fire from the Midst of You,"* 115–20.

Chapter 3: The Hard Lessons of Capitalism, pp 28–37

54. While Brown traveled far more extensively in the later 1840s, Matthew McKeever, a sheep farmer from southwestern Pennsylvania, remembered his visit in 1842. At that time, Brown was attempting to rebuild his own livestock after losing them to bankruptcy. It was his idea to partner with McKeever by caring for his ewes and splitting the profit from sale of their wools. Thus Brown had some of his own sheep when he entered into the more beneficial partnership with Oviatt. See letter of Matthew McKeever, Sept., 17, 1880, in Percy F. Smith, *Memory's Milestones: Reminiscences of Seventy Years of A Busy Life in Pittsburg* [sic] (Pittsburgh, Pa.: Murdoch-Kerr Press, 1918); interview with E. O. Randall, grandson of Heman Oviatt, Dec. 26, 1908, in JB Prior to 1859; Ohio Interviews folder, Box 5, OGV; Boyd B. Stutler, "The Shepherd and Wool Dealer," an unpublished manuscript, RP13-0186, BBS; agreement between Brown, Heman Oviatt, and Orson M. Oviatt, Jan. 3, 1842, MS01–0012, BBS.

55. John Brown to John Brown, Jr., Jan. 11, 1844, Folder 1, Box 1, JB2; Walter Jack, "Famed Leader Lived in Ohio-N.W. Pennsylvania Area," *The Jefferson Gazette* [Jefferson, Ohio] (July 5, 1949), 4; "The Perkins Company's Woolen Factory," *The Summit Beacon* [Akron, Ohio] (June 6, 1849), 3; P&B to Thomas Noble, Dec. 27, 1845, MS01–0017, BBS; John Brown to A. B. Allen, ed., Feb. 15, 1846, in "Sheep Husbandry," *American Agriculturalist* (Apr. 1846): 118–19.

56. See letter of William H. Ladd, Oct. 16, 1849, under "A Proposition to Stock Breeders," and accompanying "Remarks," *The New England Farmer* (Nov. 24, 1849): 391–92; John Brown, "Remedy for Bots or Grubs, in the heads of Sheep," *Ohio Cultivator* (Apr. 15, 1846), 59–60; "John Brown's Report. Preparing Wool for Market," *Ohio Cultivator* (Sept., 1, 1846): 134–35; Report of M. B. Bateham and letter of Samuel Lawrence to Simon Perkins, July 22, 1844, in *Ohio Cultivator* (Sept., 1, 1846): 134.

57. Edward N. Wentworth, *America's Sheep Trails* (Ames, Iowa: Iowa State College Press, 1948), 570–75; Chester W. Wright, *Wool-Growing and the Tariff* (Cambridge, Mass.: Harvard University Press, 1910), 154.

58. Stutler, "The Shepherd and the Wool Dealer," 81–82; "Convention of Wool Grow-ers," *Ohio Cultivator* (Jan. 15, 1847): 12; Wright, *Wool-Growing and the Tariff*, 153–54; "John Brown's Report," 134; Wentworth, *America's Sheep Trails*, 575.

59. "Remarks," *New England Farmer* (Nov. 24, 1849): 392; Wentworth, *America's Sheep Trails*, 571–72, 587; "Old John Brown. A Washington County Granger's Recollec-tions of 'Osawatomie,'" *The Washington Post* (Feb. 18, 1883): 6; The Tri-State Wool Growers organization was formed in 1918 to empower wool producers and get higher prices for their products, which had been P&B's objectives. See "History at a Glance," *The Mid-States Wool Growers Cooperative Association* (2005), an on-line source. Retrieved from <http://www.midstateswoolgrowers.com/history.htm> on July 27, 2005.

60. Perkins & Brown, "To Wool Growers," *Ohio Cultivator* (Apr. 15, 1846): 60. Also in *Cultivator* [Albany, N.Y.] (July 1846): 232; An associate named E. C. Leonard said: "The idea [for the wool commission operation] took, and to the surprise of [Brown], they pitched upon him as their agent. I understood that he was finally persuaded to take the agency with considerable difficulty." *LLJB*, 64–65; Stutler, "The Shepherd and Wool Dealer," 77.

61. Stutler, "The Shepherd and Wool Dealer," 78–79; Transcript of letter from Aaron Erickson to "Henry A. Wise, Govr [sic] of Virginia," Nov. 8, 1859, Tatham Papers folder, Box 17, OGV.

62. John Brown to Simon Perkins, Dec. 16, 1846, MS01–0022, BBS; Stutler, "The Shep-herd and Wool Dealer," 79–87; John Brown to Simon Perkins, Nov. 24, 1847, tran-script in "Letters of John Brown," unidentified publication (May 1900), 177–78, in "Letters through 1854" file, Box 4, OGV; Wentworth, *America's Sheep Trails*, 570.

63. Erickson to Wise, Nov. 8, 1859; letters of Samuel Lawrence, Sept., 26, 1848 and Sept., 28, 1848, under "Wool . . . Letters from S. Lawrence of Lowell," *The Plough, the Loom, and the Anvil* (Nov. 1848): 329–330.

64. "Prices that would tickle": P&B to Philo Buckingham, Dec. 29, 1849, MS03–0415, BBS; "seat of war": see P&B to Patterson & Ewing, Feb. 20, 1849, MS03–0175, BBS; P&B to Cook & Jones, Mar. 9, 1849, MS03–0189, BBS. My profile of Brown's per-ception of the manufacturers is based on reading through many pages of correspon-dence in P&B's letter books for the years 1846–49 all of which are in BBS. While there are many attesting documents, some worth noting are: P&B to Josiah Perham and Company, Jan. 14, 1847, MS03–0125; P&B to Simon Perkins, Aug. 1, 1848, MS04–0020; P&B to Samuel McFarland, Feb. 3, 1849, MS03–0158; P&B to Patter-son & Ewing, Feb. 13, 1849, MS03–0166; P&B to James Crawford, Feb. 16, 1849, MS03–0167.

65. P&B to Patterson & Ewing, Dec. 4, 1846, MS03–0065, BBS; P&B to Thomas More, Dec. 28, 1846, MS03–0117, BBS; P&B to James D. & William H. Ladd, Feb. 9, 1849, MS03–0163, BBS; P&B to Thomas Lewis & Company, Dec. 26, 1849, MS03–0408, BBS; P&B to Philo Buckingham, Dec. 29, 1849, MS03–0415, BBS; P&B to Jacob Winter, Dec. 22, 1849, MS03–0403, BBS.

66. Arthur H. Cole, *The American Wool Manufacture Vol. 1* (Cambridge, Mass.: Harvard University Press, 1926), 268, 272–74.

67. P&B to Cook & Jones, Mar. 9, 1849, MS03–0189, BBS.

68. Wright, *Wool-Growing and the Tariff*, 97, 99, 101, 111–12, 114, 116; Cole, *The American Wool Manufacture*, 338–39.

69. As to European buyers' interest, also see: P&B to W. Burroughs, Jr., Mar. 14, 1849, MS03–0193, BBS; P&B to Alexander Campbell, Mar. 29, 1849, MS03–0199; BBS; P&B to James Ewing, Mar. 30, 1849, MS03–0200, BBS; P&B to H[enry] W. T. & H. Mali, Mar. 31, 1849, MS03–0200, BBS; P&B to H[enry] W. T. & H. Mali, Apr. 7, 1849, MS03–0213 and Apr. 16, 1849, MS03–0223, BBS; Transcript of letter from John Brown to Simon Perkins, May 1, 1849, in "Letters of John Brown," anonymous publication (May 1900), 178–79, in Box 4, "Letters through 1854" file, OGV; John Brown to Simon Perkins, Apr. 7, 1849, OHS. My emphasis of "permanent . . . trade."

70. Stutler, "The Shepherd and the Wool Dealer," 88–90; Transcript of letter from John Brown, London, England, to John Brown Jr., Oct.. 5, 1849, in JB letters through 1855 file, Box 4, OGV; John Brown, Paris, France, to John Brown Jr., Aug 31, 1849, within letter of John Brown Jr. to Mary Brown, Sept., 24, 1849, Box 1, Folder 2, JB2; John Brown, London, England, to John Brown Jr., Sept., 21, 1849, Box 1, Folder 2, JB2; P&B circular, "Springfield, Mass." (ca. Oct.-Nov. 1849), Folder 3, Box 1, JB2; John Brown, London, England, to Simon Perkins, Oct. [ca. 5] 1849, in Gen. Coll. Mss. Group 1147, File F2, Beinecke Rare Book and Manuscript Library, Yale University Library. Also see P&B to Frederick Kinsman, Oct. 30, 1849, MS03–0381, BBS, which essentially reiterates the 1849 circular;

71. *LLJB*, 79–80; "News by the Mails," *New York Daily Tribune*, Feb. 7, 1853, 6; John Brown to John Jr. and Wealthy Brown, Apr. 12, 1850, Folder 4, Box 1, JB2.

72. John Brown to John Brown Jr. et al., Dec. 4, 1850 and John Brown to John Brown Jr., Dec. 6, 1850, *LLJB*, 76 and 79. Also compare the interview with Simon Perkins on pp. 57–58 (including note on page 57) with John Brown Jr.'s testimony on pp. 88–89.

73. Brown's son Salmon later claimed that Simon Perkins afterward lost a great deal more money by investing in a failed railroad scheme, a devastating loss that greatly embittered him. Salmon said further that Brown consented to work for Perkins at a diminished wage in order to help him. While Salmon's account cannot be taken at face value, there may be something to it. According to John Brown in 1850, Perkins had "expressed a strong desire to have our flock of sheep remain undivided to become the joint possession of our families when we have gone off the stage," which suggests that he wanted Brown to be a permanent shareholder in the flocks. This being the case, Perkins's subsequent ruin may well explain why Brown did not continue in partnership after 1854. See Salmon Brown to Franklin B. Sanborn (transcript), Sept., 10, 1909, in F. B. Sanborn II file, Box 16, OGV; Brown to John Jr. and Wealthy Brown, Apr. 12, 1850; DeCaro, *"Fire from the Midst of You,"* 186–87, 205–06; undated letter excerpt from Allen Nevins to Louis Filler, in Filler to Boyd Stutler, June 12, 1949, RP04–0191, BBS.

Chapter 4: The Making of a Radical Reformer, pp 38–42

74. William F. M. Arny, who first met Brown in the mid-1840s among the wool-growers in western Virginia, later testified that he remembered Brown as having been a firm abolitionist "non-resistant." Arny was probably mistaken, having associated his conservative ways with that of the pacifist Quakers and other non-resistant anti-slavery Christians with whom Brown associated in the region. Furthermore, since Arny

considered himself a "peace man" and came to sharp difference with Brown in the 1850s, he more likely portrayed him as something of an ideological turncoat. *CHFI*, 72, 75; Cf. James D. Ladd, "The Immortal John Brown; His Wool Meeting at Steubenville," *Herald-Star* [Steubenville, Ohio] (June 13, 1904), where Brown is remembered as arguing against the pacifism of his Quaker friends.

75. See Judah Colt to Thomas Astley, Feb. 1, 1826, MS06–0038, BBS. Boyd Stutler recovered agent Colt's complaint about the "evil and unprincipled" John Brown, and after some investigation felt assured that this was indeed a reference to abolitionist John Brown. Boyd B. Stutler to Frederick P. Seely, Mar. 20, 1950, RP13–0134, BBS; "A Visit to John Brown," *Crawford Journal* [Meadville, Pa.] (Nov. 29, 1859), CCH clipping files; "Resume of Pamphlet: *A Tribute of Gratitude to the Hon. M. B. Lowry, Erie State Senator, Pennsylvania* (Philadelphia: J. B. Rodgers Co., 1869)," in Lowry file, John Brown Collection, Pelletier Library, Allegheny College, Meadville, Pa.

76. DeCaro, *"Fire from the Midst of You,"* 111–12; Salmon Brown, "My Father, John Brown," *The Outlook* (Jan. 25, 1913), 217; M.H.F., "A Brave Life," *Atlantic Monthly* (Oct. 1885): 360–67.

77. For extensive treatment of Brown's relationship to black leaders and the African American community in Springfield, see Benjamin Quarles, *Allies for Freedom & Blacks on John Brown* (New York: DaCapo, 2001; rpt. 1974), 15–36, and DeCaro, *"Fire from the Midst of You,"* 146–59, and 190; see also Frederick Douglass to [William C.] Nell, Feb. 5, 1848, in "Editorial Correspondence," *North Star* (Feb. 11, 1848), 2, and Frederick Douglass, *Life & Times of Frederick Douglass* (Hartford, Conn.: Park, 1881; rpt. Secaucus, N.J.: Citadel, 1983), 277.

78. For a fairly comprehensive account of Brown's involvement in the black colony experiments in the Adirondacks, see DeCaro, *"Fire from the Midst of You,"* 163–188.

79. John Brown to Henry Thompson, May 10, 1853, MS01–0043, BBS.

Chapter 5: Kansas, pp 43–54

80. Douglass, *Life & Times*, 279–80; DeCaro, *"Fire from the Midst of You,"* 213–15, 224.

81. Frank A. Rollin [Frances E. Rollin Whipper], *Life and Public Services of Martin R. Delany* (Boston: Lee and Shepard, 1883; rpt. New York: Arno Press and the New York Times, 1969), 87–88. Delany may have conflated the events of 1858 with earlier statements by Brown. This is evident in that Delany claimed to have suggested the term "Subterranean Pass Way" to Brown in 1858; but Brown had already appropriated that term nearly a decade before in Springfield, Massachusetts.

82. John Brown Jr. to John Brown, care of Henry and Ruth Thompson, May 20, 1855, Dreer Collection, Historical Society of Pennsylvania, Philadelphia.

83. "Convention of Radical Political Abolitionists; Third Day-Morning," *New York Tribune* (July 2, 1855), 6, col. 3; DeCaro, *"Fire from the Midst of You,"* 225; Interview with Lucy Brown Clark by Clarence S. Gee, Nov. 17, 1925, in Jeremiah R. Brown folder, Box 1, Series II, GEE.

84. Villard, *John Brown*, 108; John Brown to Mary Brown, Nov. 30, 1855, transcribed by Katherine Mayo in Letters through 1859, Box 4, OGV; John Brown to Owen Brown, Dec. 5, 1855, GLC 02454, GLC; John Brown to Mary Brown, Dec. 16, 1855, #299, Folder 15, Box 1, KSHS; John Brown to *Summit Beacon* [Ohio] (Dec. 20, 1855), in

Will Clemens, "John Brown, the American Reformer," *The Peterson Magazine* (Feb. 1898), 216–18; John Brown to Mary Brown, Feb. 1, 1856, #299, Folder 16, Box 1, KSHS; John Brown to Mary Brown, Feb. 6, 1856 (transcription), in Letters through 1859 folder, Box 4, OGV.

85. Villard, *John Brown*, 111, 136; John Brown to Orson Day, Feb. 21, 1856, RH MS P2 V.L.T., John Brown Letters, Kansas Collection, Kenneth Spencer Research Library, University of Kansas, Lawrence; John Brown to Owen Brown, Mar. 26, 1856, GEE; see letters of Henry Thompson to Ruth Brown Thompson, Mar. 23, 1856 and Jan. 26, 1856 (transcriptions), in Henry & Ruth Thompson folder, Box 17, OGV; John Brown to Charles Adair, Apr. 22, 1856, in File 25, Box 1, GEE; John Brown to Mary Brown, Apr. 24, 1856, #929.01, GLC.

86. Villard, *John Brown*, 130–31, 137–38; Brown expressed concern over Pierce's policies and the possibility of fighting U.S. troops in a letter to Congressman Joshua Giddings, Feb. 20, 1856, the text of which is found in Villard, *John Brown*, 131. Also see Document 12.

87. *LLJB*, 260, n.; Katherine Mayo's interview with Wealthy Hotchkiss Brown, Nov. 30-Dec. 3, 1908, in Mr. & Mrs. John Brown Jr. file, Box 6, OGV; Eldrid Herrington, "Introduction: The Anguish None Can Draw," in *The Afterlife of John Brown*, edited by Andrew Taylor and Eldrid Herrington (New York: Palgrave Macmillan, 2005), 5; Michael Kelly, "77 North Washington Street," *Atlantic Monthly* (Nov. 2001), 8; Villard, *John Brown*, 151.

88. Stephen Oates made a careful study of the Pottawatomie killings but admits that the evidence and testimony concerning the Pottawatomie incident make it a difficult case to evaluate with complete certainty, and that his "'retaliatory blow' thesis" is his best interpretation. Cf. Oates, *To Purge This Land With Blood*, 130 and note 3, p. 384, and DeCaro, *"Fire from the Midst of You,"* 233–36 and 324, n. 12.

89. See Katherine Mayo's interview with Henry Thompson, Aug. 22 and Sept., 1, 1908, in Henry and Ruth Thompson folder, Box 17, OGV, and letter from Thompson's granddaughter, Adeline Towne Bryant, to "Mrs. Mackenzie," Apr. 28, 1966, file 68, box 2, Edwin Cotter Jr. Papers, Special Collections, Feinberg Library, State University of New York, Plattsburgh, N.Y.

90. Barbara Youree, "Looking 'From Below Up,' a Profile of Russell Banks," *Potpourri* 14:1 (2002); regarding Brown's attitude toward Lawrence, Kansas, see the testimony of Horace White, Feb. 27, 1860, in *CHFI*, 248–49; Anne Brown Adams to Oswald G. Villard, Mar. 25, 1908, in Annie Brown Adams file, Box 1, OGV; Samuel Lawrence to Charles Hovey, editor, Oct. 30, 1874, in *Contributions of the Old Residents' Historical Association Vol. 1, No. 4* [Lowell, Mass.], (May 1879), 286; William Lawrence, *Life of Amos A. Lawrence* (Boston: Houghton Mifflin, 1888), 130.

91. See Finkelman's insightful introduction in Peggy A. Russo and Paul Finkelman, *Terrible Swift Sword: The Legacy of John Brown* (Athens, Ohio: Ohio University Press, 2005), xxv-xxvi; Salmon Brown to William E. Connelley, May 28, 1913, MS05–0039, BBS; Mahala Doyle to John Brown, Nov. 20, 1859, in Villard, *John Brown*, 164; "Questionnaire Filled Out by John C. Doyle" (transcription), undated, from the Tennessee Archives, Nashville, Tenn., RP10–0137, BBS; Mahala Doyle to David N. Utter (transcription), June 18, 1883, RP10–0138C, BBS.

92. John Brown to John Brown Jr., [Aug.] 9, 1858, MS02–0027, BBS.

Chapter 6: The Road to Virginia, pp 55–69

93. John Brown, along with John Jr. and Jason and their wives, as well as Owen, Watson, and Salmon, were in Hudson over the holidays in 1856–57 and had Christmas dinner at the home of Brown's younger half-brother, Jeremiah. See Wealthy Brown to Ruth Brown Thompson, Jan. 4, 1857, Jeremiah Brown folder, Box 3, Clarence S. Gee Papers, Hudson Library & Historical Society, Hudson, Ohio; Jean Libby, "The John Brown Daguerreotypes: A Leader Uses His Likeness for Remembrance and Promotion," *The Daguerreian Annual*, 39–40. I differ with her only in that she sets the date for the Hudson daguerreotype in the summer of 1856, which I find highly improbable if not impossible, given events as they were at the time. Since we can document that Brown was back in Ohio in Dec.-Jan. 1856, it seems likely that this was when the portrait was made in Hudson; John Stauffer, *The Black Hearts of Men: Radical Abolitionists and the Transformation of Race* (Cambridge: Harvard University Press, 2002), 57–58.

94. Testimony of Horace White, Feb. 27, 1860; *"Fire from the Midst of You,"* 240–43.

95. Brown's letters are full of references to "the fever and the ague," and in one case he was so sick that he required an amanuensis to complete his correspondence. See Brown to William Hutchinson, Aug. 3, 1858, #299, Box 1, Folder 32, John Brown Collection, Kansas State Historical Society, Topeka, Kan.; also see "The Companion of Your Choice," *Private Letters: The Correspondence of Rev. James S. Griffing & J. Augusta Goodrich*. Retrieved from <http://www.griffingweb.com/the_companion_of_your_choice.htm> on Jan. 6, 2006; "Descriptions of the Effects of Fever and Ague," *Center for Columbia River History*. Retrieved from <http://www.ccrh.org/comm/slough/primary/descript.htm> on Jan. 6, 2006; Libby, "The John Brown Daguerreotypes," 42–43; DuBois, *John Brown*, 172; Robert W. Taylor, "An Appeal for the Harriet Tubman Old Folks' Home," *Colored American Magazine* (July 1901): 237; Kate Clifford Larson, *Bound for the Promise Land: Harriet Tubman, Portrait of An American Hero* (New York: One World/Ballentine, 2004).

96. The best narrative on the Forbes case is Oates, *To Purge This Land With Blood*, 200–01, 206–18; see undated entry, ca. 1858, in John Brown's diary (no. 2, 1856–59), in the Boston Public Library, Boston, Mass.; Villard, *John Brown*, 53–55, 317–18; see testimony of Richard Realf, Jan. 21, 1860, in *CHFI*, 96; Schamyl quoted in T. H. Huxley, "Schamyl, The Prophet-Warrior of the Caucasus," *Westminster Review* (1854), retrieved from <http://aleph0.clarku.edu/huxley/UnColl/WestRev/Schamyl.html> on Jan. 10, 2006; William Fellows, "Saw John Brown Hanged," *New York Sun* (Feb. 13, 1898), in Box 3, OGV; Douglass, *Life & Times*, 321; Franklin B. Sanborn, "The Virginia Campaign of John Brown," *Atlantic Monthly* (Mar. 1875): 328; Thomas W. Higginson, "Cheerful Yesterdays," *Atlantic Monthly* (May 1897), 673.

97. DeCaro, *"Fire from the Midst of You,"* 244–51; Villard, *John Brown*, 332–38, and 401; Ralph R. Gurley, *Life of Jehudi Ashmun* (James C. Dunn, 1835; rpt. New York: Negro Universities Press, 1969); compare Boyd B. Stutler's preface with the publisher's afterword in *Provisional Constitution and Ordinances for the People of the United States by John Brown* (Weston, Mass.: M&S Press, 1969). Brown's original draft, which he called a "skeleton," is in the Yale Collection of Western Americana, Beinecke Rare Book and Manuscript Library, Yale University, New Haven, Conn.

98. Rollin, *Life and Public Services of Martin R. Delany*, 85–93; Victor Lauriston, "Samson in the Temple," *The Canadian Magazine* (June 1932), 40; Jane Rhodes, *Mary Ann Shadd Cary: The Black Press and Protest in the Nineteenth Century* (Bloomington, Ind.: Indiana University Press, 1998), 130; *Provisional Constitution*, Article XLI, 15; Richard Realf recalled that Delany disputed and debated Brown while largely supporting his efforts. See *CHFI*, 99; *AVHF*, 9–13, including John H. Kagi's minutes from the Chatham convention; Villard, *John Brown*, 330–38; "African Members of John Brown's Constitutional Convention of May 8, 1858, in Chatham, Canada, with Corresponding Black Conventions and Organizations, U. S. Civil War Service, and Election to Reconstruction Governments in the Defeated Southern States," an incomplete, unpublished draft, copyright 2003 by Jean Libby, Palo Alto, Calif.; Against the record of Brown's black contemporaries and formidable Brown specialists like DuBois and Quarles, Vincent Harding surprisingly disdains Brown as a rebel "with a strong streak of paternalism" rather "than as an exemplary white hero of the struggle for black freedom." See *There is a River: The Black Struggle for Freedom in America* (New York: Vintage, 1981, 1983), 206.

99. Libby, "The John Brown Daguerreotypes," 43; William A. Phillips, "Three Interviews with Old John Brown," *Atlantic Monthly* (Dec. 1879), 743–44; Oates, *To Purge This Land With Blood*, 250–51; Villard, *John Brown*, 340; DeCaro, *"Fire from the Midst of You,"* 254–55; Brown's pseudonym, Shubel Morgan, may have been invented, particularly because of its biblical meaning. However it is also possible that he had also known someone by that name, in part or whole.

100. Richard J. Hinton, *John Brown and His Men* (New York: Funk & Wagnalls Company, 1894), 227–28; John C. Dancy, "The Negro People in Michigan," *Michigan History Magazine* [Lansing] (Spring 1940): 226; Quarles, *Allies For Freedom*, 60–61; Henry Mayer, *All On Fire: William Lloyd Garrison and the Abolition of Slavery* (New York: St. Martin's Griffin, 1998), 374. Also see John R. McKivigan, "The Frederick Douglass-Gerrit Smith Friendship and Political Abolitionism in the 1850s," in *Frederick Douglass: New Literary and Historical Essays*, edited by Eric J. Sundquist (Cambridge: Cambridge University Press, 1993), 207; Douglass, *Life & Times*, 282; Philip S. Foner, *Frederick Douglass* (New York: Citadel, 1964, 1969), 177.

101. Douglass, *Life & Times*, 322–24, 319; see "Fred. Douglass," *Valley Spirit* (Aug. 24, 1859), under "Newspapers," on *John Brown and the Valley of Shadows*, an electronic source retrieved from <http://www3.iath.virginia.edu/jbrown/spirit.html#8/24> on Jan. 14, 2005; G. M. Philips, "A John Brown Story," *The Outlook* (Mar. 1, 1913), 504; F. B. Sanborn, *Recollections of Seventy Years, Vol. 1* (Boston: The Gorham Press, 1909), 153; see Katherine Mayo's interviews with Anne Brown Adams, Oct. 2–3, 1908 and Salmon Brown, Oct. 11–13, 1908, both in Frederick Douglass folder, Box 7, OGV, and with Henry Thompson, Aug. 22 and Sept. 1, 1908, in Henry & Ruth Thompson folder, Box 17, OGV. Also see Mayo's notes on "Owen Brown's Story of taking Shield's Green to Kennedy Farm," in Oliver Brown & Martha His Wife folder, Box 6, OGV; in 1976, Jean Libby interviewed Beatrice Keesey, a descendant of John Brown, and found her to be quite bitter toward Douglass for withdrawing his support from her famous progenitor. Libby to author, 15 Mar. 2001.

102. William S. McFeely, *Frederick Douglass* (New York: W. W. Norton & Co., 1991), 196; Sanborn, *Recollections of Seventy Years,*153–54; *Autobiography of Dr. William Henry Johnson* (Albany, N.Y.: The Argus Company, 1900), 194–96.

103. Interview with Anne Brown Adams, Oct. 2–3, 1908; John Brown Jr. to Franklin B. Sanborn, Apr. 21, 1885, Box 4, The Alfred Anthony Collection, Rare Books and Manuscripts Collection, New York Public Library; Katherine Mayo's transcript of speech by Nellie Russell at the Bussey Institute, Jamaica Plains, Jan. 11, 1908, in Judge Thomas Russell folder, Box 15, OGV; undated portion of letter from Annie Brown Adams [to A.M. Ross?], 3007, GLC. Anne Brown Adams frankly and repeatedly contended that Douglass had essentially bribed Shields Green into going to Harper's Ferry on his behalf, claims that are as cranky as they are unfair. Yet there is substance to the Brown family's sense of betrayal, and Anne's testimony regarding this alienation cannot be dismissed wholesale. I have observed the conspicuous absence of Douglass's letters in the various Brown family repositories, especially the papers of John Brown Jr., who was the eldest spokesman in the Brown family and well-connected with black leaders. This lack of correspondence from Douglass reinforces the idea that he avoided the Browns from either a sense of shame or offense. See the John Brown Jr. Papers (FR-5), Charles E. Frohman Collection, Rutherford B. Hayes Presidential Center, Fremont, Ohio.

Chapter 7: The Raid Considered, pp 70–89

104. See Katherine Mayo's chronology in Villard, *John Brown*, 678; Henry B. Stanton, *Random Recollections* (New York: MacCowan & Slipper, 1886; first edition 1885, privately printed), 100–01; Douglass, *Life & Times*, 281; Letter of Edwin N. Cotter to Clarence S. Gee, Feb. 11, 1966 and Cotter to Velma West Sykes, Dec. 12, 1972, in Gee-Cotter correspondence, GEE.

105. Jean Libby et al., *John Brown Mysteries* (Missoula, Montana: Pictorial Histories Publishing Company, 1999), 20; Testimony of John H. Allstadt, Jan. 6, 1860, in *CHFI*, 42; Katherine Mayo's undated note, based on interview with Anne Brown, Anne Brown Adams folder, Box 1, OGV; for instance, see ad for Isaac Smith & Co., Manufacturers, *Springfield Republican* (July 20, 1849), 3; "I. Smith" to "Mary Smith," July 5, 1859, in Villard, *John Brown*, 404–05; Mary D. Smith to "Deare [sic] Husband," June 29, 1859, in Ferdinand J. Dreer Papers, Historical Society of Pennsylvania, Philadelphia; Statement of Annie Brown, Daughter of John Brown, Written Nov. 1866, typewritten transcript, Box II, Annie Brown Adams file, GEE.

106. *AVHF*, 18; George Sigler, *A Brief History of My Life and Labors* (ca. 1890), unpublished, typewritten manuscript provided to the author by Natalie and Richard Smith; "Dr. George Sigler—Churches of God Minister was John Brown's Pastor," *The Church Advocate* [Harrisburg, Pa.: The Church of God] (July 1976): 4–7; Virginia Ott Stake, *John Brown in Chambersburg* (Chambersburg, Pa.: Franklin County Heritage, Inc., 1977), 17, 23–24, 65–66; Larson, *Harriet Tubman*, 174. Larson speculates that this mysterious agent was possibly Harriet Tubman, but this is unconvincing. It is more likely that the agent was another of Brown's many associates; *From Slavery to Salvation: The Autobiography of Rev. Thomas W. Henry of the A.M.E. Church*. Edited by Jean Libby (1872; rpt. Jackson: University Press of Mississippi, 1994), 103–05;

DeCaro, *Fire from the Midst of You*, 261–62 and 329, n. 7; Lewis B. Sperry, "At Las Cacitas; Recollections of a Visit to the Late Owen Brown, in California," *The Inter-Ocean* [Chicago, Ill.] (Feb. 3?, 1889), Reel 5, BBS-MIC.

107. This sketch of the raid is based largely on Jean Libby's helpful chronology in *John Brown Mysteries*, 20–22.

108. Ott Stake, *John Brown in Chambersburg*, 108; Boyd B. Stutler, "John Brown's Last Visit to Western Virginia," *The West Virginia Review* (Apr. 1926): 228–41. For the record, Stutler later reversed his opinion about Brown's presence in western Virginia, most likely because he was himself a Lodge man and found it increasingly difficult to reconcile his fraternal affinities with his admiration for Brown, especially if other brethren were particularly offended by the idea that Brown had fleeced the Masons after renouncing the movement himself. Stutler backed away from his brilliant article by making much to do about the length of Brown's beard and the direction he was traveling on horseback, but neither argument is very persuasive in arguing against his 1926 analysis.

109. Following the estimation of Boyd Stutler, it is also my belief that the single best work on Brown by a biographer to date is Barrie Stavis's *John Brown: The Sword and the Word* (New York: A. S. Barnes and Company, 1970). Stavis wrote this work for a popular reading audience, however he effectively engages the issues surrounding Brown's raid and its impact on the enslaved community, recognizing the political nature of original reports and descriptions surrounding the raid. In the same decade, a California-based photographer and college professor, Jean Libby, delved deeply into the raid and its black participants, even staying in the vicinity of the raid to study the layout and local history, including local black oral traditions. Her self-produced, limited edition publication, *Black Voices From Harpers Ferry* (Palo Alto, Calif., 1979), provides an essential analysis of the accepted reading of the raid and persuasively defends the trustworthiness of the testimony of Brown's black raider, Osborne Anderson.

110. See Louis A. DeCaro, Jr., "Black People's Ally, White People's Bogeyman: A John Brown Story," in *The Afterlife of John Brown*, 11–26.

111. Hannah N. Geffert, "John Brown and His Black Allies: An Ignored Alliance," *The Pennsylvania Magazine of History and Biography* (Oct. 2002): 601 and 605.

112. The majority and minority senate opinions are found in *CHFI*, 1–19 and 21–25, respectively; Andrew Hunter, "John Brown's Raid; Recollections of Prosecuting Attorney Andrew Hunter," *Times Democrat* [New Orleans] (Sept. 5, 1887), transcribed in Andrew Hunter file, Box 10, OGV; Joseph Cephas Carroll, *Slave Insurrections in the United States 1800–1865* (New York: Chapman & Grimes, 1938; rpt. New York: New American Library, 1969), 187–99; "John Brown's Death," an undated clipping reiterating an article by Passmore Williamson in the *Philadelphia Press*, in Christian Cackler folder, Box 7, OGV.

113. John Brown Jr.'s testimony in *Gerrit Smith vs. the Tribune Company of Chicago* (Sandusky, Ohio, July 19, 1867) in Mr. & Mrs. John Brown, Jr. folder, Box 6, OGV; Alfred M. Barbour to Roger A. Pryor, Apr. 2, 1860, *Pennsylvania Magazine of History and Biography* (1918), 175–76; "John Brown's Raid; Related by a Kentucky Gunsmith Who was Master Armorer at Harper's Ferry," *The Courier-Journal* [Lexington, Ky.], undated transcript, in the Gunther Collection folder, Box 8, OGV; Annie

Brown Adams to editor, *Springfield Republican* (June 6, 1908), in GEE; Philips, "Three Interviews with Old John Brown," 743–44; interview with George B. Gill, Nov. 12, 1908, in George B. Gill folder, Box 8, OGV; David H. Strother's speech in Cleveland, Ohio, Dec. 23, 1868, transcribed and edited by Hilary Attfield from the original manuscript, A&M 2894, Box 8, FF16, West Virginia and Regional History Collection, West Virginia University Libraries. Retrieved from <http://www.libraries.wvu.edu/theses/Attfield/HTML/DHS_frameset2.html> on May 26, 2004.

114. "Verbatim Report of the Questioning of Old Brown by Senator Mason, Congressman Vallandigham, and Others," *New York Herald* (Oct. 21, 1859), 1; transcription of Brown's statement to the Court, Nov. 2, 1859, in *JBR*, 126; John Brown to Andrew Hunter, Nov. 22, 1859, in *CHFI*, 67–68; Sperry, "At Las Cacitas."

115. Over twenty-five of the fifty-five whites killed by Nat Turner's men were children. See Herbert Aptheker, *Nat Turner's Slave Rebellion* (New York: Grove Press, 1966), 151; John Brown to Mary Brown, Mar. 31, 1857, in Letters through 1859, Box 5, OGV; John Brown's final written statement, Dec. 2, 1859, in *JBR*, 159; Jean Libby, "The Slaves Who Fought with John Brown and Thoughts About Their Absence in U.S. History Textbooks" (draft, Apr. 2005), 11; *AVHF*, 29.

116. Douglass, *Life and Times*, 325; Larson, *Harriet Tubman*, 174; *AVHF*, 15; See Daniel C. Littlefield, "Blacks, John Brown, and a Theory of Manhood," in *His Soul Goes Marching On: Responses to John Brown and the Harpers Ferry Raid* (Charlottesville: University of Virginia Press, 1995), 67–89.

117. Robert M. Copeland, "My Man Antony," *Putnam's Magazine* (Apr. 1869), 444–55; correspondence from Copeland biographical scholar Patricia McGinnis to author, Apr. 12 and 23, 2004; Interview with Anne Brown Adams, Oct. 2–3, 1908.

118. See listing for Robert M. Copeland in Massachusetts Soldiers and Sailors in the Civil War, M544, Roll 9. Retrieved from <http://www.itd.nps.gov/cwss/soldiers.htm> on Jun. 30, 2004; Census of 1870, Chapline Township, Jefferson County, West Virginia, p. 36; correspondence from Hannah Geffert to author, 9 Apr. 2004; Census of 1870, Shepherdstown, Jefferson County, Virginia, pp. 82–83; Slave Schedule for 1860, Jefferson County, Virginia, p. 9.

119. Geffert, "John Brown and His Black Allies," 601, 595, and 610.

120. Libby, *Black Voices From Harpers Ferry*, 111, 119–20; Geffert, "John Brown and His Black Allies," 604–05.

121. Libby refers to the reminiscence of Randolph A. Shotwell, who records that "a party of twenty brave railroad men" attempted to batter in the engine house door on Monday at about 3 p.m. Though they were able to break through and kill one of Brown's men and wound one of his sons, they were repelled with heavy wounds, and the failed skirmish "somewhat subdued the ardor of the militia and citizens." She also shows that *Harper's Weekly* likewise noted Monday's attack. Compare *AVHF*, 44–45, and Libby, *Black Voices From Harpers Ferry*, 154 and n. 13.

Chapter 8: John Brown—For the Record, pp 90–94

122. Libby, *Black Voices From Harper's Ferry*, 131 and 134; *AVHF*, 41 and 59.

123. *AVHF*, 59 and 61.

124. Ibid., 61.

125. Ibid., 37 and 38; "John Brown's Life: Recalled By a Surviving Son Who at One Time Resided in This Section," *The Fortuna Advance* [Fortuna, Calif.] (Aug. 16, 1905): 2.

126. *AVHF*, 62.

127. Transcript of interview conducted by *the Spirit of Jefferson*, reprinted in the *Baltimore American and Commercial Advertiser*, Oct. 24, 1859, in JB First Days in Charlestown Jail folder, Box 4, OGV.

128. John Brown to "E.B.," Nov. 1, 1859, in James Redpath, *The Public Life of Capt. John Brown* (Boston: Thayer and Eldridge, 1860), 348–49; John Brown to Mary Brown, Nov. 10, 1859, in JB Jail Letters 1859, Box 5, OGV; John Brown to Reverend H.L. Vaill, Nov. 15, 1859, *JBR*, 135–36; Interview with "Captain Cockerell" in F. A.B., "Poor Old John Brown; People Who Witnessed His Brave Raid and Execution," *The Press* [Cleveland, Ohio?], Jan. 27, 1884, in the John Brown clipping files of the New York Historical Society.

129. John Brown to Heman Humphrey, Nov. 25, 1859, *LLJB*, 603–05.

130. John Brown to Andrew Hunter, Nov. 22, 1859, in *CHFI*, 67–68.

131. Frank I. Fisher, "John Brown; The Pottawatomie Martyr and His Sons," *Los Angeles Times* (June 12, 1886), 4.

132. John Brown to his jailer, quoted from an unidentified Southern source in *LLJB*, n. 572.

Chapter 9: John Brown's Body Revisited, pp 95–99

133. "Lincoln, Abraham," *Microsoft® Encarta® Encyclopedia 99*. © 1993–1998 Microsoft Corporation. All rights reserved. Lincoln twice denounced Brown's raid, the first time while in Kansas in December 1859, and then at the Cooper Union in Feb. 1860. His statements about Brown can be found in the on-line version of *The Collected Writings of Abraham Lincoln, Vol. 5*, at: http://www.classic-literature.co.uk/american-authors/19th-century/abraham-lincoln/the-writings-of-abraham-lincoln-05/ebook-page-30.asp; and http://www.classic-literature.co.uk/american-authors/19th-century/abraham-lincoln/the-writings-of-abraham-lincoln-05/ebook-page-44.asp.

134. "John Brown's Remains," *New York Tribune* (Dec. 5, 1859), 5, col. 3; *Historical Address Delivered . . . 12th of January, 1908, by Horace Howard Furness* (Philadelphia: First Unitarian Church, 1908), in JB Funeral & Burial folder, Box 3, OGV. Also see reference to the "tumult of excitement" that took place during a meeting in Philadelphia on Dec. 2, 1859, the day of Brown's execution, in "What the Union-Saving Meeting in Philadelphia Was Made Of," *New York Tribune* (Dec. 12, 1859), clipping in the John Brown file of the Sophia Smith Collection, Smith College, Northampton, Mass.

135. See "John Brown's Clothes," *Brooklyn Eagle* [Brooklyn, N.Y.] (Apr. 6, 1890), 19.

136. Brown's hanging and funeral: see notes from *New York Herald* (Dec. 6, 1859), 8; and anonymous, undated [New York?] newspaper clipping, "Tilton As He is Now," both of which in JB Funeral & Burial folder, Box 3, OGV; and Clarence Gee's notes in folder 2, Box 9, GEE (which includes details about the New York undertakers, including transcripts of the letter of Louisa Williamson to Jedidiah Williamson, Dec. 8, 1859, etc.). The original undertaker bill and Williamson's letter are, respectively, MS12–0054 and MS10–0050, in BBS; entries for Dec. 4 and 9, 1859 in *The*

Diary of George Templeton Strong. Vol. 2, edited by Allan Nevins and Milton H. Thomas (New York: Macmillan, 1952), 474, 476.

Document Section Notes, pp 106–147

1. See Gee's documentary note, Nov. 6, 1969, accompanying the photocopy, Box 31, GEE.

2. See receipt of John Brown, June 15, 1839, West Hartford, Conn., in the Miscellaneous Manuscripts Collection of the Library of Congress. The receipt, written in Brown's own hand, states that the $2800 had been conveyed to him by Samuel Whitman for "the purchase of wool in Ohio."

3. The original letter from Brown to George Kellogg dated August 27, 1839 is in the Miscellaneous Manuscripts Collection of the Library of Congress, and was reproduced in *JBR,* 46. Also see DeCaro, *"Fire from the Midst of You,"* 103–05.

4. "John Brown and the Fugitive Slave Law," *The Independent* [New York], Mar. 10, 1870, 6.

5. Two other later transcriptions are found in Richard Hinton, *John Brown and His Men* (1894), and [Harry Andrew Wright], "John Brown's Fugitives," *The Republican* [Springfield, Mass.], June 17, 1909, 13.

6. "Branded hand" is a reference to Jonathan Walker, a ship captain who attempted to assist seven fugitives from slavery in their escape to the Bahamas from Florida in 1844. After the escape was thwarted and Walker was convicted of being a "slave stealer," his right hand was branded with the letters "SS" and he was imprisoned. Walker was afterward celebrated in a poem by John Greenleaf Whittier. Elijah Lovejoy was a clergyman and abolitionist publisher who was killed in an exchange of gunfire in Alton, Ill., on Nov. 7, 1837, while defending himself from a racist mob. In the same year of Walker's arrest, the Reverend Charles Torrey also attempted to aid fugitives from slavery in Maryland, where he was convicted and imprisoned, unfortunately dying while serving sentence in 1846. All three figures became powerful symbols of martyrdom for the abolitionist movement, and evidently to Brown himself.

7. In 1957, Clarence Gee made a transcription of Brown's letter to Giddings from the original, which at the time was privately owned.

8. Samuel C. Pomeroy (1816–91) was a leader in the anti-slavery movement and an agent of the New England Emigrant Aid Company. Pomeroy was residing in Lawrence at this time and Brown looked to him for financial support. August Bondi, "With John Brown in Kansas," *Transactions of the Kansas State Historical Society 1903–04* (Topeka: Clark, 1904), 278, n.

9. Orson Day was the elder half-brother of Brown's wife, Mary Day Brown. Day moved to Kansas from New York state and the Browns assisted in helping to build his first home. There are two letters from Brown to Day in the collections of the University of Kansas and the Kansas State Historical Society.

10. Michael A. Bellesiles, *Arming America: The Origins of A National Gun Culture* (New York: Alfred A. Knopf, 2000), 381.

11. According to a note in the Villard papers, Stearns replied as directed to Brown's son Watson on May 6, 1857, informing him that Carter had agreed to provide the desired weapons and only needed directions for sending them. Stearns also mentions the

efforts of Brown's associates to pay for Brown's home in North Elba by getting a mortgage and raising the money to finance a mortgage. He closes by admonishing Brown to "go to Kansas as soon as possible, and give Robinson and the rest some Backbone," referring to the waning leadership of the free state cause. See "Letters Through 1859," Box 5, OGV.

12. Given his former life as a sheep farmer and breeder, it is no wonder that Brown would refer to his young family at home as "that little company of Sheep." The child he dubbed "my big Baby" was probably his second youngest daughter, Sarah, born on Sept. 11, 1846. "Mums Baby" would then have been little Ellen, born on Sept. 25, 1854.

13. "Hariet [sic] Tubman hooked on *his* whole team at once. He Hariet is the most of a man naturally: that I ever met with." John Brown to John Brown Jr., April 8, 1858, MS02–0019, BBS.

14. Robert W. Taylor, "An Appeal for the Harriet Tubman Old Folks' Home," *Colored America Magazine* (July 1901):237.

15. Redpath, *The Public Life of Capt. John Brown*, 348.

16. Brown refers to the scene in the Gospel of St. Luke 22: 36–38.

17. Brown alludes to St. Paul's words in the epistles to the Ephesians 6:17 and 2 Corinthians 6:7.

18. Brown's daughters-in-law were Isabella Thompson, who married his son Watson in 1856, and Martha Brewster, who married his son Oliver in 1858. The latter was pregnant at the time of the raid but died shortly after the death of her infant in early 1860.

19. Besides the two Thompsons who had married into his family, Brown enlisted William and Dauphin Thompson from the same family to join his men at Harper's Ferry. Both men lost their lives, and William's wife is the widow to whom Brown refers.

20. George H. Hoyt was a Boston lawyer retained by northern friends to represent Brown on trial in Virginia. Hoyt was young and inexperienced and those who sent him actually intended to use him as a spy in the hopes of making a rescue attempt. The latter never materialized and Hoyt was suspect in the eyes of Virginia authorities. See Villard, *John Brown*, 484–85.

21. After Brown's arrest, trial, and conviction, his wife Mary traveled southward to see him in jail. Worried for her safety, Brown urgently demanded that she not come, and Mary—who had gotten as far as Baltimore, Maryland— retreated to the homes of anti-slavery well-wishers in Pennsylvania and New Jersey until Dec. 1, 1859, the day before his hanging.

22. There are a number of scriptural allusions here, particularly Matthew 14:27, Psalm 129:4, Matthew 6:9, Mark 7:37, and Daniel 2:23, in the King James version.

23. Brown refers to their two sons who died at Harper's Ferry, Watson (b. 1835) and Oliver (b. 1839).

24. See Document 19.

25. Brown refers to Jeremiah Root Brown (1819–74), his younger half-brother back in Hudson, Ohio, who wrote to him on Nov. 9, 1859. See James Redpath, *Echoes of Harper's Ferry* (Boston: Thayer and Eldridge, 1860), 430.

26. H. L. Vaill to John Brown, Nov. 8, 1859, in Redpath, *Echoes of Harper's Ferry*, 388–89; Carolyn Thomas Foreman, "The Foreign Mission School at Cornwall, Connecticut,"

Chronicles of Oklahoma 17:3 (Sept. 1929), retrieved from: <http://digital. library.okstate.edu/Chronicles/v007/v007p242.html> on Jun. 18, 2006.

27. Brown's references are either direct quotations or allusions to the following biblical texts: Psalm 57:4, 2 Chronicles 6:18, 2 Corinthians 7:4, Hebrews 11:25, and Psalm 40:9–10.

28. For insights into Brown's millennial thought implicit in this phrase, see DeCaro, *"Fire from the Midst of You,"* 59–60.

29. Here Brown makes reference to one of his favorite hymns, "I'll Praise My Maker," by Isaac Watts (1719), a chorus of which reads: "The Lord has eyes to give the blind; The Lord supports the sinking mind; He sends the labr'ing conscience peace; He helps the stranger in distress, The widow, and the fatherless, And grants the pris'ner sweet release."

30. Deacon John Brown, born in 1767, was Brown's uncle, being the older brother of his father Owen. Deacon John died of dysentery in 1849. See Abiel Brown to Owen Brown, Mar. 7, 1850 (transcription), in Gray Box #5, GEE.

31. Sarah Mills Woodruff was an aunt of John Brown, being the younger sister of his mother Ruth Mills Brown. During his brief stint as a student back east, John Brown stayed with the Woodruffs in Connecticut.

32. Luther Humphrey's letter, dated, Nov. 12, 1859, is transcribed in Redpath, *Echoes from Harper's Ferry*, 431–32; Heman Humphrey's letter, dated Nov. 20, 1859, is transcribed along with Brown's response in *LLJB*, 602–05.

33. Brown alludes to Judges 13:5, referring to the story of the Samson the Israelite liberator, to whom he also refers to as "a poor, erring servant."

34. Brown refers to the pre-Christian activity of St. Paul who, as Saul of Tarsus, violently persecuted the early Jesus movement according to the biblical book of Acts. In other words, Brown suggests that he has at least used militancy for the sake of a righteous cause.

INDEX

A Voice from Harper's Ferry, see Osborne Anderson

Allen, A. B., 128

Allstadt, John, 71

American Agriculturalist, 128

American Colonization Society, 8-9

Anderson, Osborne, 62, 75
declines command position at Harper's Ferry, 84
his testimony vindicated, 88-89
quoted, 90-92

Andrew, John (Gov.) (quoted), 49

Anthon, George, 99

Banks, Russell (quoted), 50

Barbour, Alfred, 81

Bateham, M. B., 29 (*also see Ohio Cultivator*)

Blakeslee, Levi (foster brother), 19-20

Blunt, James (quoted), 14

Brewster, Byron, 70

Brown Adams, Anne (daughter), 126, 132
criticism of Frederick Douglass, 66, 69
quoted, 51, 69, 86

Brown, Edward (half-brother) (quoted), 14-15

Brown, Ellen Sherbondy (daughter-in-law, Jason's wife), 143

Brown, Frederick (brother), letter to, 121-23

Brown, Frederick (son), 49, 137, 141

Brown, Jason (son), 49, 72, 137, 140, 146

Brown, Jeremiah R. (half-brother), 55

Brown, John
admiration of freedom fighters, 58
anti-slavery plan, 43-44, 80, 81
autobiographical sketch, 10-12, 114-20
association with blacks, 40
deaths of loved ones, 42
cultural and religious orientation, 3-5
distorted interpretations of
by Chester Hearn, 3-4
by Allen Guelzo, 16
by Edward J. Renehan Jr., 17
by Allan Nevins, 37
and economic crises of 1830s-40s, 24-27
expertise in sheep and wool, 28, 29-30
conflict with Frederick Douglass (1859), 64-65
European tour (1849), 35-36
failures contrasted with Lincoln's, 17-18
financial indiscretions, 23, 77
fund raising in 1857-58, 55-56
errs at Harper's Ferry, 92-94
health problems, 19, 56-57
as "Isaac Smith," 71, 72-73, 75

not an insurrectionist, 82-83
justice orientation, 14-15, 30,
39-40
failed Ohio business ventures,
21-27
as "Nelson Hawkins," 13
as "Old Brown," 46
Missouri raid and trek (1858-
59), 63-64
Pennsylvania years, 20-21
Provisional Constitution, 59-
60, 83
a modern man, 16-17
and pacifism, 6, 38
and P&B lawsuits, 36
personality traits, 12-13, 18
and phrenology, 129
preparations for family while
absent, 70-71
pre-raid clandestine activities,
75-77
not racially prejudiced, 84
Pottawatomie killings, 45,
48-54, 140, 141, 143
proposes school for black
youth, 4, 121-23
as "Shubel Morgan," 63, 170,
n. 99
alleged terrorism, 48-49
efforts on behalf of wool
growers, 30-36
Brown, John Jr.
captured by pro-slavery forces,
140
regarding Frederick Douglass,
69
letter to, 28
not at Harper's Ferry, 72
regarding raid plans, 81
writes from Kansas, 44
and Pottawatomie incident, 49
and phrenology, 129
Brown, Mary Ann Day (wife),
writes as "Mary Smith," 71

letters from Brown to, 27, 47,
51-53, 82-83, 93, 126-27,
131-32, 132-33, 139-43,
144-46, 149-51
goes to Virginia to collect husband's body, 95
Brown, Martha Brewster (daughter-in-law), 72
Brown, Oliver (son), 49, 72, 132,
137, 146
Brown, Owen (father)
biographical profile, 7-8
concern over his son in Kansas,
44
and Guinean Sam, 9-10
Brown, Owen (son), 133
Pottawatomie incident and
aftermath, 49, 141
on his father's intentions at
Harper's Ferry, 82
Brown, Salmon (son), 49, 66, 126,
132, 137, 146
Brown, Sarah (daughter), 12, 132
Brown, Watson (son), 72, 126,
132, 144, 146
Brown, Wealthy Hotchkiss
(daughter-in-law, John Jr.'s
wife), 48, 143

Carter, T. W. (Massachusetts
Arms Co.), 138, 144
Clark, Lucy Brown (niece)
(quoted), 45
Collamer, Jacob (Sen.), 78-79
Copeland, Robert Morris, 84
Cotter, Edwin (Jr.), 71, 110 (cap-
tion)
Cowper, William (quoted), 131
Cromwell, Oliver (quoted), 131

Day, Orson (brother-in-law), 140,
143
Delany, Martin, 44, 61-62
Depeyster, George B., 125
Dorsey, Thomas J., 67

Douglass, Frederick
   autobiographical stylizations
      regarding Brown, 65-66
   Brown's friendship with, 13, 41
   Brown's letter to (1858), 146-
      48
   hosts Brown in 1858, 59-60,
      144-46
   on Brown's plan, 43, 66, 71
   at Albany conference (1855),
      44
   absence from Chatham confer-
      ence (1858), 61
   denies Detroit conflict with
      Brown, 64
   resented by Browns after
      Harper's Ferry, 66
   discourages black participation
      in raid, 67-69
   postscript in Brown's 1858 let-
      ter, 146
   pre-raid meetings with Brown,
      66-68, 92
   suspicious of Hugh Forbes, 59
Doyle, Mahala, 53-54
Drucker, Peter (quoted), 17
DuBois, W.E.B. (quoted), 56, 68

"E.B." (Rhode Island), 148-49
Emerson, Ralph W., 56
Erickson, Aaron, 32, 33

Finkelman, Paul (quoted), 53
Forbes, Hugh, 57, 58-59, 63, 68
Fowler & Wells, 129, 130
Frank Leslie's Illustrated
   Newspaper, 105 (caption)
Fugitive Slave Act (1850), 6, 40,
   131-36

Garibaldi, Giuseppi, 57
Garnet, Henry Highland, 41
Garrison, William Lloyd, 9
Geffert, Hannah
   quoted, 78

describes Shepherdstown, Va.,
   86
reveals black support of
   Brown, 87
Giddings, Joshua R., Congress-
   man, 6, 138
Gill, George, 81
Gloucester, James, 41
Greeley, Horace, 59
Green, Shields, 68

H. W. T. Mali, Inc., 35
Hamilton, Charles, 54
Harding, Vincent, 62
Harper's Ferry Raid described,
   74-75
   prejudiced analysis of Oswald
      Villard, 78
   pre-raid conditions in South,
      79-80
Harper's Weekly, 90
Harris, Charlotte, 76
Hawkins, Nelson (the real), 13
Heaton, William (Rev.), 73
Henry, Thomas (Rev.), see Jean
   Libby
Herrington, Eldrid (quoted), 48
Hodges, Willis, 41
Hopper, Jacob, 96-98
Hoyt, George H. (Esq.), 149, 176,
   n. 20
Huidekoper, Harm Jan
   profile, 123-24
   Brown's letter to, 124
Humphrey, Heman (Rev.), 93,
   153-55
Hunter, Andrew, 94
Hunter, Antony (Anthony), 84-86

Jackson, Thomas "Stonewall," 4
Johnson, William H. (Rev.), 66-67

Kelly, Michael (quoted), 49
Kent, Zenas, 21

Lawrence, Larry (quoted), 24

Lawrence, Samuel
   praises Brown's expertise, 30
   quoted, 33
   capitalist opponent of Brown,
   33-34

League of Gileadites, United
   States, 133-36

Lee, Robert E., 75

Liberator, *see* William Lloyd Garrison

Libby, Jean
   Brown's Hudson daguerreotype
   (1856),55
   Brown's Kansas daguerreotype
   (1856), 103 (caption)
   Brown's so-called "mad"
   daguerreotype, 57
   on Chatham convention attenders, 62
   corrects record of Harper's
   Ferry raid, 77, 83, 88-89, 172,
   n. 109
   on David H. Strother's cartoon
   distortions of blacks, 90
   on Thomas Henry and Brown,
   73

Lincoln, Abraham
   his colonization leanings, 8
   dismisses Brown at Cooper
   Union (1860), 95
   his "House Divided" speech, 4
   his failures contrasted with
   Brown's, 17-18

Loguen, Jermain (Rev.), 41, 61

Long, Henry (fugitive), 6, 132,
   135

Lovejoy, Elijah (Rev.), 39, 134,
   175, n. 6

Lowry, Morrow B. (quoted), 39

Lusk Brown, Dianthe (first wife),
   20

Mason, James (Sen.), 79, 81

"Mason Report," 77-78, 79

Mayer, Henry (quoted), 64

McFeely, William S., 66

McKim, James Miller, 96, 110
   (caption)

"moral suasion" ideology, 6

National Kansas Committee, 55

Nevins, Allan, 37

New York Tribune, 98

Nixon, Malvina, 76

Oberlin Institute, 6

Ohio Cultivator
   Brown quoted in, 17, 31
   editor praises Brown's expertise,
   29-30

Oviatt, Heman, 28

Painter, Nell Irvin (quoted), 5

Panic of 1837 (Crisis of 1839),
   25-27

Parker, Theodore (Rev.), 144

Pennsylvania Population Company, 39

Perkins, Simon Jr., 19
   absorbs business losses kindly,
   36, 130
   subsequent business losses, 37
   critical of Brown's anti-slavery
   activity, 37
   partnership with Brown, 28-
   29, 31-32, 36

Phillips, William A. (quoted), 63,
   80-81

phrenology, *see* Fowler & Wells

Pomeroy, Samuel C., 175, n. 8

"Popular Sovereignty," 43

Postman, Neil, 4

Quakers, *see* John Brown and
   pacifism

Quarles, Benjamin (quoted), 40,
   64

Rankin, John (Rev.), 7

Reynolds, J. G., 61
Russell, Nellie, 12, 13, 56

Sanborn, Franklin, 66, 67, 70
Shaw, Robert Gould, 84
Sigler, George (Rev.), 72, 73
Simons, J. J., 67
Slavery issue, 5-6
"The Solitude of Alexander Selkirk," 131
Smith, Gerrit, 41, 70, 143
Smith, Isaac (the real), 71, 102
Spirit of Jefferson, 92
Springfield Republican, 71, 131
Stavis, Barrie, 77, 172, n. 109
Stearns, George L., 10, 56
    Brown's letters to (1857), 120-21, 143-44

Stewart, Anne, 21
Strong, George Templeton, 98-99
Strother, David Hunter, 90
Stutler, Boyd B.
    on Brown as businessman, 18, 23, 32
    on Brown and wool reform, 32
    on *Provisional Constitution*, 61

Thirion Maillard Inc., 35
Thompson, Henry, (son-in-law), 44
    subsequent disdain toward Frederick Douglass, 66
    not at Harper's Ferry, 72
    troubled by killing role in later years, 50
    wanted by Brown for Harper's Ferry raid, 145

Thompson, Ruth Brown (daughter), 66, 72, 145
Thompson, Seth, 20, 22, 24, 26
Thoreau, Henry D., 56
Tilton, Theodore, 96-97
Torrey, Charles (Rev.), 134, 175, n. 6
Tubman, Harriet
    Brown's letter on behalf of, 146-48
    meets Brown, 57
    not at Harper's Ferry, 83-84

Uncle Tom's Cabin, 7
Utter, David (Rev.), 53-54

Vaill, Herman L. (Rev.)
    Brown's letter to, Nov. 15, 1859 (Doc. 19), 151-53
    mentioned in Brown's letter of Nov. 10, 1859 (Doc. 18), 151

Villard, Oswald Garrison, 78, 88
Vince, Thomas (quoted), 24

Wallis, John (quoted), 25, 26-27
Walker, Jonathan, 134, 175, n. 6
Webb, William, 64
Western Reserve College, 6, 16
Wiener, Theodore, 49
Williamson, Louisa, 97-98
Williamson, Passmore (quoted), 80
Wise, Henry (Gov.), 79
Woodruff, Sarah Mills (aunt), 153, 177, n. 31
wool industry in U.S., 30-31, 34-35